W9-AQF-523

Philadelphia's Old Ballparks

BASEBALL IN AMERICA (BIA)
In the series *Baseball in America*, edited by Rich Westcott

Philadelphia's Old Ballparks

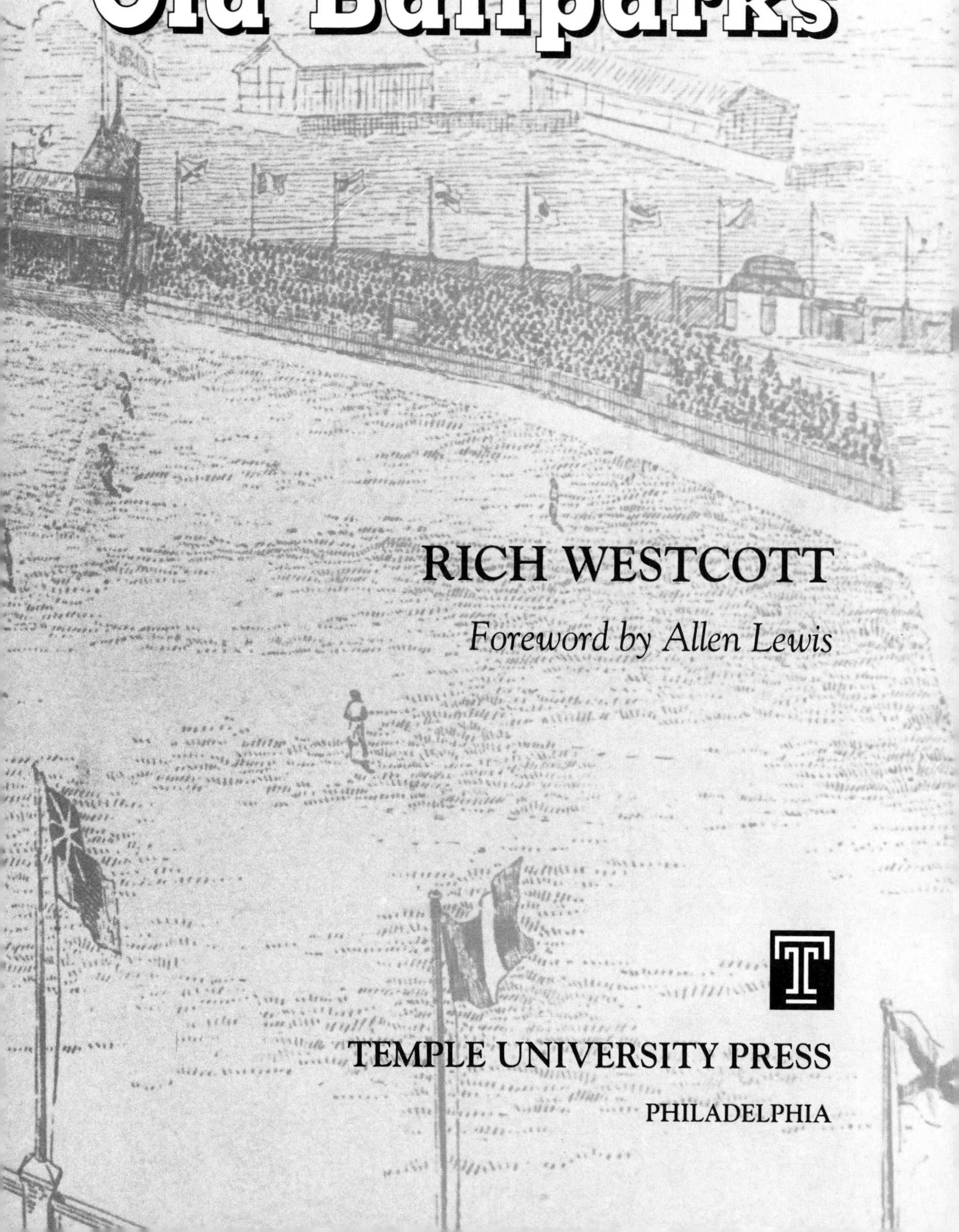

RICH WESTCOTT

Foreword by Allen Lewis

TEMPLE UNIVERSITY PRESS

PHILADELPHIA

To my father, the late W. Norris Westcott,
who not only introduced me to my first big league ballpark,
but was instrumental in helping to launch
my lifelong passion for the game of baseball.

Temple University Press, Philadelphia 19122

Copyright © 1996 by Temple University

All rights reserved

Published 1996

Printed in the United States of America

♾ The paper used in this publication meets the requirements of the American National Standard for Information Sciences—Permanence of Paper for Printed Library Materials, ANSI Z39.48-1984

Text design by Robert Freese

Library of Congress Cataloging-in-Publication Data

Westcott, Rich.
    Philadelphia's old ballparks / Rich Westcott.
       p.   cm. — (Baseball in America)
    Includes bibliographical references (p.).
    ISBN 1-56639-454-6
    1. Baseball fields—Pennsylvania—Philadelphia—History.
    2. Stadiums—Pennsylvania—Philadelphia—History.   I. Title.
    II. Series.
    GV879.5.W47   1996
    796.357'06'874811—dc20   96-485
                                      CIP

ISBN: 1-56639-454-6 cloth

Contents

Foreword by Allen Lewis   *vii*

Introduction   *xiii*

Early Parks   **1**
     Philadelphia's Oldest Pro Baseball Fields

Recreation Park   **9**
     Birthplace of the Phillies

Columbia Park   **15**
     First Home of the Athletics

Philadelphia Park/Baker Bowl   **27**
     Unusual in Almost Every Way
     A Grand Opening   31
     The Wall of Horrors   32
     A Hitter's Paradise   37
     Special Effects   42
     Not Much Was Ever Constant   48
     Outside the Park   51
     The Paying Customers   57
     Gentlemen of the Press   65
     The Best of Times   68
     Some Other Memorable Days   71
     The Great Catastrophes   74
     A Touch of Comedy   79
     Beautifully Decrepit   83
     Not Just a Baseball Park   87
     The End Finally Arrives   91

Shibe Park/Connie Mack Stadium   **99**

An Enduring Favorite

A Park for the Masses   103

The Big Day Arrives   108

Some Things Changed   111

Idiosyncrasies   117

A Wall of Its Own   123

A Player's Park   127

The Phillies Arrive   133

The World Series   135

All-Star Games   145

Great Games by the Visitors   147

Other Memorable Games   150

Around the Edges   161

Inside Jobs   163

As Tough As There Is   169

The Fourth Estate   176

A Park for Many Occasions   181

Farewell to a Ballpark   188

Bibliography   197

About the Author   199

Index   201

Foreword

*T*his book will delight any baseball fan. In addition to the many interesting pictures, Rich Westcott has intertwined countless interviews with ballpark history to make *Philadelphia's Old Balllparks* fascinating reading.

Sports played a major role in the life of any red-blooded boy growing up in the first half of the twentieth century. And if you grew up in the Philadelphia area, sports were undoubtly important. Until 1934, Pennsylvania's blue laws prevented any commercial activity on Sundays. The only stores open were drug stores; there were no movies, no baseball or football games for which admission was charged, and, of course, no television. Radio was in its infancy.

Those restriction made trips to big league ballparks a special treat. On a Saturday afternoon, after half a day at his office, your father would take you to Shibe Park to see the Philadelphia Athletics play. The A's were recovering from the breakup of the team which had won four pennants in five years (1909–1914). In the mid-1920s, the A's were on their way to becoming one of baseball's really dominant teams for the third time, winning three American League pennants in a row (1929–1931) with a roster of future Hall of Famers that has seldom been matched, and which made this teenager a rabid baseball fan forever more.

The Athletics were by far the most popular team in the city, and they played in what seemed to a young fan a baseball palace, Shibe Park. The green double-decked stands were huge, and the perfectly groomed grass field, with its similar distances down the foul lines and great expanse of 450 feet to the center field corner, was truly a field of dreams.

When the game was about to begin, and with no numbers on the uniforms until the 1930s, the lineups for both teams were chalked on a board in right field near the bottom of a 12-foot-high fence. That fence was more than tripled later to put an end to the small stands residents on 20th Street had erected atop their row homes. Residents charged a modest admission price, cutting attendance at the park, and that didn't sit well with the Shibes. Squatty Babe O'Rourke would use a large megaphone to announce the batteries to the fans on both side of the grandstand. That's the way is was when I first went to Shibe Park.

I remember the game on Saturday, September 14, which won the 1929 American League pennant. Big George Earnshaw shut out the Chicago White Sox, 5-0. The A's Lefty Grove, Mickey Cochrane, Jimmie Foxx, Al Simmons, and others had compiled such a huge lead over the second-place New York Yankees that there was almost no celebration by the players or fans.

The A's went on to beat the Chicago Cubs that year in the five games played in the World Series. The third game, won by the Cubs, 3-1, was the first of almost 200 World Series games I have attended, 158 of which I covered for the *Philadelphia Inquirer*.

Back then, watching the venerable Connie Mack, part owner of the A's whom he managed for half a century, sitting stiffly in the dugout wearing a high collar and tie and using his scorecard to position his outfielders for each opposing batter, was always a unique sight.

There were fans in those days who wouldn't even think of attending Phillies games and many who felt the same way about the A's despite their success. But to a young fan old enough to go to games alone, the Phillies were too interesting to ignore.

Playing at the old Baker Bowl with its famed right field wall, the Phillies games were a sight to see. Their powerful offense, fueled by Chuck Klein, Lefty O'Doul, Don Hurst and Pinky Whitney, made high-scoring games the norm, but inept pitching usually made losers of the Phillies.

Because the Phillies won more games than they lost only once between 1917 and 1949, finding a good seat in old Baker Bowl was never a problem. In the 1920s and 1930s, the Phillies never averaged more than 4,000 fans at a home game. Except on Saturdays or when playing a doubleheader, games usually started at 3:15. Excessive scoring and the many pitching changes often made this young fan late for dinner in suburban Philadelphia.

Sitting in the first row of Baker Bowl on the upper deck at first base was always a favorite, offering an unobstructed view and, because of the minimal crowd noise, an opportunity to hear clearly what the players were yelling to each other. Another favorite seat was in the upper deck behind home plate where only chicken wire separated fans from the press box. Sitting alongside the writers was a real treat for someone who some day hoped to be a baseball writer.

Baker Bowl, which seated only 18,000 compared to 33,000 at Shibe Park, was not only outdated but falling apart with the ownership financially unable to maintain it to major league standards. As a result, the Phillies became tenants of the A's on July 4, 1938, and later the only occupants after the A's moved to Kansas City in 1955. Prior to that, the A's played host to the 1943 All-Star Game and the Phillies the 1952 game, which ended after five innings because of rain.

After watching the Phillies win their second pennant in their 68-year history in 1950, watching their two one-run losses to the New York Yankees in the World Series from the Shibe Park press box was painful. But that couldn't match the 1964 debacle of the first seven games of their 10 game losing streak played at Connie Mack Stadium (renamed in 1953). It cost the Phillies a pennant they seemed to have wrapped up two weeks from season's end. A 1-0 loss began the swoon and even a three-homer game by Johnny Callison couldn't halt it.

Memorable games played in Philadelphia's old parks include 13 no-hit games and two games in which an opposing player hit four home runs. One Phillies pitcher and one opposing hurler pitched no-hitters in both Recreation Park and Baker Bowl, four A's pitchers and two opponents had no-hitters in Shibe Park, and three opponents performed the feat after the name was changed to Connie Mack Stadium. New York's Lou Gehrig and Chicago's Pat Seerey each hit four homers in a game against the A's in Shibe Park.

One of the most memorable Shibe Park games involved the National Football League's Philadelphia Eagles, who played at the park for many seasons. In 1948, the Eagles beat the Chicago Cardinals, 7-0, with Steve Van Buren powering his way to the score that gave the Birds their first title in the championship game. A snowstorm had made getting to the park that day an adventure. Clearing the field of snow had delayed the start of the game.

Philadelphia's fourth big league ballpark, Connie Mack Stadium, closed on a memorable night, October 1, 1970, when the Phillies beat Montreal in 10 innings, 2-1, and many of the 31,822 souvenir-hunting fans practically tore the place apart during and after that final game. The park had been host to more than 6,800 major league games, several hundred Negro League games, and other sporting events. Veterans Stadium opened in 1971.

The two old ballparks illustrated and remembered here, Baker Bowl at 15th Street and Lehigh Avenue and Shibe Park–Connie Mack Stadium at 21st Street and Lehigh Avenue, will always hold important places in the history of Philadelphia sports. This book documents that history in a way that will delight all.

Allen Lewis

ALLEN LEWIS is a member of the writers' wing of the Baseball Hall of Fame at Cooperstown, New York. Inducted in 1982, he covered baseball for more than 30 years for the Philadelphia Inquirer *during a distinguished newspaper career that began in 1940. Lewis was the beat writer covering the Phillies for more than two decades before retiring in 1979. During that time, he served for 12 years as chairman of baseball's Scoring Rules Committee. A baseball historian of considerable note, Lewis is a long-standing member of the Veterans Committee of the Hall of Fame and the author of four baseball books.*

Acknowledgments

Writing a book of this kind is a task that is not done easily. Nor is it done alone. Many people contributed to the material contained herein, and it is with particular gratitude that I thank them for their generosity and willingness to help.

I am especially indebted to the late Ed (Dutch) Doyle, who before his untimely passing on November 27, 1995, not only provided a wealth of information and expertise, but helped in a variety of other ways in the collection of material. Without his enthusiastic help and limitless support, this book would not have been possible.

I also wish to express my deepest appreciation to the more than 80 people who were interviewed and whose names can be found throughout these pages. Unfortunately, some of those interviewed have since passed away. The insights and experiences that have been related, all so cheerfully and unhesitatingly, are the most valuable elements of this book.

Finally, for help in a variety of other ways, I would like to express my most sincere thanks especially to Dick Miller of Cincinnati, who probably knows more about old baseball parks than any living soul; to Barry Morrill of Temple University Press; to my good friend Bob Armbruster for his editorial advice; to Jimmy Gallagher, Allen Lewis, Ernie Montella, Robert Shoemaker, and Gene Weinert; and to my wife, Lois Westcott, for her unwavering support and encouragement and her willingness always to listen when I needed to talk about this sometimes difficult project.

Photo Credits

I would like to acknowledge the following for their photographic contributions to this book: The National Baseball Hall of Fame and Museum, Urban Archives of Temple University, the City of Philadelphia's department of records, the Free Library of Philadelphia, the Historical Society of Pennsylvania, the Philadelphia Eagles, *Phillies Report*, Alan Kravetz, and Dick Miller.

Introduction

*P*hiladelphia has an enormously rich professional baseball history that dates back to the Civil War days. That history has been embellished not only by memorable games and events, but by scores of outstanding and sometimes colorful individuals and by teams that have run the gamut from tremendously successful to hopelessly inept.

One other significant contributor to Philadelphia's marvelous baseball tradition has been the ballparks on which the city's professional teams have played. These parks are every bit as important to Philadelphia baseball history as any other part of the sport.

They may lack the human characteristics of a player, a manager, or a team. But probably no segment of Philadelphia baseball has more character or invokes more sentiment than the city's ballparks of yesteryear. And nothing has been more durable.

To this day, Philadelphia's old ballparks—particularly Baker Bowl and Shibe Park—linger prominently in the minds of those who went to them. Despite their eventual shortcomings, the old parks are still remembered fondly. And even among those who didn't have the thrill of experiencing them, there is a strong sense of nostalgia—indeed, a fascination with the old parks—that is seldom seen in other areas of baseball.

Like one's old homestead, no matter what kind, an old ballpark has an allure that cannot be dismissed. It evokes warm memories while suggesting another era when baseball was a kinder, gentler game. One cannot simply forget it. Its grip is far too strong.

Who among us doesn't remember his or her first view of a major league ballpark? Most of us were children at that point, and our first glimpse of a major league ballpark was probably overwhelming.

I will never forget mine. My dad took me to Shibe Park to see the Philadelphia Athletics, his favorite team, meet the Boston Red Sox. It was late in the season in 1946, and the Athletics were rooted deep in last place in the American League. The Red Sox were running away with the pennant.

Despite being a mere tyke, I already had a growing familiarity with big league baseball and its players. But I had no conception of what a big league ballpark looked like. An incident a few weeks earlier proved how clueless I was. I had seen some teams playing on a sandlot field, and because one team had red on its uniforms, I was sure it was the Phillies, who were playing at home that day.

As my dad and I approached 21st and Lehigh, I could feel the excitement building. Traffic got heavier, and by the time we reached the park, cars and people filled the streets. And the dull murmur of the crowd, pierced intermittently by the whistles of policemen and the shouts of vendors, grew louder as we reached the gate.

After purchasing our tickets, we climbed the steps to our seats. Suddenly, as we did, the interior of the ballpark came into view. To an impressionable eight-year-old, it was absolutely breathtaking.

Everywhere I looked, I saw green. Green seats. Green walls. And the most beautiful sight of all—green grass. To me, that marvelously exquisite playing field, surrounded on three sides by a formidable two tiers of grandstands, was far beyond any level of my comprehension.

I knew instantly that I was hooked on baseball for life.

The game itself was equally magnificent. The downtrodden A's, getting three home runs from Sam Chapman and one from Pete Suder, rode to a 5–3 victory. Luther Knerr pitched a rare complete game to get the win, one of only three he would have that year to go along with 16 losses.

With that game, Sam Chapman became my first baseball hero. And Shibe Park became a place that in the years ahead not only would be my second home, but would play a significant role in shaping my future.

The following season, I saw one of the most memorable games of my viewing days when pitcher Carl Schieb hit a grand slam home run and the A's pulled a Suder–to Eddie Joost–to Ferris Fain triple play in a 16–1 victory over the Chicago White Sox. Years later, I would learn that my future wife, Lois, attended the same game, a discovery that doubtless was an influential part of our courtship.

As a 12-year-old, I stood in line along Somerset Street for five hours so I could buy a bleacher ticket for one dollar to the 1950 World Series opener. My 7:30 A.M. arrival and long wait were rewarded when I saw the Phillies and Jim Konstanty lose a memorable 1–0 game to the New York Yankees.

Over the years, there were other great events at Shibe Park, later to be named Connie Mack Stadium. Collectively, they form an indelible feeling of affection for the old ballpark that will never disappear.

That's what old ballparks do to you. That is also one reason that writing this book has been an enormously appealing project. It has been a continuous series of pleasurable experiences.

Basically, the book is intended to be a combination oral history and documentary on the old major league ballparks of Philadelphia. I have relied heavily on the recollections and eyewitness accounts of many people who have had exposure to the old parks, especially former players, front office employees, media people who covered games, people who worked at the parks during games, neighborhood residents, and just plain fans.

Naturally, the discussion is most heavily focused on Baker Bowl and Shibe Park, two very special parks that while they housed big league teams had a combined lifespan of some 113 years. They are the parks most closely associated with Philadelphia's major league baseball teams, and their histories are deeply ingrained parts of the city's long baseball history.

Along with looks at the evolution, events, and effects of those parks, the book offers a brief discussion of Recreation Park and Columbia Park, the original homes of the National League Phillies and American League Athletics, respectively. Although their histories were short, both were important elements of major league baseball in Philadelphia.

An additional chapter cites some of the other ballparks in which professional teams played. These parks may be mostly forgotten and less important in the broad view of Philadelphia baseball, but they, too, need to be acknowledged.

Overall, it is hoped that this book adds another dimension to the rich tradition of Philadelphia major league baseball history and, equally important, provides enjoyment to those who have soft spots in their hearts for the old ballparks.

Rich Westcott

Early Parks

Philadelphia's Oldest Pro Baseball Fields

*P*hiladelphia has been endowed with a rich history of baseball parks, particularly in the northern section of the city where ball fields have been an indelible part of the landscape since the mid-19th century.

Although four primary major league parks—Recreation Park, Columbia Park, Baker Bowl, and Shibe Park—dominated the city's past, numerous other ball fields played brief roles in the local big league scene.

That was especially true in the late 1800s when teams described as being in the major leagues came and went with dependable regularity. At one point, in fact, three teams, all playing in what were considered major leagues, performed within a few blocks of each other. The Phillies of the National League were doing battle at Philadelphia Park at Broad Street and Lehigh Avenue, the Athletics of the American Association held forth at Jefferson Park at 25th and Jefferson Streets, and the Quakers of the Players' League contested the opposition at Forepaugh Park at Broad and Dauphin Streets.

The American Association, represented by the Athletics from 1882 until its collapse after the 1891 season, and the Players', or Brotherhood, League, a circuit for players who had bolted the National League in a labor dispute and existed for just the 1890 season, were two of the so-called major leagues that performed in Philadelphia in the late 1800s. The

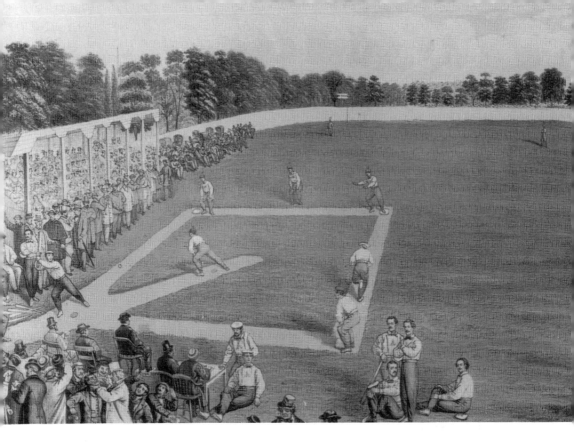

The Athletics and the Brooklyn Atlantics battled for the mythical national championship in 1866 at 15th Street and Columbia Avenue.

Union Association, which lasted just the 1884 season, and the National Association, which operated from 1871 to 1875 as the forerunner of the National League, also fielded teams in Philadelphia.

The various Philadelphia teams played at an assortment of fields, amazingly many of them within the same general area of North Philadelphia. The city's first professional team, the Athletics, played in the 1860s at a park at 15th Street and Columbia Avenue. In 1865, having by then become a quasi-pro team, the Athletics—with future Phillies owner Al Reach playing second base and getting paid $1,000 for the season—lost to the Brooklyn Atlantics, 21–15, in a widely anticipated game played before an estimated crowd of 12,000. Newspaper accounts claimed that 20,000 people actually saw the game, with the additional 8,000 who did not get onto the grounds watching it from trees, from rooftops, or through the windows of nearby buildings.

One year later, on October 1, 1866, the two titans of baseball squared off again at the Columbia Avenue park in what was billed as a "true" baseball championship match. The game generated more excitement in Philadelphia than even the most fervent political conventions.

The Athletics were the toast of the town, and according to author

Charles Peverelly, "have done more to advance the popularity of the game by visits to towns and villages where base ball was previously unknown than almost any other Club in the United States."

Before the game, some 8,000 tickets had been sold at 25 cents apiece. By game time, fans were paying five dollars for elevated seats outside the park. Many more brought their own wagons and coaches and plunked down on their roofs to watch the action; others climbed virtually every tree surrounding the park or roosted on the roofs of nearby houses. A special detail of police was unable to keep the huge crowd under control.

As game time approached, gamblers walked through the stands waving fistfuls of bills and accepting bets from all comers, while a frenzied crowd, estimated to have eventually reached 30,000, including many Brooklyn fans, packed the grounds both inside and outside the park. Spectators were jammed so tightly around the playing field that when they spilled over onto the diamond, it became impossible to play. After one inning, by mutual consent of the teams, the game was postponed.

The series shifted to Brooklyn for a game won by the Atlantics, 27–17, then returned to Philadelphia for an October 22 contest. This time, the Athletics erected a large fence around the field and hired a huge special police force. Some 20,000, including 3,000 who paid one dollar each to get inside the ballpark, saw the game. Scoring 22 runs over the last three innings of the seven-inning game, the Athletics emerged with a 31–12 victory. Because the teams could not agree about the division of gate receipts, a deciding game in the series was not played. With more wins than any other team in the league, the Athletics then claimed the mythical championship of baseball, a title they would successfully defend in each of the following two seasons.

The Athletics played at the 15th and Columbia park until 1870. One of their last significant games there occurred June 22, 1870, when they lost, 27–25, to the touring Cincinnati Red Stockings, baseball's first professional team, before an estimated crowd of 20,000. At the time, the Red Stockings were nearing the end of a 2,500-mile, 15-city, 23-game tour.

Managed by Harry Wright, later to become skipper of the Phillies, the Red Stockings one week earlier had their 81-game winning streak come to an end in an 8–7 defeat by the Brooklyn Atlantics. Their game against the Athletics was anxiously awaited by baseball fans in Philadelphia, who began filling the streets several hours before game time.

In the book *The First Boys of Summer* by Greg Rhodes and John Erardi, an account of the game noted that "wagons and carriages filled the streets adjacent to the park, many backed up to the fence with temporary seats upon them so people could see into the enclosed field." So great was the crowd surrounding the park that the Red Stockings had to scramble over a low fence to enter the field.

Jefferson Park was the home of the Athletics during their time in the National Association from 1871 to 1875.

The park was not an easy place on which to play a game. Outfielders had to look into the sun to catch a ball. And infielders had to throw uphill to first base because the field was higher at the initial sack than it was around the rest of the infield.

The field, however, was sold later in 1870, and by the time the Athletics entered the National Association the following year, they had moved to another field at 25th and Jefferson Streets. It was a field that had already seen a fair share of baseball games. In fact, in 1865, the Athletics had dropped a 28–13 decision there to a team called the Actives in a game in which the Athletics blamed the defeat on a lost ball. The ball had been hit over the fence and into the grounds of the adjoining Wagner Free Institute of Science, whose principal refused to return it. A substitute ball was apparently not quite satisfactory for the indignant Athletics.

Called Jefferson Park, or sometimes Athletic Park, the field was the first fully enclosed grounds in Philadelphia. The field had short fences down the foul lines, but it was 500 feet to straightaway center field. A swimming pool was located behind the right field fence. The park seated 5,000.

The Athletics played at Jefferson Park for the duration of the National Association, which extended from 1871 to 1875, even winning the league's first championship with a 22–7 record. From 1872 to 1875, one of their top players was the legendary Adrian (Cap) Anson, a future Hall of Famer, who hit .352 in his four years with the Athletics before going on to a 22-year career in the National League with Chicago.

The grounds were also the home field of the Philadelphia Quakers, also called the White Stockings as well as the Pearls, of the National Association during their term in the league from 1873 to 1875, and the American Association's Athletics, who played there from 1883 to 1890.

Jefferson Park's most celebrated use, however, came from none of those teams, but from another team called the Athletics, members of the new National League. On April 22, 1876, the first National League game was played at Jefferson Park between the Athletics and the Boston Red Caps.

Playing under cloudy skies with 3,000 spectators watching, Boston, managed by the ubiquitous Harry Wright, scored two runs in the ninth inning to gain a 6–5 triumph. Joe Borden, a Yeadon, Pennsylvania, native who is buried in West Chester, Pennsylvania, and who was later to become the first National League pitcher to hurl a no-hitter, got the win. Three days later, the teams met again at Jefferson Park. This time, with 2,000 in attendance, the Athletics avenged their opening day loss with a 20–3 victory over Borden and Boston.

The Athletics did not linger long in the National League. Despite having the league's first home run champion, George Hall with five, the club won just 14 of 59 games and was mired in seventh place as the end of the season approached. Scheduled for a final western road swing, the Athletics, having insufficient funds and not anxious to waste any more time playing in a futile season, refused to make the trip. The team was expelled immediately from the league.

Jefferson Park, however, remained the site of a considerable amount of baseball activity. After the American Association was formed in 1882, another team called the Athletics moved to the grounds the following year. They played their first game there on April 7, 1883, defeating Yale University, 12–0. The Athletics then played games against teams from Huntsville, Auburn, and Trenton before losing to the Phillies in what was most likely the first City Series game. Throughout the regular season and until the seats and grandstands were sold to pay for past debts after the 1890 season, the Athletics continued to play at Jefferson Park, except on Sundays, when from 1888 to 1890 they played their home games at a field in Gloucester, New Jersey.

In 1883, the Athletics, under manager Lew Simmons, won the American Association pennant with a 66–32 record. Harry Stovey, one of the league's premier players, won his first of five home run crowns while holding down first base for the Athletics. Stovey, who would lead the league in scoring four times and in slugging average three times while a member of the Athletics, also captured the batting title in 1884 with a .326 average.

All the while, other parks housing major league teams had surfaced in Philadelphia. Oakdale Park, at 11th and Cumberland Streets, was used by the Athletics in their maiden year in the American Association in 1882. Oakdale Park had been a baseball ground used by amateur teams since shortly after the conclusion of the Civil War. It was sold and converted to other uses following the 1882 season.

Keystone Park, at Broad and Moore Streets in South Philadelphia and the original grounds of the Forepaugh Circus, was used in 1884 by the Keystones of the short-lived Union Association, a seven-team circuit that included a team in Altoona, Pennsylvania. Forepaugh Park, at Broad and Dauphin Streets, was the home of both the Philadelphia Quakers of the Players' League in 1890 and the American Association Athletics in 1891.

On April 30, 1890, 17,182 fans jammed Forepaugh Park, by then the new home of the circus, to watch the Quakers in a game with the Boston Reds.

Several other fields were used by professional teams. In 1894, when their own Philadelphia Park was destroyed by fire, the Phillies played at the University of Pennsylvania's Varsity Grounds at 37th and Spruce Streets. The Phillies compiled a 5–1 record during their short stay on the Penn campus.

In the eight-team Union League, which lasted during 1908 only, the Philadelphia entry, also known as the Quakers, staged its home games at a field called 62d Street Grounds at 62d and Walnut Streets in West Philadelphia. The Quakers defeated Brooklyn, 1–0, before a crowd of 2,500 in the opening game April 27. By June 3, the league had disbanded, leaving the Philadelphia club in seventh place with a 10–24 record.

Two other noteworthy baseball stadiums in the Philadelphia area were the home fields of Negro League teams, which were a prominent part of the city's baseball history.

One of them, which never had a formal name, was located at 44th and Parkside in West Philadelphia. It was home base for the Philadelphia Stars from 1935 to 1952. Built in the 1920s by the Pennsylvania Railroad, it had originally been used by a company team. Later, a semipro team called the All-Phillies and operated by Eddie Gottlieb used the 5,000-seat field.

The Stars, league champions in 1934, began playing at 44th and Parkside after performing at Passon Field at 48th and Spruce Streets. Until 1948, the Stars were members of the Negro National League. They then played in the Negro American League until 1952.

Dense smoke often billowed onto the Parkside field as trains passed in and out of the nearby roundhouse, frequently causing fly balls to be lost and games to be delayed, sometimes for as long as 15 minutes. "Every time we played, we would have to stop the game until the smoke cleared from a train passing by," Stars player Mahlon Duckett recalled.

One of the most memorable games at 44th and Parkside was played in 1947. Toiling for the Kansas City Monarchs, Satchel Paige pitched a perfect game against the Stars for eight innings. In the ninth, he intentionally walked the first three batters, then ordered the seven fielders behind him to sit down. Paige proceeded to strike out the next three hitters on nine pitches to finish his no-hitter.

The other primary Negro League field was Hilldale Park in Yeadon, Pennsylvania, just a few miles from the Philadelphia border. The field was home to the Hilldale Club, which played as both the Giants and Daisies as members of first the Eastern Colored League, then the Negro American League from 1923 through 1932.

Hilldale, which featured such top players as Biz Mackey and Hall of Famer Judy Johnson, won the Eastern Colored League championship three straight years from 1923 to 1925 and won its division title in the Negro American League in 1931.

Recreation Park

Birthplace of the Phillies

Of all the major league ballparks that graced the terrain in Philadelphia, none was quite as unusual as Recreation Park.

It was not only one of the first ballparks of any kind in the Philadelphia area, but also the original home of the Phillies. What made it unusual, though, was the lot on which it stood.

Located in what was then the outer region of the city, it sat on the oddest possible kind of plot. Bordered by Columbia and Ridge Avenues and 24th and 25th Streets, the plot was the most irregularly shaped piece of land imaginable. In fact, today's viewers of that plot can do nothing but wonder how a baseball park was ever located there.

So misshapen was the plot that when the Phillies established Recreation Park as their home base in 1883, the dimensions of the playing area defied belief. It was 300 feet down the left field line and 331 feet to straightaway center field. But the park jutted out into Ridge Avenue, reaching 369 feet in right-center before receding to an incredibly short 247 feet down the right field line. It was 79 feet from home plate to the grandstands behind it.

Despite its strange dimensions, Recreation Park was the home of the Phillies for four years. That period extended from the team's arrival in Philadelphia to its shift in 1887 to the widely heralded new stadium originally known as Philadelphia Base Ball Park, later to become Baker Bowl.

Recreation Park had a long history of activity well in advance of the Phillies' arrival. Although it wasn't known as Recreation Park then, the land was used as a baseball field as early as 1860 and perhaps even before that.

Teams known as Winona, Equity, Swiftfoot, and Pennsylvania competed there. On June 26, 1860, Equity defeated Pennsylvania in a rousing battle, 65–52, in what author Charles Peverelly, writing about "the national game," called the first game ever played in the state of Pennsylvania.

According to ballpark historian Jerrold Casway, writing in *Phillies Report*, the field at the time "was not enclosed, and women spectators were encouraged to attend." Games started at 4:00 P.M.

The park was located next to a terminal for a horse trolley traction company. Presumably, spectators from center city could ride to the games with ease.

During the Civil War, the park was occupied by a cavalry of the Union Army. In 1866, with new houses bordering the grounds, which were then called Columbia Park, the field was put back in shape for baseball and a nine-foot fence was erected around the entire field. Baseball playing resumed on the site for amateur teams—with names such as Swiftfoot, Hatters, and Alert—as well as a prominent team of black players called the Philadelphia Pythians.

By 1871, however, with the site having been poorly maintained, the park was used less and less frequently. It remained in that state until 1875 when the Philadelphia Centennials of the newly formed National Association made the park their home. The Centennials leveled and resodded the field, erected a 10-foot fence around it, built a clubhouse, and put up grandstands. They called the field Centennial Park.

"The most distinctive feature of the new ballpark was a mammoth sign advertising the *Sunday Item* newspaper," wrote Casway. "It could be seen throughout the city."

Crowds of up to 5,000 attended games at the park. The National Association, however, folded after the 1875 season. The Centennials disbanded, leaving the park to be used by the White Stockings and the Athletics, each of which had also been franchised in the original National Association but had dropped out and become semiprofessional teams.

By the late 1870s, even those teams stopped playing there, as neglect turned the park into a rundown dump with overgrown weeds and deteriorating grandstands blighting the landscape. Much of the site of the old ballpark was converted into a horse market.

But help was just around the corner. It came in the form of Alfred J. Reach, a resourceful Philadelphia resident with a keen interest in baseball.

Reach, a native of Great Britain, had been a star lefthanded second baseman for the Athletics, a team that traveled the country playing baseball games in the 1860s. His chief claim to fame then was that in 1864 he had become the first baseball player known to have accepted a salary.

The sport's first professional had led the Athletics to the pennant in the first year of the National Association in 1871. Later, he managed the team and also opened a sporting goods store in Philadelphia. Eventually, Reach and Benjamin F. Shibe, a leather expert and manufacturer of whips, formed a partnership to manufacture sporting goods at a plant at Palmer and Tulip Streets in North Philadelphia.

Reach never surrendered his passion for baseball, and in 1882, hoping to attract a National League franchise to Philadelphia, he formed an independent team called "Fillies" and obtained the grounds on the peculiar lot at 24th and Columbia, which he renamed Recreation Park, as the home field.

The new owner cleared the grounds, leveled and resodded the playing surface, and built a three-section wooden grandstand. The main section contained folding chairs and private boxes in the rear. Benches lined the outfield. Dressing rooms and offices were built along the sides of the grandstand, and a press box was located on top of it.

The park had a total capacity of about 6,500, which included 1,500 in the grandstands, another 2,000 in bleachers in the outfield, and the rest standing.

The Fillies played their first game at Recreation Park on April 8, 1882. Major league baseball arrived one year later.

In late 1882, Reach was approached by an old friend, Colonel A. G. Mills, a former player who had become president of the National League, about operating a team in Philadelphia. Mills told Reach that he would move the ailing Worcester (Massachusetts) Brown Stockings franchise to Philadelphia if the now highly successful sporting goods manufacturer was interested.

Citing Philadelphia and New York, where he wanted to move the Troy, New York, franchise, Mills said, "We've got to get these big cities back into our league. Both New York and Philadelphia have tremendous futures, and some day their populations will be in the millions."

Mills had no trouble convincing Reach of the merits of his plan. "I'm in," Reach responded. "Let's get going."

Reach enlisted the aid of Colonel John I. Rogers, a Philadelphia lawyer and member of the governor's staff, and the two formed a partnership in which each owned 50 percent of the team.

Because no players were involved in the shift of franchises, the partners had to recruit minor leaguers and others they were able to lure away from existing major league teams. They named the group the Phillies, after the city in which the team would play, and started work on turning Recreation Park into a major league stadium.

The brand new Phillies conducted their first spring training at Recreation Park. Their first game was played April 2, 1883, when they faced the

Ashland Club, a semipro team from Manayunk. The Phillies won as John Coleman pitched a no-hitter.

A few weeks later, the Phillies played the Athletics of the American Association in what may have been part of the first real City Series. Some 10,000 bugs (fans) squeezed into every available space to watch the contest.

Opening day was approaching, and to prepare for it, Reach had his crew go to work sprucing up the park. They added a small upper deck to the stands behind home plate, placed an awning over the press box, installed a large clock on wooden supports near home plate, and painted the seats red and the outfield walls white.

Unfortunately, the white fence proved to be bothersome to the vision of batters. So did the setting sun, which shined directly into batters' eyes as they stood at home plate. Actually, the park wasn't much of a place for hitters anyway. In the four years that the Phillies played there, the club collected a mere 21 home runs, 5 of them by second baseman Charlie Bastien, hardly a noted power-hitter.

Such drawbacks notwithstanding, the Phillies opened their first season May 1, 1883, at Recreation Park against the Providence Grays. Facing Charles (Old Hoss) Radbourne, who went on to win 48 games that year, the Phillies had a 3–0 lead after seven innings, but Providence rallied with four runs in the eighth to hand the Phillies and Coleman a 4–3 defeat. Coleman, who would lose 48 games that season while pitching 65 games and 538 innings, gave up just six hits.

The 1883 Phillies were a curious collection of fringe major leaguers who were managed by their second baseman, Bob Ferguson, a veteran player with a hot temper and the unusual nickname of "Death to Flying Things," a label hung on him because of his ability to catch anything hit in the air near him. The team's first baseman was a gent named Sid Farrar, who not only batted ninth most of the time, but became much more familiar to the public as the father of famed opera star Geraldine Farrar.

The first Phillies team was subjected to all kinds of atrocities during the season. It lost one game to Boston, 29–4, another to Providence, 28–0, in the highest scoring shutout victory in major league history, and was no-hit by Cleveland's Hugh Dailey, 1–0. Ferguson quit as manager after the team won just four of its first 17 games. Then under Bill (Blondie) Purcell, the Phillies went on to their most dismal record, winning 17 and losing 81.

During the season, the Phillies were a distant second to the neighboring Athletics in the minds of local baseball fans. The Athletics, on their way to the American Association pennant while playing at nearby Jefferson Park at 25th and Jefferson, far outdrew the Phillies. What's more, they charged just 25 cents for admission.

Recreation Park was the original home of the Phillies. Here is a partial view of the park and the 1884 Phillies.

National League teams were required to charge 50 cents. To offset that and to try to lure fans away from the Athletics, Reach gave away two free horse-trolley tickets worth 12 cents to every fan who bought a 50-cent ticket to a Phillies game. The ploy didn't work. Reach then persuaded the league to allow him to charge 25 cents for game tickets. That still didn't help much, and eventually Reach was obligated to rent Recreation Park for other sporting events, particularly bicycle racing and college football.

The Phillies, meanwhile, improved their status in 1884. Of critical significance was Reach's hiring of legendary manager Harry Wright, one of baseball's brightest pioneers and a man who came to be known as the Father of Professional Baseball because of his many innovations.

Wright, who served as the Phillies pilot until 1893, led the club to respectability during its remaining years at Recreation Park, not only because of his managerial skills but because of the influx of solid players he was able to sign. Included in this group were such early Phillies stars as third baseman Joe Mulvey; outfielder Jim Fogarty; lefthanded catcher Jack Clements; and pitchers Ed Daily, Dan Casey, who until his death in 1943 steadfastly claimed that he was the subject of Ernest Thayer's legendary poem "Casey at the Bat," and particularly Charlie Ferguson.

Ferguson was the most popular and most successful Phillies player to perform at Recreation Park. Between his rookie year in 1884 through 1886 he won 77 games, highlighting his stay with a 30–9 record in 1886. On August 29, 1885, at Recreation Park, Ferguson pitched the first

Phillies no-hitter, defeating Providence, 1–0, while striking out eight and walking two. And when he wasn't pitching, he played second base and was considered one of the team's best hitters.

Tragically, Ferguson died of typhoid fever at the age of 25 in the spring of 1888, one year after the Phillies had moved to their new grounds at Philadelphia Park. His passing not only left a huge void in the Phillies' lineup, but sent the whole city into a state of prolonged mourning.

As Wright shepherded the Phillies up the National League ladder, the club began to attract more fans, even outdrawing the rival Athletics. By 1886, Recreation Park was packed for each game, and Reach was getting anxious to move to a larger ballpark.

"We are having difficulty finding space for all the people who want to pay to see us play," Reach said. "Our Ridge Avenue park isn't big enough to handle our crowds. We've got a real team now, and we've got to get a park worthy of our team."

The 1886 season turned out to be the Phillies' last at Recreation Park. After four years, the park had become obsolete, and the Phillies were moving to a new stadium.

Recreation Park was returned to local sandlot teams. They would play there for a few more years. Eventually, houses were built on the field. There are no signs today that a ballpark—a significant one at that—ever stood on the site. Its place, now part of a rundown section of the city, is occupied by a few homes, a storefront church, and mostly a decayed collection of abandoned houses and businesses.

Columbia Park

First Home of the Athletics

*F*or a ballpark that had such a short lifespan, Columbia Park played a prominent role in the evolution of major league baseball in Philadelphia.

The park functioned as a major league stadium for just eight seasons. During that period, however, it gave birth to a new league, was the site of a World Series, and was the field upon which numerous future Hall of Famers launched their careers.

Located on a rectangular lot bordered by 29th Street, Columbia Avenue, 30th Street, and Oxford Street in North Philadelphia, Columbia Park was the first home of the Philadelphia Athletics. As such, it was therefore also the first American League stadium in Philadelphia.

Although there had been earlier teams in Philadelphia called the Athletics, the Athletics who played in Columbia Park were newcomers to the city in 1901. They had arrived as a new team in the new American League, which had been started by an enterprising former Cincinnati sportswriter named Byron Bancroft (Ban) Johnson.

Johnson was the longtime president of an independent minor league called the Western League. Desiring major league status for his league, Johnson had renamed it the American League in 1900. In 1901, he reorganized the league and declared it a true major league, the equal of the National League.

In reorganizing, Johnson placed a team in Philadelphia (as well as ones in Chicago and Boston) to go along with existing teams in Baltimore, Cleveland, Detroit, Milwaukee, and Washington. And he persuaded a former big league catcher, whose real name was Cornelius McGillicuddy but who was called Connie Mack, to come to Philadelphia to organize the new team.

Mack had been a light-hitting but highly respected catcher with Washington and Pittsburgh in the National League before becoming manager of the Pirates in 1894. After getting fired by the Pirates following the 1896 season, he resurfaced as manager and part owner of the Milwaukee team in Johnson's Western League.

Johnson was highly impressed with the way Mack operated, and by the time he made his move into the big time, the slender ex-catcher had become one of the league president's top supporters. Mack was a natural candidate to establish a new team in Johnson's ambitious enterprise.

Mack, appointed manager and minority stockholder by Johnson, arrived in Philadelphia with no players and no stadium. Moreover, he also had to raise operating capital, which meant he had to find investors in the team.

Mack was led to Benjamin F. Shibe, a partner of Phillies owner Al Reach in a sporting goods business. With the blessing of Reach, Shibe became the Athletics' principal investor.

The next step was to build a ballpark. Although several other plots were considered, Mack found a suitable property in the Brewerytown section of Philadelphia. Taking a 10-year lease on the grounds—at the time a vacant lot with houses surrounding it on the adjacent streets—Mack soon initiated construction of a ballpark.

Columbia Park was erected at a cost of $35,000. It had a seating capacity of 9,500 with covered, wooden grandstands extending on either side of the field from home plate to first and third bases. A wire screen ran along the top of the grandstand roof, an apparent attempt to keep foul balls from leaving the park. Open bleachers continued from the grandstands down both foul lines. Another small bleacher section ran across left field. A small press box sat atop the bleachers behind home plate.

Home plate at Columbia Park was at the corner of Oxford and 30th Streets. Above the right field wall bordering 29th Street, 25-foot-high chicken wire extended from the right field bleachers to center field.

The Athletics dressed in a small clubhouse under the stands. Visiting players changed into their uniforms at their center-city hotel and generally rode trolleys or horse-drawn carriages to the ballpark. There were no dugouts. Players sat on wooden benches in front of the grandstands.

When games were taking place at Columbia Park, the aroma of hops and freshly brewed beer from nearby breweries often wafted across the stadium. Beer, of course, was not sold at the ballpark.

While his team played at Columbia Park, Connie Mack lived in a house across the street from the field at 2932 Oxford Street. Eventually, many players moved into the neighborhood, too.

Columbia Park (looking in from left field) featured an enclosed wooden grandstand with a tiny press box on the roof.

Emil Beck, now 100 years old but then a youth living in the neighborhood, clearly remembered those days. "Rube Waddell, Chief Bender, and a lot of others lived in the area," he said. "You could often see Connie Mack and some of the players walking through the neighborhood. We used to chase after them as they walked to the ballpark.

"It cost a quarter to see a game," Beck added. "You had to pass through big steel turnstiles to get into the park. There weren't many vendors in there, but you could get a hot dog and a soda.

"The crowd was pretty refined. Everybody rooted for the Athletics. It was a good park for watching a game. The playing field was always in very good shape."

The playing field was put to its first test on April 26, 1901. That's when the first game was played at Columbia Park.

By then, Mack had filled his roster with an assortment of players culled from other major as well as minor league teams. Several, including Napoleon Lajoie, Chick Fraser, and Bill Bernhard, had been lured away from the Phillies in what had been part of a major effort by American League teams to raid the rival National League of some of its leading players (other Phillies would be pirated the following year).

The opening game had been postponed twice because of rain. But it was finally held, and with an overflow crowd of 10,524 in attendance, including people standing atop the outfield walls and on the roofs of neighborhood houses, the First Regiment Band playing fervently before the game, and mayor Samuel Ashbridge striding through the stands to throw out the first ball, the Athletics lost to the Washington Nationals, 5–1. Lajoie had three hits, and Fraser was the losing pitcher.

Despite the loss, an account in the Philadelphia *Public Ledger* gushed ecstatically about the event.

"Another epoch in the history of local baseball was written yesterday afternoon at Twenty-ninth and Columbia Avenue when the stamp of public approval was inscribed upon the escutcheon of the American League, the occasion being the opening championship game between the Athletics and Washington," the article babbled. "The latter won by the score of 5 to 1, but considered purely from a local point of view, it is doubtful if the great national game ever received such a tribute from the sport loving populace."

The lead article in the Philadelphia *Inquirer* was more subdued. "The game itself will never be recalled as a sample of the National pastime at its best estate," it said, "and yet but for the fact that it was witnessed by such a tremendous crowd, the chances are that it would have been voted a pretty entertaining affair."

Curiously, the locals' enthusiasm was not maintained. Despite a winning record (74–62) and fourth place finish by the Athletics, just 206,329 fans had passed through the turnstiles, an average of slightly less than 3,300 per game.

That would turn out to be by far the Athletics' lowest season's attendance at Columbia Park. They drew 442,473 in 1902, and only one other year attracted less than that during their eight-year stay at the park. The crowd reached a high of 625,581 in 1907.

Meanwhile, the A's for the most part were fielding excellent teams made up of outstanding players. Second baseman Lajoie, who in 1902 would be banned from playing for the A's by the Pennsylvania Supreme Court (as were Fraser and Bernhard), won the triple crown in 1901, setting a still-standing American League record with a .422 batting average, 14 home runs, and 125 RBI. In one of the greatest single seasons ever staged, he also led the league in runs scored (145), hits (229), slugging average (.635), total bases (342), and doubles (48).

While they played at Columbia Park, Athletics players won six home run titles. Right fielder Ralph (Socks) Seybold led the league with 16 home runs in 1902, and team captain and first baseman Harry Davis won the home run crown four straight seasons, between 1904 and 1907, and twice led the circuit in RBI. Little five-foot-five left fielder Topsy Hartsel topped the league in bases on balls five times.

As good as they were with the bat, the Athletics had equally fine pitching. Their Columbia Park days were marked by the outstanding hurling of Waddell and Eddie Plank. Waddell, the eccentric lefthander with the crackling fastball and the penchant for chasing fire trucks, won more than 20 games four years in a row, and in 1904 set a major league strikeout record by blowing away 349 batters. That record stood for 42 years. The southpaw Plank, the first 20th-century pitcher to win 300 games, also enjoyed his best seasons at Columbia Park, five times winning 20 or more games.

Chief Bender and Jimmy Dygert also produced outstanding seasons on the mound while Columbia Park was their home field. Bender, as well as Plank, Waddell, Lajoie, second baseman Eddie Collins, who got his major league start at Columbia Park in 1907 as a skinny shortstop out of Columbia University playing under the name of Sullivan, and Frank (Home Run) Baker, who played in nine games in 1908, all ascended to the Hall of Fame.

Shoeless Joe Jackson launched his career at Columbia Park. Signed originally by Mack out of the backwoods of South Carolina, the ill-fated batting titan played briefly in 1908 with the Athletics before jumping the club and returning home, a stunt he repeated the following year.

The Athletics had an assortment of other fine players while they performed at Columbia Park. Included in the group were second baseman and later right fielder Danny Murphy, center fielder Rube Oldring, catcher Ossee Schreckengost, pitcher Jack Coombs, and third baseman Lave Cross, who had the unusual distinction of having played with four Philadelphia major league teams in the National League, American Association, Players' League, and American League.

During their residence at Columbia Park, the Athletics won two American League pennants and finished second twice. The first flag flew in 1902 when the A's posted an 83–53 record and danced home five games ahead of the St. Louis Browns. Because the National League still refused to recognize the American League, there was no World Series that year.

A World Series was held, however, at Columbia Park in 1905. That year, with the capacity of the park increased to 13,600, the Athletics rumbled to the American League pennant with a 92–56 record, edging the Chicago White Sox by two games.

The Athletics went into first place to stay on August 2 as Waddell struck out 14 and beat the Chicago White Sox, 4–3, at Columbia Park. Then, in a thrilling three-game series at Columbia Park one week before the season ended, the Athletics took two games from the White Sox to establish a lead they never relinquished. Plank captured a 3–2 victory in the opener. Bender followed with an 11–1 decision in the second game.

Waddell, who had won 10 straight games earlier in the season, was injured and unable to pitch. One week earlier, on a train bringing the A's

An estimated 30,000 fans watched from all angles when the
Athletics and Detroit Tigers played in a memorable 17-inning game
in 1907.

back to Philadelphia, he had engaged in a scuffle with pitcher Andy Coakley. Plank was forced to take the mound for the third game. The weary southpaw lost a 4–3 verdict to George Owen and the White Sox with a ballpark record of 25,187 in attendance, but Chicago left town trailing the Athletics by one and one-half games.

The World Series opened October 9 at Columbia Park with the Athletics facing the New York Giants in what was the first best-of-seven series format. Haughty Giants manager John McGraw had refused to let his team meet the Boston Pilgrims in the 1904 Series, but this time consented to send his club against the rival American League.

The Giants arrived at Columbia Park wearing black uniforms, an attempt on McGraw's part to intimidate the opposing A's. The ploy was probably unnecessary, as the Giants' record of 105–48 for the season was intimidating enough.

New York featured 31-game winner Christy Mathewson, 22-game winner Red Ames, and Iron Man Joe McGinnity, who had won 21. The Giants' best hitter was Mike Donlin, who had hit .356.

Although the Athletics had no .300 hitters, Davis had won the home run and RBI titles and the club had a marvelous pitching staff, led by three 20-game winners, Waddell (26-11), whose injured shoulder prevented him from taking the mound in the Series, Plank (25–12), and Coakley

(20–7). The 21-year-old Bender, a part Chippewa Indian in his third year with the A's, had a 16–10 mark.

In perhaps the most magnificently pitched Series in history, the Giants won, four games to one, with all five games being won by shutouts. The redoubtable Mathewson, who had signed a contract in 1901 with the Athletics but jumped to the Giants before ever playing a game in Philadelphia livery, hurled three of them.

Mathewson, a Bucknell graduate, defeated his old college rival, Gettysburg's Plank, 3–0, with a four-hitter in the first game. After Bender four-hit the Giants for a 3–0 decision at the Polo Grounds in the second game, Mathewson came back with two days' rest and hurled the Series' third-straight four-hitter, beating the Athletics, 9–0, at Columbia Park. First baseman Dan McGann drove in four runs with two singles and a double.

Plank fired a four-hitter in the fourth game, which was played back in New York. But an unearned run on errors by infielders Monte Cross and Lave Cross gave the Giants and McGinnity a 1–0 victory. The final game, also played at the Polo Grounds, ended with Mathewson allowing six hits to Bender's five but with the Giants on top, 2–0.

Although they lost the Series, the Athletics were feted with a massive parade along Broad Street when they returned to Philadelphia. Amateur and semipro players from Pennsylvania, New Jersey, and Delaware took part in the parade. The A's and some of the Giants players rode in open cars.

"Broad Street was an impassable mass of human beings when the parade started," wrote H. Walter Schlichter in the Philadelphia *Evening Item*, "and the greatest difficulty was experienced by the police, which headed the procession, in forcing a passage for the marchers and floats. It was past midnight when the route laid out was covered by the great army of marching fans, but the crowd waited to the end, and the enthusiasm was kept up to the last."

An estimated 300,000 fans lined the parade route. When the players came into view, fans broke past the police barriers in a frenzied effort to get closer to their heroes.

There were no other World Series at Columbia Park. But there had been and would continue to be plenty of excitement. Brilliant individual performances and memorable games were common at the ballpark.

Seybold once hit a ball that was said to have hit a telegraph pole on Hollywood Street, which ran behind Columbia Avenue. Waddell made his debut in 1902 with a two-hit shutout of the Baltimore Orioles in a game in which he faced just 27 batters (one was caught stealing, the other was picked off first base). Center fielder Ollie Pickering hit a dramatic 14th-inning home run on June 12, 1903, to give Waddell a 2–1 victory over Addie Joss and the Cleveland Naps. Waddell set a one-game strikeout record on July 14, 1903, by fanning 14 Chicago batters. And on September 10, 1904, Plank pitched and drove in the only run in a 13-inning, 1–0 victory over Boston and Cy Young.

On September 20, 1902, Columbia Park had one of its biggest crowds when 23,897 fans watched the Athletics defeat Boston, 7–2, to clinch the American League pennant. Thousands were turned away at the gate.

No doubt the most memorable game occurred at the park on September 30, 1907. At the time, the Athletics, Detroit Tigers, and White Sox were locked in a tense battle for the pennant. The A's were in first place three points ahead of the Tigers when Detroit came to town for a crucial three-game series starting Friday, September 27. The New York *Times* said it would be "the greatest struggle in the history of baseball."

In the first game, the Tigers beat Plank, 5–4, before a crowd of 17,926. Rain canceled the game the next day, and with no Sunday baseball permitted, a doubleheader was scheduled for Monday, September 30.

A huge crowd that included 24,127 who paid to watch and another 2,000 who got in free by climbing the fences jammed the grandstands and the outfield. Thousands more stood on ladders, hay bales, and the roofs of nearby houses to watch the battle. "If it had been possible to accommodate them, 50,000 people would have attended the game," said the Philadelphia *North American*. What the massive throng saw was a fiercely

Avid fans paid two dollars to watch from rooftops along Columbia Avenue as the A's and Tigers battled.

played 17-inning game that ranks as one of the most memorable in Philadelphia baseball history.

The Athletics jumped on Philadelphia native Wild Bill Donovan, later to become a Phillies manager, taking an early 7–1 lead. Waddell replaced an ineffective A's starter Jimmy Dygert in the second inning, but slowly the Tigers narrowed the deficit to 7–5. Finally, in the ninth inning, Detroit's emerging star Ty Cobb socked a Waddell pitch over the right field wall to tie the score at 9–9.

Plank replaced Waddell as the game went into extra innings. Donovan, with a large contingent of family and friends in the stands, continued to pitch for Detroit. Then in the 14th inning, the Athletics' Davis hit a drive into the crowd behind the ropes in left-center field. Although such a hit would normally have been ruled a ground-rule double, Detroit center fielder Sam Crawford claimed that a policeman interfered with him, preventing him from making the catch.

Umpire Silk O'Loughlin deliberated for several minutes, and as he did, a fight broke out after the opportunistic Cobb told teammate Claude Rossman that the Athletics' Monte Cross had called him a "Jew bastard." Other players soon joined the melee before order was restored by the police. Finally, O'Loughlin called Davis out. The Athletics were outraged, and even normally mild-mannered manager Connie Mack, who from the start of his A's career had piloted the team while wearing street clothes, protested vigorously. The decision, of course, was upheld, and when Murphy followed with a single that would have scored Davis with the winning run, the A's were even more chagrined. The game clamored on for three more innings before it was called because of darkness. After nearly four hours and 17 innings, the score was still tied at 9–9. Naturally, the second game was not played.

Many fans scrambled over the wall to get inside Columbia Park for the 1907 game.

"A victory for the Athletics in this great game would have brought to Philadelphia the American League pennant for the third time," wrote Ray Ziegler in the Philadelphia *Record*. "Wouldn't it have been grand to have a record of three championships in eight years to point back to the old field where the American League was so successfully launched?"

"Crawford," Ziegler added, "had never gotten up to the ball, and Davis should have been allowed a two-base hit under the ground rules."

Mack was so incensed that for one of the rare times in his career, he issued a blistering statement. "If ever there was such a thing as crooked baseball, today's game would stand as a good example," he said, asserting that he thought the umpires had conspired against him.

No other game at Columbia Park ever produced such controversy. But there was another set of games that annually generated widespread interest among the local fans. The games were called the City Series, and they pitted the Athletics and the Phillies against each other.

The first modern City Series game was played April 6, 1903, at Columbia Park. In it, Fred Mitchell pitched a four-hitter to lead the Phillies to a 2–0 victory in 10 innings. Waddell took the loss, allowing just two hits and striking out 11.

Altogether, 26 City Series games were played at Columbia Park, with each team winning 13.

The Phillies briefly used the park as their home field in 1903 after a balcony collapsed at the club's Philadelphia Park. The disaster killed 12 fans and injured 232. Forced to find new quarters while their park was being repaired, the Phillies relocated to Columbia Park.

Nine consecutive rainouts prevented the Phillies from making their debut at Columbia Park until August 20. From then until September 10, they played 16 games there, winning 6, losing 9, and tying 1.

Although the Athletics drew well at Columbia Park, the little wooden stadium didn't hold enough people to suit Mack and Shibe. Often, as the park filled to capacity, the gates had to be shut, leaving thousands of fans on the outside. Envisioning higher profits based on larger crowds at a bigger park, the A's owners dumped their original site after the 1908 season, moving to the newly constructed Shibe Park.

"Columbia Park stood for another three or four years after the A's left," recalled Emil Beck. "The circus and a few other events were held there. But finally the park was knocked down, and houses were built on the site."

An era that had been brief but eventful had become just a memory.

Philadelphia Park/ Baker Bowl

Unusual in Almost Every Way

*I*n the 51½ years that it served as the home of the Philadelphia Phillies, Baker Bowl was one of the most eccentric ballparks in major league baseball.

Located on an odd-shaped plot bounded by Broad Street, Lehigh Avenue, 15th Street, and Huntingdon Avenue in North Philadelphia, not only was the ballpark a peculiar configuration itself, but its existence was fraught with events and situations that ranged from bizarre to absurd.

The park was the site of high humor and awful tragedy, of performances that ranged from the brilliant to the wretched, of drama, deceit, death, and destruction. Three major disasters and numerous smaller ones occurred at the park.

Adding to its checkered history, Baker Bowl probably suffered more abuse than any other professional baseball park. Usually brought on by its own failures or shortcomings, the park was often damned but rarely praised. Especially in its later years, players, fans, and writers all directed a steady flow of insults at the withering old stadium.

Yet, despite its many flaws, Baker Bowl was as fascinating as it was unusual, and it commands an important place in the history of Philadelphia major league baseball.

It was the place where the Phillies went to their first World Series. Remarkably for the Phillies, it was also the place where the club once staged nine consecutive first division finishes. And it was the site of some of the most extraordinary performances and events ever witnessed on a baseball field.

Baker Bowl was the home field of Hall of Famers Ed Delahanty, Grover Cleveland Alexander, Chuck Klein, Billy Hamilton, Sam Thompson, Nap Lajoie, Dave Bancroft, and Eppa Rixey. Other fine players such as Sherry Magee, Roy Thomas, Gavvy Cravath, Cy Williams, Fred Luderus, Dick Bartell, Johnny Moore, and Jimmie Wilson also called it home. Jack Clements, baseball's most enduring lefthanded catcher, and Bill Hulen, the only regular lefthanded shortstop in baseball history, also played for the Phillies at Baker Bowl. So did Earle (Greasy) Neale, who would later coach the Philadelphia Eagles to two NFL championships, future Hall of Fame manager Casey Stengel, and Billy Sunday, who played his last game there before embarking on a career in which he became a world-renowned evangelist.

It was a ballpark that had character. It had a long and colorful history. And, many decades after it has been gone, it still exists vividly in the minds of those who saw it.

"It's not a park you could easily forget," recalled Claude Passeau, the Phillies starting pitcher in the last game at Baker Bowl in 1938. "It was about as unique a park as I ever played in."

Originally built at a cost of $101,000, Baker Bowl when it opened in 1887 was regarded as the finest stadium in the nation, a magnificent showplace that was the pride of Philadelphia and the envy of other cities. By 1938, when the Phillies moved out, the enigmatic park was not only the oldest in baseball, but also the laughingstock of the game, an obsolete relic that was damned and discredited and derisively called such names as "toilet bowl," "cigar box," and "bandbox."

The park was initially known as the Philadelphia Base Ball Park or Huntingdon Street Grounds. It was built on a dump that was lower than street level, with Cohosksink Creek running through it. It took some 100,000 wagon-loads of dirt to fill the gullies on the field and another 20,000 loads to bring the site even with the adjacent streets.

The master plan for the park, devised by Phillies president and principal owner Al Reach, was the most modern and advanced of the era and unlike that of any other stadium that had been previously built. It incorporated brick, instead of the commonly used wood, and pavilions for seating.

The outside of the stadium, which at the main entrance looked more like a castle than a ballpark, was all brick. Paneled brick with ornamental moldings also enclosed the playing field. The seating capacity was 12,500, with 5,000 seats in a pavilion rising 23 rows on one side of home plate and

An artist's rendition of the original Philadelphia Base Ball Park
when it was opened in 1887.

16 rows on the other and 7,500 seats in grandstands that extended down
the left and right field lines. No seats were in the outfield.

Each end of the pavilion was topped by two 75-foot-high turrets. Another turret, located over the main entrance, was 165 feet high and 39 feet
in diameter. Sheds for 55 horse-drawn carriages were located beneath the
grandstands.

Although the main entrance of the park was at 15th and Huntingdon,
there were six other entrances. One was along 15th Street, one was along
Huntingdon, and one allowed access to the left field bleachers along
Lehigh Avenue. The other three entrances were kept closed except for
emergencies.

Reading Railroad tracks paralleled the park across Broad Street. A train
tunnel ran under the center field section of the park, making that area
some 10 feet higher than home plate. Often, locomotives would billow
smoke or spray sparks on the grandstands, occasionally starting small fires
on the wooden floors or seats.

Perhaps the most unusual characteristic of the park was its lopsided dimensions. In the original park the distance was more than 400 feet from
home plate to the wall in left field, 408 feet to straightaway center, and a

The main entrance of the park at 15th and Huntingdon resembled an old castle.

tantalizingly short 300 feet down the right field line. In later years, those distances would change several times, with left field eventually becoming 341.5 feet and right field closing to 272 feet before it was pushed back to its final distance of 280.5 feet.

Because of the small space in which the park was situated, the playing field was extremely close to the stands. That not only meant that foul balls that would have been caught in most parks fell safely into the stands, it also put the paying customers and the players close together. To fans, that was an asset.

"One of the great things about Baker Bowl was that you could sit in the stands and see the expressions on the guys' faces on the field," said Ed (Dutch) Doyle, a prominent Philadelphia baseball historian who began going to games at the park in the late 1920s. "You could hear them yelling to each other; you could almost shake hands with them, you were so close to the field."

From a player's standpoint, the proximity to the fans had other implications. "We could sit in the dugout and smell the peanuts in the stands," pitcher Bucky Walters said. It was also possible to hear more clearly the insults hurled by the often-disgruntled fans.

A Grand Opening

The first game at Philadelphia Park was played April 30, 1887. The whole city of Philadelphia celebrated the event, which started when the Phillies and opposing New York Giants were escorted up Broad Street in open carriages.

A crowd estimated to be close to 20,000, one of the largest throngs ever to attend a baseball game and including some 3,000 specially invited guests of the Phillies, jammed the ballpark far beyond its capacity. Phillies management was forced to rope off the outfield to allow standing room for the overflow.

Although baseball crowds of the era usually consisted mostly of men and boys, spectators at the inaugural were evenly divided between men and women. Among those in attendance were Mayor Edwin Fitler and most other prominent city officials, plus a large contingent of socialites, another rarity in the era of rough-and-tumble baseball fans who were then often referred to as cranks or bugs.

The game was such an important event that the Athletics, playing Brooklyn in an American Association game that day at 25th and Jefferson Streets, moved their starting time up several hours so their fans could see both games.

Beck's Military Band gave a concert before the game. Then came the official opening of the park.

"The formal ceremony of raising the club's flag was a picturesque scene, all of the players and the visiting and home teams participating," reported the *Evening Bulletin* the next day, "and as manager Harry Wright raised the big flag to the breeze, three mighty cheers that must have been heard for miles rent the air."

The cheering continued as the game got under way as the first nine Phillies batters in the first inning all hit safely and nine runs were scored.

During the game, the crowd that had been herded behind the ropes in the outfield occasionally surged forward. Numerous hits went among the spectators and were declared ground-rule doubles. The game was called because of darkness in the eighth inning, with Ed Andrews getting the first hit, George Wood slugging the first home run, and Charlie Ferguson posting the win as the Phillies marched off with a 19–10 victory in what would launch the club's most successful season up to that point. Engaged in a spirited pennant race all season long with the Detroit Wolverines and the Chicago White Stockings, the Phillies finished in second place. Fans flocked to the park in huge numbers, and the stadium received countless testimonials to its beauty and modern design.

In the years that followed, the Phillies heavily outdrew the rival Athletics. But Reach and his partner, Colonel John Rogers, searched constantly for ways to help pay for their ballpark. One way was to capitalize on the popularity of bicycle racing by building a quarter-mile track around the edge of the field. The track was 15 feet wide and had banked turns. Often outfielders were forced to run up the banks to catch fly balls.

The Wall of Horrors

Nothing at Baker Bowl compared to the infamous right field wall, an instrument of heartbreak for pitchers and jubilation for hitters. If there is one oddity for which the park is remembered, it's the extraordinarily close wall that loomed bigger than life along Broad Street.

Unlike the legendary "Green Monster" of Fenway Park, Baker Bowl's wall had no catchy nickname. But just as Wrigley Field was noted for its ivy, Yankee Stadium for its monuments, and Sportsman's Park for its rock-hard infield, Baker Bowl and its right field wall were synonomous. It was merely a long, black, ugly wall that extended from the right field grandstands to the center field bleachers, but it was the park's most prominent characteristic as well as its most enduring feature.

Originally 300 feet from home plate and 40 feet high with a stone base, the wall eventually became 280.5 feet from home and 60 feet high with a 20-foot screen on top. Lazy fly balls that would have normally been caught invariably went for home runs, and often scorching line drives that should have been four-baggers dropped for mere singles or doubles.

The wall was so close that it once prompted the fabled sportswriter Red Smith to note, "It might be exaggerating to say the outfield wall casts a shadow across the infield. But if the right fielder had eaten onions at lunch, the second baseman knew it."

Many times, home run balls cleared Broad Street and landed on the railroad tracks of the Reading line. Cars being driven along Broad Street during a game were always at risk of having balls crash into their windshields. The Phillies reimbursed drivers for any such mishap.

Several generations of lefthanded batters, most notably the Phillies' Cy Williams, Chuck Klein, Don Hurst, Fred Luderus, Dolph Camilli, and Johnny Moore, as well as Mel Ott and Bill Terry of the Giants, Babe Herman of the Dodgers, Jim Bottomley of the Cardinals, and Paul Waner of the Pirates, saw their home run totals soar at Baker Bowl. In 13 years of playing there, Ott hit 40 home runs at the park.

But no one hit more home runs at Baker Bowl than Klein. With the

Baker Bowl's short right field wall was a tin relic that was full of pockmarks.

wall looming within such close range, he hit 164 of them there, including 156 as a Phillie. Williams, who exploded for 23 of his league-leading 41 home runs in 1923 at Baker Bowl, followed with 140. Predictably, 9 of the Phillies' top 12 home run producers at Baker Bowl were lefthanded batters.

"It was an easy target," said outfielder Lefty O'Doul, who hit 32 homers there in two years with the Phillies. "Every time I went to bat, I looked at that high fence and I felt sure I could hit it. That old fence sure gave me some confidence."

First baseman Camilli had a somewhat different view. "Sometimes I wonder if that park was much of an advantage for me," he said. "I liked big parks better because the line drives I hit at Baker Bowl were singles, while they would have been home runs in some of the bigger parks. But I guess it all evened out."

Although the nearby wall favored lefthanded batters, it was a highly inviting target for righthanders, too. And that included visiting players, especially sluggers such as Rogers Hornsby, Hack Wilson, and Joe Medwick.

"Everybody aimed for right," said the National League's first All-Star Game shortstop Dick Bartell in his book *Rowdy Richard*. "I've seen high fly balls the second baseman could go out and catch come down against the fence for doubles. But if you hit it with a hard drive, you had to run like the devil to get to second or the right fielder would throw you out. A few times Ernie Lombardi hit the fence, and was thrown out at first."

Right fielders, especially the Phillies' Klein and Moore, learned the nuances of the tin wall and played it to their advantage. Although he possessed one of the strongest throwing arms in Phillies' history, Klein's National League record of 44 assists was greatly enhanced by the short length of right field and his ability to play the wall. "He played that wall like a violin," said Joe Holden, a Phillies catcher in the 1930s.

"Playing right field in Baker Bowl was the softest job in baseball," said Casey Stengel, who patrolled right field for the Phillies in the early 1920s. "I had the wall behind me and the second baseman in front of me. The foul line was on my left, Cy Williams, the center fielder, was on my right. The only time I had a chance to catch the ball was when it was hit right at me."

Johnny Moore, who played right field with skill and dexterity in the 1930s, once revealed his secret for playing the wall. "Telegraph poles held up the fence in right field," he remembered. "If a ball hit the fence, it would drop straight down. If it hit a pole, it would bounce all the way back to the infield. I knew where every pole was, so I could tell how to play each ball that was hit out there. Of course, if you were the batter and you hit a line drive to right field, you'd have to run like hell to make it to first base. If you didn't you were liable to get thrown out because the right fielder was playing so close."

The wall, however, not only changed the way hitters approached each at-bat, it altered the way pitchers worked. Most of them got little enjoyment out of drawing a starting assignment at Baker Bowl. "When visiting teams came in, all their pitchers would always come up with lame arms," said Bucky Walters, who launched a fine pitching career with the Phillies in the mid-1930s. "But it wasn't the home runs that hurt you the most. It was those damn outs that hit the fence that gave you the most trouble. An ordinary fly ball would hit the fence, and the guy would get a double."

"You had to pitch altogether differently than you would at any other field," said Claude Passeau. "I didn't have a curveball, so I pitched high inside, low inside. But it was never any fun. Even the righthanders would square off against you and hit to right. They could pepper that wall.

"Often, you'd have a situation where the first man up in the first inning would hit an easy fly ball to right. It'd hit the wall, and he'd end up on second. Then the next man up would do the same thing. The third man up would do the same. Now, you should have three outs, but instead you had two runs in against you and a man on second base."

Hugh Mulcahy, a hard-luck Phillies pitcher in the team's final years at Baker Bowl, once had a no-hitter broken up there in the eighth inning by the Boston Braves' Vince DiMaggio. He also tried to keep his pitches away from the hitters' strengths. "I was a low ball pitcher, and usually low ball pitchers were better off," he recalled. "They could get more loft on the balls that were hit so that you had a better chance of them being caught. My mentality was such, though, that I never thought much about the wall. I could just block it out."

Whenever he came to town with the Brooklyn Dodgers or the Boston Braves, catcher Al Lopez said he would always give special instructions to his pitchers: "Pitch the lefthanded hitters low and away. Try to keep them from hitting that wall.

"All the lefthanded hitters stood on top of the plate," Lopez added. "They all tried to pull the ball to right. You had to pitch them outside. Of course, we always tried to save our lefthanded pitchers for the Phillies when we came to town because they had some great lefthanded hitters."

In the declining years of Baker Bowl, when it was, as Moore recalled, "in very bad shape and about to fall down," the wall was littered with pockmarks in spots where balls had hit. The wall was rusty, too, and sometimes a line drive would bore a hole right into the tin.

The wall had one other feature that had nothing to do with playing baseball. "If you played right field at Baker Bowl," said Holden, "you didn't have to go to Atlantic City to get a suntan. That tin wall held in the heat, and when you played right field in the summer, the sun would burn you to a crisp. You came away red as a beet."

Throughout much of the 20th century, the wall was also noted for its advertising signs. The most famous was the huge Lifebuoy sign that extended much of the way across the wall from 1928 until 1938. "The Phillies use Lifebuoy," the sign proclaimed. Underneath, some unhappy soul had painted, "And they still stink."

Before the Lifebuoy sign, the most prominent advertisements in the outfield were the Schmidt's Beer sign that reached from the clubhouse to the flagpole in right-center field and the Bull Durham tobacco sign in right field. Showing a picture of a huge bull ripping through the fence, the latter sign, which stood for many years, offered $50 to any player who hit a ball against a cutout on the bull. Another prominent advertisement that

Even in the early 1900s, advertising signs were common along the right field wall.

preceded the Bull Durham sign was an ad for a fly-catching product. "Dode Paskert caught 209 flies last season," the sign said in 1915. "Our fly-catcher caught 1,237,345."

Over the years, numerous other products were advertised on signs on the wall, according to noted ballpark historian Dick Miller. One of the most prominent was the Flying White Horse of Sacony Vacuum Co. Another was an advertisement for Fatima cigarettes. Businesses also hung billboards on the outside of the wall along Broad Street.

As inviting to hitters as right field was, left field at Baker Bowl was just the opposite, despite its low three-foot-high wall. Even after the distance down the line was reduced to 341.5 feet in 1925, hitting a home run to left was still a noteworthy accomplishment.

And to hit the ball clear out of the park in left was an even greater challenge. During the park's entire existence only four batters ever hit balls out of the stadium in left field. The first was the Phillies' Cliff Lee in 1922 off Giants pitcher Art Nehf. Wally Berger of the Boston Braves in 1931, the Phillies' Hal Lee in 1932, and the Cardinals' Medwick in 1937 also cleared the left field barrier, dropping balls onto Lehigh Avenue.

(Jimmie Foxx was also said to have hit a ball over the left field wall during a City Series game, but there is no authentic record of his having done

The Lifebuoy sign on the right field wall was one of Baker Bowl's most noteworthy features.

that. Several eyewitnesses claim that Foxx hit a home run that landed on top of the wall behind the bleachers and bounced out of the park.)

No one ever hit a ball out of the park in center field, although Hornsby crushed a ball through a window in the Phillies' clubhouse.

A Hitter's Paradise

Because the right field wall was so close and posed such an inviting target, hits and runs were an easy commodity at Baker Bowl. Some of the highest-scoring games and some of the most spectacular individual hitting achievements were accomplished there.

"It was interesting going to Baker Bowl, because you knew you would see a lot of action " said retired *Inquirer* baseball writer Allen Lewis, who first attended a game at the stadium as a boy in the mid-1920s. "I can remember going to doubleheaders that would end up something like 13–10 and 18–16 . . . and I'd still get home in time for dinner."

The Phillies won a 24–0 game at Baker Bowl. They lost games of 28–6 and 20–16. And in one 20–14 Phillies' victory over the Cardinals, the teams combined to hit 10 home runs.

Ed Delahanty hit his way into the Hall of Fame with the fifth-highest batting average (.346) in baseball history while playing much of his career

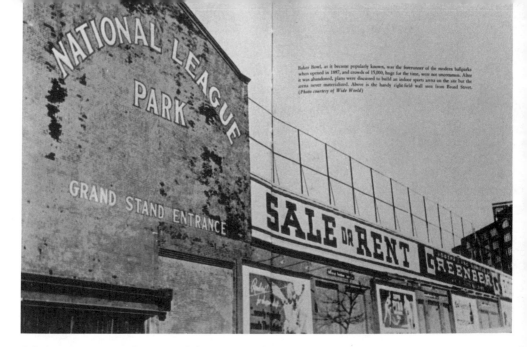

Baker Bowl, as it became popularly known, was the forerunner of the modern ballparks when opened in 1887, and crowds of 15,000, huge for the time, were not uncommon. After it was abandoned, plans were discussed to build an indoor sports arena on the site but the arena never materialized. Above is the handy right-field wall seen from Broad Street. *(Photo courtesy of Wide World)*

Advertising signs decorated the right field wall outside the park, too.

at Baker Bowl. Likewise, Chuck Klein entered the baseball shrine with a big boost from his glittering Baker Bowl statistics, which included the finest first five years any player ever enjoyed.

The highest-hitting outfield in baseball history—the 1894 Hall of Fame trio of Delahanty (.407), Sam Thompson (.407), and Billy Hamilton (.404), plus substitute Tuck Turner (.416)—played for the Phillies at Baker Bowl. So did Lefty O'Doul when he tied a National League record with 254 hits and won the batting championship with a .398 mark in 1929.

In the dead-ball era, the lefthanded Thompson was the first National League player to hit 20 home runs when he led the league in that category in 1889 while making Baker Bowl his home park. Gavvy Cravath won six National League home run crowns, Klein captured four, and Cy Williams was a three-time winner while performing at Baker Bowl. Klein was also the last Phillie to win a Triple Crown, performing the rare feat in 1933. Thompson in 1894 and Klein in 1931 hit for the cycle at the park. Delahanty slammed six hits in an 1894 game against Cincinnati, and Cravath drove in eight runs in a 1915 game against Pittsburgh. And Butch Henline in 1922, Williams in 1923, and Johnny Moore in 1936 each hit three home runs in one game, the only Phillies players to do that at Baker Bowl.

Between 1911 and 1938, Phillies players led or tied for the National League lead in most home runs hit at home 19 times. Starting with Fred Luderus, the group included Cravath, Williams, Dode Paskert, Emil Meusel, Klein, and Camilli.

A look at the playing field of Baker Bowl in 1916.

Even notoriously weak hitters hit home runs at Baker Bowl. Phillies pitcher Bill Duggleby got his first major league hit with a grand slam home run at the park in 1898. Forty years later, a real oddity occurred when on opening day in 1938 Brooklyn Dodgers outfielder Ernie Koy and Phillies infielder Emmett Mueller both hit first-inning home runs in their first major league at-bats.

Overall, 187 Phillies players hit a total of 1,314 home runs at Baker Bowl. No hitter enjoyed more success there than Klein, the big, rawboned slugger who spent much of his career slamming one hit after another on or over the right field wall, including one that went through the rusted barrier.

Klein's batting proficiency at Baker Bowl later proved to be a detriment. For years, he was kept out of the Hall of Fame by critics who claimed that the short right field wall allowed him to embellish his statistics and placed him at a level at which he would not have been if he'd played his home games at more normal stadiums.

There was more than a little truth to that contention. In 1933, for instance, when he became the only Phillies player ever to win the Triple Crown, Klein hit .467 at Baker Bowl and .280 when the team was on the road. Baseball researcher Bill Deane also figured out that Klein had hit .391 at home and .321 away in 1929, .439 at home and .332 on the road

With the right field wall so close, Baker Bowl (with the Reading Railroad tracks and station in the background) was a hitter's park.

in 1930, .407 at Baker Bowl and .266 in away games in 1931, and .423-.266 in 1932.

Nevertheless, when Klein stepped up to the plate in games at Baker Bowl, kids in the upper stands rushed to the corner to peer out over the wall so they could watch if the slugger clouted a drive onto Broad Street. So frequent were such blows that in 1929 Phillies owner William Baker added 12 feet of screen to the top of the 40-foot high wall. It was an effort, many believed, to thwart Klein's home run assault and thus reduce the chance of what could be the slugger's higher salary demands. Few believed Baker when he said, "Home runs have become too cheap at the Philadelphia ball park."

Klein went on to hit 43 home runs, a new National League record, that year. It was a year in which the Phillies hit .309 as a team, with only one regular hitting less than .300. The Phils had a team batting average of .340 at Baker Bowl, and the rest of the league collectively hit .339 there. Klein hit .393 at home, but that average took a back seat to the mark compiled by teammate O'Doul, who, on his way to a batting title, hit .453 with 144 hits at Baker Bowl.

At one point in 1929, the Phillies scored 88 runs in 12 games. The following year, they had a team average of .315 but still lost 102 games and finished in eighth place, 40 games out of first. The Phils' pitching staff had a team earned run average of 6.71.

Because of the wall, pitching at Baker Bowl was never a very enjoyable experience. ERAs ballooned and losses were plentiful. "Those who could win in Baker Bowl were magicians," Joe Holden said. "If a guy could go nine innings there, he should be in the Hall of Fame."

In 1930, the average score of a game during the 77-game home schedule was opponents 8, Phillies 7. There wasn't a shutout tossed all season, and 71 home runs were hit in the first 41 games. In 1934, in a six-game series with the Dodgers and Braves, the Phillies outscored their opponents, 63–55.

"The games always seemed to wind up with three on and a lefthanded hitter up," said Bucky Walters. "The game was never over at Baker Bowl because somebody was always likely to poke one over that short right field fence. It was a hitters' paradise, and the hitters always fattened up their averages at Baker Bowl. As a pitcher, you just had to learn to contend with it."

Because they usually had an ample number of strong hitters in their own lineup, the Phillies went through the decades facing quality pitching at Baker Bowl. "We always faced tough pitchers in that park because the other teams knew we had good hitting," said Dolph Camilli. "They didn't pitch humpty-dumpties against us. They threw their best at us, and often they were lefthanders."

"I wasn't thrilled about pitching in that old park," remembered ex-pitcher Joe Bowman, who hurled both for and against the Phillies during his career. "A fly ball would scrape the right field fence as it was coming down, and it would go for a double or triple."

Some pitchers claimed to be less affected. "You could take a little 30-inch bat and poke it over the fence in that place," said former pitcher Pete Sivess. "I never gave it a thought. It [pitching at Baker Bowl] showed whether or not you could pitch. Any fool can pitch when the fence is 400 feet away. But in a small park like that, you better know what you're doing."

No pitcher was less affected at Baker Bowl than the great Grover Cleveland Alexander. Old Pete won 30 or more games in three straight seasons, and in his finest campaign in 1916, when he won 33 and hurled a record

16 shutouts, nine of his whitewashings were achieved at Baker Bowl. While pitching there that year, Alexander also gave up just 33 earned runs in 205 innings for a remarkable earned run average of 1.45.

In later years, manager Jimmie Wilson addressed his concern about sending a pitching staff to work at Baker Bowl. "A pitcher goes along for four or five innings, and then a couple of pop flies, which would be easy outs in other parks, hit that wall for doubles or triples," he said. "I have to yank my pitcher and use maybe a couple more during a game. After one home stand, the staff is coming apart at every seam."

About the only way a pitcher had any success was to keep the ball low and try to get the batters to hit to center field. Center field wasn't spacious by modern standards, but there was plenty of room for a fleet fielder to roam.

"It was a very easy park to play center field in," said Terry Moore, who played that position with the St. Louis Cardinals. "There wasn't too much playing area in center to right because of the short wall, so you could play a short center field. That made it easy to throw out runners going from first to third. If a ball went to right and hit the tin wall, it would drop straight down. You just had to run right to it and pick it up."

Appropriately, only two nine-inning no-hitters were ever thrown at Baker Bowl. Francis (Red) Donahue won a 5–0 decision for the Phillies over the Boston Braves in 1898, and Jeff Tesreau pitched the New York Giants to a 3–0 victory in 1912.

Special Effects

There was never anything ordinary about Baker Bowl. It was a park that featured the unusual, although that was not always a condition that could be considered positive.

One of the park's most unusual features was the location of the clubhouse in center field. Only two other major league stadiums have had clubhouses located in center field—Robison Field in St. Louis, where the Cardinals played from 1893 to 1920, and the Polo Grounds, the home of the New York Giants.

Originally, the Phillies dressed in a first-level clubhouse in center field. Visiting teams dressed in their hotels downtown and rode to the park in horse-drawn carriages. Groundskeeper Sam Payne, who worked for the team until he was 80, took up residence with his wife in the upper level clubhouse, maintaining an apartment there until about 1918. Payne's wife often cooked dinner for the unmarried players, and if the game was still in progress while she was preparing the meal, outfielders could usually tell what was on the menu as the smell drifted out the windows.

Soon after the turn of the century the Phillies moved out of the lower-level clubhouse and into the one upstairs with the Payne's maintaining an apartment on the side. It was a big improvement, not only because numerous windows overlooked the playing field but because it had a pool table, used mostly for playing craps and poker, and a large swimming pool located in the middle of the clubhouse. It was a place where Grover Cleveland Alexander and Mike Doolin frequently engaged in underwater "rassling" matches while the more urbane Eppa Rixey enjoyed leisurely daily swims.

Around the start of World War I, the swimming pool, having badly deteriorated, was drained. But it remained in the center of the clubhouse, an ominous cement tank with a fading green bottom.

"One time," remembered 1920s Phillies pitcher Huck Betts, "Hugh Jennings—he was a coach then—came in after a game. There was a lot of steam from the showers, and you couldn't see too well. He jumped into the pool, but there wasn't any water in it. Hughie landed right on his head."

The lower clubhouse became the domain of the visiting team. Cramped and dingy and with the bleachers blocking off the ventilation from a few windows, it was little more than a glorified toolshed.

Wrote one wag in a moment of high sarcasm, "National League players will be pleased to learn that the visiting dressing room at Baker Bowl is being completely refurbished next season. Brand new nails are being installed on which to hang their clothes."

"It was just terrible," remembers the Cardinals' Terry Moore. "It was small and dingy. There was no air. And they only had one or two spigots in the shower. It was just like the rest of the ballpark—awful. The whole place was more like an old minor league park."

The Phillies' clubhouse, called "just a hole in the wall" by Claude Passeau, wasn't that much better. Although more roomy and better ventilated because of the windows, it still had its faults.

"You had to stand in line to take a shower," said Pete Sivess, the losing pitcher when Carl Hubbell won his 16th straight game with a 5–4 victory over the Phillies at Baker Bowl. "They had one shower room with only four shower heads."

Because the home and visiting clubhouses were so close to each other, players had frequent contact entering and leaving their respective locker rooms. "I remember there being some pretty good fights," said Dick Bartell.

Austin (Doomie) Aria, who served the Phillies as a batboy in the early 1930s, remembered a clubhouse with few frills.

"The locker room had a wooden floor," he said. "It had open lockers, like bins. The players hung their clothes on nails.

The Phillies' clubhouse (shown here in the late 1930s) was described by one player as "just a hole in the wall."

"There were no washers in the clubhouse. Players had two uniforms—a new one that they got at the beginning of the season and the one from the year before. They hung up their wet shirts to dry them out for the next day. It was crude, but that's the way they did it in those days.

"There was a little trainer's room and a separate room—more like a big closet—for the manager. They didn't have food or beer in the clubhouse under Burt Shotton. When Jimmie Wilson became manager, he allowed two cases of beer for each game."

To get to the street from the clubhouse, Phillies players descended a flight of rickety wooden stairs to a door that opened onto Broad Street (another less-used exit opened onto Lehigh Avenue). Fans would line up along Broad Street to seek the players' autographs.

The players used the same steps to get to the field but would turn in the opposite direction and walk to the playing level alongside the bleacher section of stands. Being so close and depending on their mood, fans would shower the players with either praise or condemnation.

As unusual as the clubhouses were, the bullpens at Baker Bowl were somewhat strange, too. The left field bullpen used by the Phillies was located just a few steps beyond the far end of the third base dugout and, because of the shortage of foul territory, was right on top of the foul line. The visitors' bullpen in right field was farther down the foul line. Little benches for the players rested against the grandstand wall in left field and, on the other side of the field, against the right field wall.

"The fans could shake your hand, you were so close to them," said Joe Holden, the ex-catcher. "You used to have to tell them to move back when a pitcher started to warm up because the seats were only about two feet from the plate. Sometimes guys warming up would hit the seats with their throws. If a fan got hit in the puss with one of those throws, he'd feel it."

The small confines of the bullpens presented other problems.

"One day," outfielder Ethan Allen remembered, "one of our pitchers, Snipe Hansen, had been sent down to the bullpen just before the game was to begin and had just gotten himself settled on the bench when he saw a ball rolling toward him. He reached down, casually picked it up, and threw it back toward the infield, thinking it was a loose ball. Unfortunately, the game had begun, and what Hansen retrieved was an overthrow."

"The bullpen had one real advantage," Holden added. "When a ball was hit to right field, players in the bullpen down the right field line would be able to tell if it was going to hit the wall. Because it was usually so hot, they had large white towels with them. They'd wave a towel if the ball was going to hit the wall to let the runners know to take off and get an extra base. And the hitters would see them waving the towels as they ran down the first base line and would be able to stretch the hits into doubles a lot of times. If the ball wasn't going to hit the wall, they wouldn't make a signal."

Dugouts at Baker Bowl were as crude as the rest of the park. Wooden boards served as benches on which the players sat. The dugouts were small and cramped with none of the facilities found in modern dugouts.

"If you had to go to the bathroom, you had to run all the way across the field to the clubhouse," remembered Al Lopez, who became a Hall of Famer. "Sometimes that would happen in the middle of the game."

When a player was ejected or otherwise removed from the game, he'd also have to make his way across center field to the clubhouse, usually during the break between innings.

The Phillies' dugout was originally on the third base side of the diamond. When he became manager, Wilson moved it to the first base side because he wanted to be closer to the runners at first.

Because players left their gloves on the field between innings, there were no special facilities for storing gloves in the dugouts. Nor were there such things as bat racks.

"The bats were stored in a special room behind home plate," said former batboy Aria. "Every player had at least one dozen bats. They didn't break as many then as they do now. When they did, I'd just throw them out.

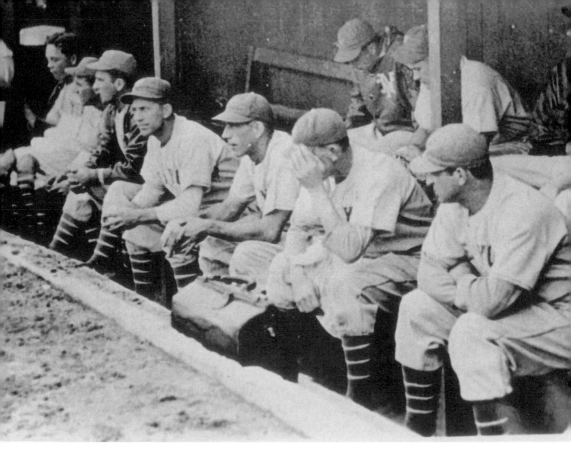

Dugouts were pretty spartan, too, as this uninspired group of 1930s New York Giants seems to attest.

"Before batting practice each game, I'd put the bats in a wheelbarrow and bring them out to the front of the dugout. Then I'd lay them out in a row on the playing field right in front of the dugout. When a player went to bat, he'd come out and pick up his bat and a weighted bat and take them both to the plate."

Generally, the playing field at Baker Bowl was regarded as being more than satisfactory. "The infield and the outfield were fine," said 1930s pitcher Ray Benge. A proud line of groundskeepers worked hard to maintain the field despite the club's limited funds.

"The groundskeepers always did a very good job," said Hugh Mulcahy. "They always kept the playing field in top shape."

Early in the 20th century, Sam Payne took over as head groundskeeper. For a number of years, he kept two ewes and a ram under the left field bleachers. Roaming the field when there was no game, the sheep served as grass cutters, which for the penny-pinching Phillies saved the expense of hiring workers and buying equipment to keep the grass trimmed.

Baker Bowl housed the livestock until 1925 when the ram charged club

The playing field at Baker Bowl was considered satisfactory by most players.

official Billy Shettsline. The ponderous Shettsline escaped the ram's wrath, but soon afterward the sheep received their outright releases.

Not long after that, Payne added people to his staff. The ground crew eventually grew to 10 full-time members, including a couple of local characters nicknamed South Street and an albino known as Sky Joe Plover, who sewed bank bags into each of the front pockets of his pants and smuggled balls out of the park, which he sold to neighborhood teams for 50 to 75 cents. A group of 20 to 25 neighborhood kids also held part-time jobs, helping to maintain the field and performing other miscellaneous duties.

"We used big hand mowers to cut the grass," recalled Aria. "We'd mow the grass, then bag it and put it under the bleachers. We didn't get paid. It was all gratis. Once in a while they gave us an old green ball, and we'd take it home and play with it in the street."

After Payne retired, his top assistant, Woods Lukens, who lived in the neighborhood, became the Phillies' head groundskeeper. Later, Tommy Lancaster became the head groundskeeper until the park closed.

Although their main office was in center city, the Phillies maintained a small office at the ballpark for the groundskeepers and others who worked at Baker Bowl. There was also a small umpires' locker room under the stands on the third base side of the field where the umpires would dress and rub game balls with mud.

After fire destroyed the park in 1894, the stadium looked this way
when it was rebuilt.

Not Much Was Ever Constant

The Phillies' record in 51 1/2 years of playing at Baker Bowl was 1,957
wins, 1,778 losses, and 29 ties.

That included seasons with one first-place finish, five seconds, six
thirds, and ll fourths. It also included 28 second-division finishes, 12 of
which were in last place.

The early years at the park were mostly successful for the Phillies. Between
1887 and 1917 the club finished in the first division 22 out of 31 times. Conversely, the years between 1918 and 1938 were disastrous, with the Phillies
placing in the first division only once but ending in last place nine times.

During their years at Baker Bowl, the Phillies were led by 18 full-time
managers and several interim pilots. The most noteworthy were Harry
Wright, a legendary pioneer who has often been called the Father of Professional Baseball, and Pat Moran, who led the club to its only pennant
in its first 67 years of existence. Billy Shettsline, Charlie (Red) Dooin, Art
Fletcher, Burt Shotton, and Jimmie Wilson also managed for lengthy pe-
riods, although with less than spectacular results. Shettsline spent 43 years
with the Phillies, rising from a handyman and ticket taker to club president.

In their more than five decades at Baker Bowl, the Phils had 10 presidents. Only three of them presided for more than three years—Alfred J. Reach, who held the reins from the team's beginning in 1883 until 1902, William F. Baker (1913–1930), and Gerald P. Nugent (1932–1943).

Shortly after he became president, Baker gave the ballpark the name by which it was known for the longest part of its existence. The name was one of the few constants in the park's history.

Changes were always being made in the park itself. The most significant one came in 1894 when the park was virtually rebuilt after it had been destroyed by fire. The new park, utilizing steel and brick for the first time in a stadium, was vastly different from its predecessor. One major difference was the extension of the third base side of the grandstands 27 feet onto the playing field, which shortened the distance to the right field wall to 272 feet.

Around the turn of the century, a small section of bleachers was added atop the clubhouse in center field. In the early 1920s, it was removed after being condemned by the city.

The park underwent another significant change in 1910 when new bleachers were installed in the outfield, extending from the left field foul line to the clubhouse in center field. At the same time, the grandstands beyond third and first bases were also extended, and the original bleachers along the left field foul line were curled to meet the new bleachers in the outfield. The curved bleachers became known as field seats.

The additions had a pronounced effect on the playing field. The left field line was reduced from 415 feet to 335, and the right field line became one foot longer at 273 feet.

With a seating capacity that now accommodated 18,800 fans, Baker Bowl stood without further change until 1925 when home plate was moved back seven feet closer to the stands. This put the left field wall 341.5 feet away, and the right field wall 280 feet from home plate. "I'm tired of hearing about pop-fly home runs," said manager Fletcher, who had ordered the change. "And the pitchers won't have a chance to yell about the short right field fence and claim they are laboring in a bandbox now."

When 10 rows of stands down the right field line collapsed in 1927, the damaged sections were remodeled. Two years later, Baker added a 12-foot screen to the 40-foot-high right field wall.

"Our lefthanded hitters weren't too happy about that," recalled pitcher Ray Benge. "But as a pitcher, I was glad to see the fence raised. In fact, it would have suited me if they had made it even higher.

"The line drives that were hit off of you didn't hurt," Benge added. "It was the bloop flies that went over the fence that hurt."

After the screen went up, Baker Bowl underwent no major changes. The only other significant alteration was the addition in the late 1920s of a new scoreboard in right-center field. Placed at ground level and extending part of the way up the wall, it replaced a series of three small scoreboards that had been in use since 1910. In the old setup, there had been a small scoreboard in right-center that gave the batteries of all the teams playing that day, another small scoreboard in right field that provided the score of the game, and a third scoreboard down the right field foul line that listed the Phillies' lineup.

Austin Aria worked in the new scoreboard after leaving his job as the Phillies batboy.

"You had to go up a ladder to get into the scoreboard," he said. "The place you entered was about 20 feet high. Once you got inside, you were all closed in. On a hot day in the summer you would really cook.

"Two people worked in the scoreboard. We had a telephone connected to the press box. A guy would call us with the information. Everything was operated manually using disks and pulleys. I got one dollar a game."

Games at Baker Bowl started at either 3:00 or 3:15 P.M. While Sunday blue laws were in effect, prohibiting games on the Sabbath, doubleheaders drawing packed houses were often held on Saturdays. On Sundays, Phillies players often went to the Northeast section of the city or to New Jersey to participate in sandlot games.

The first Sunday major league baseball game at Baker Bowl was held April 29, 1934. The Phillies lost to the Brooklyn Dodgers, 8–7, with the winners overcoming a six-run Phils' second inning with four-run innings in the fifth and eighth. Along with a game in Pittsburgh the same day, it was the National League's first Sunday game played in the state of Pennsylvania.

Long before Sunday baseball became popular at Baker Bowl, the park was annually the site of another major attraction in Philadelphia—the City Series pitting the Phillies and the Athletics.

Played sometimes before, sometimes after, and sometimes during the season—depending on the year—it was enormously popular with local baseball fans and always attracted huge crowds, whether it was played in Baker Bowl or in Shibe Park.

"The teams took it very seriously," recalled Allen Lewis. "One year [1912], Alexander had won 19 games going into the last week of the season, but the Phillies didn't pitch him all week because they were saving him for the City Series."

The first City Series game at Baker Bowl was held April 9, 1903. The Phillies won, 6–5, in 10 innings en route to a four-games-to-one triumph in the series. The Phillies also won the last City Series game at Baker Bowl, defeating the A's, 9–7, in 1937 in their only victory in the five-game series.

The Phillies had a 30–38-1 overall record in City Series games at Baker Bowl.

In a somewhat more unusual statistic, the Phillies pulled off 10 triple plays while they played at Baker Bowl, and their opponents matched that total with 10 triple plays of their own.

Outside the Park

Although it was originally a somewhat rural area when the ballpark was built, the neighborhood surrounding Baker Bowl eventually grew into a combination of businesses and private homes.

At first, the main landmark in the neighborhood was the Junction Hotel on Broad Street. There, Ed Delahanty often held court after games. The hotel, a somewhat seedy, decaying hostelry, had once been the main stopping place for farmers on their way to market along the Delaware River in downtown Philadelphia. Later, it lodged many of the unmarried Phillies players before and shortly after the turn of the century. Crushed oyster shells littered one side of the hotel's yard, thrown there by cooks through an open window in the adjacent kitchen.

Later, the Reading Railroad and its tracks, huge station, and rail yard were added to the landscape across the park on Broad Street. The Ford building was located at the corner of Broad and Lehigh Avenue. Moore

In its later years, Baker Bowl was stashed snugly behind businesses and homes in North Philadelphia.

and White Machine and Tool Company extended all the way from Broad to 15th along Lehigh. A cigar factory was located at 15th and Lehigh. And in 1924 construction began on a new subway that would run north underneath not only Broad Street, but also the railroad tunnel that crossed it.

Homes and small businesses punctuated the rest of the area, and a trolley track ran down the center of 15th Street. A grocery store and a saloon usurped two of the corners at 15th and Huntingdon Avenue. The block from 16th to 17th on Huntingdon housed some 20 retail stores.

"It was a solid neighborhood of Catholics and Protestants," said Dutch Doyle, who grew up in the area and, like most other kids, spent much of his time playing halfball in the street when he wasn't watching a game or hustling a buck at Baker Bowl. "There were good schools, churches, and plenty of stores. Most of the people worked downtown, commuting to work on public transportation."

In the later years of Baker Bowl many of the single players on the Phillies lived in rooms in the houses around the ballpark. Married players often rented small apartments in the area. When players walked to the park,

Broad Street, along Baker Bowl's right field wall (*right*), was a bed of wooden planks while the subway was being built in 1924.

gatherings of neighborhood kids would usually accompany them. Often, players would stop and take a few turns at halfball with the young localites.

"One of the things that stands out most in my mind," said Jack Bulman, who grew up near Baker Bowl and who with his brother Paul spent many hours at the ballpark, "was that as soon as school was out, we'd tear over to the park. On summer days, we'd get there early, and we'd see the players as they walked along Broad Street from the train station to the park. We'd always ask them if we could carry their bags. Chuck Klein and Jumbo Elliott were especially good about letting us do that. We'd walk along with them, chatting about baseball. We'd take the bags into the clubhouse, and there was a door that led from the clubhouse into the bleachers. The players would say, 'Go ahead, kid,' and we'd go through the door and into the bleachers to see the game for free."

Single players who didn't live near the park stayed for the most part in either the Majestic or the Lorraine Hotel farther south on Broad Street. At times, as many as eight or 10 players lived in one of those places.

"Those of us who lived in the hotels would ride to the ballpark on the subway," remembered infielder Gene Corbett. "Nobody had a car because we couldn't afford one. My top salary was $500 a month."

And even if someone did have a car, driving to the park posed a serious problem. There were no parking lots at Baker Bowl. People who drove sometimes had to park two or more blocks from the park.

"If you drove, you just parked as close to the park as you could," said Taylor Grant, one of the Phillies' first broadcasters who began going to games in the 1920s. "You'd park on the street and you made sure the cops knew who you were."

During the Depression, parking cars was virtually the private domain of a group alternately known as The Unholy Seven or The Big Seven. The group not only handled parking—taking the cars of fans as well as judges, city officials, and other "big shots" who came to the games and finding parking spots for them in what was a kind of early valet service—but controlled it. The operation provided the participants, three of whom were the Kennedy brothers, Norman, Moon, and Francis, with their main source of income.

"They were all neighborhood guys in their 30s," said Jimmy Cochrane, then a local kid who worked both inside and outside of Baker Bowl. "You'd drive into an open space, and they'd take your car and either park it on a side street or out in the middle of Broad Street, where they double-parked the cars.

"They'd pay off the cops with a couple bucks, so nobody would bother them. Of course, just about the only ones who had cars were the gamblers and the politicians who came to the games."

On game days, it was a typical scene outside of Baker Bowl. Fans would be lined up for tickets, most of them at the main gate at 15th and Huntingdon, kids would be begging to be let in, vendors would be hawking their goods, and hustlers would be on the prowl.

Most of the vendors were located at the corners of the ballpark. For 10 cents a fan could buy a cushion or a hot dog, and for 5 cents a scorecard or a lemonade. Scorecards, purchased mostly by the gamblers, were printed by the Phillies at a nearby school, St. Joseph's Home for Boys. Newspapers—particularly the *Evening Bulletin*, but also the *Public Ledger* and *Daily News*—were also available. Souvenirs, a commodity that had yet to become popular, were generally not sold.

"The *Bulletin* had a branch around the corner at 15th and Oakdale," said Doyle, who as a youth worked his way up from selling cushions to scorecards and then to hot dogs and finally to being in charge of cushion sales while also running errands for the players. "If you sold papers and didn't have the *Bulletin* on top, you never sold papers again at a game. In hot weather, the *Bulletin* gave a brick of ice cream to every kid who sold papers."

For the youthful salesmen on the streets, the big items to hawk were cushions. A kid made one penny for every cushion he rented. He could earn a whole one dollar on weekends. And if he sold cushions inside the park, he did even better because he would first dust the fan's seat. That usually brought a tip of a nickel.

On game days, the area outside of the main entrance was always bustling with activity.

Disgruntled fans occasionally pitched their cushions on the field in protest of an umpire's decision. The kids would have to make sure all their cushions were properly returned each night before they were permitted to go home.

"Usually, only people in the box seats bought cushions," Cochrane said. "One time, we sold a cushion to George Raft, the actor. The game got rained out. Raft's bodyguard gave us the ticket stubs. We cashed them in. That was a big payday."

According to Cochrane, several adult vendors manned posts on the street for a number of years. They became part of the lore of the ballpark.

"There was a guy named Harry Martin who sold hot dogs and lemonade out of his truck at 15th and Huntingdon," Cochrane said. "Another guy named Sharky sold hots dogs off a truck at 15th and Lehigh. Then there was a one-legged fellow who sat on a blanket on Lehigh. He had peanuts lying out on an old burlap cloth and sold them for five cents a bag."

Once the game started, a different scene occurred. Men appeared along 15th Street to get a glimpse of the game through holes bored into a wooden gate, while boys lay flat on the pavement to peer under the gate for what little they could see happening on the field (they could see only the center fielder and the scoreboard). Kids and adults also congregated

After passing through the vendors, fans lined up at the windows to purchase their tickets.

to track down balls that flew out of the park. For returning a ball, the lucky person received 50 or 75 cents.

Most of the action took place along either 15th or Huntingdon, the sides of the stadium where foul balls were hit.

"Huntingdon was made of cobblestones, so you didn't know where the ball would bounce," recalled Cochrane. "I remember one time I caught a ball that bounced off the mayor's car."

The most famous ball chaser was a Baker Bowl legend known as Ball Hawk George. A large, middle-aged, weather-beaten adult who lived in South Philadelphia, he attended every game, positioning himself at 15th and Huntingdon Streets behind home plate. Able to determine where a foul ball would land from the sound of the bat, the nimble George was relentless in his pursuit of balls that flew out of the park, using whatever means he could to beat his youthful competitors to the ball, even if it meant knocking them down. Sometimes his opponents would fight back, banding together to block his path to the ball while others pursued it. George sold his booty mostly to sandlot teams, who gave him as much as 75 cents for a clean ball.

Before games, the batboy Aria, who was paid one dollar a game for his services, was a frequent visitor to the streets, too, running errands for the players.

"I'd get to the clubhouse around 10 o'clock and the players would come in at about ll," he said. "After I helped the clubhouse man shine shoes, I'd go to the drugstore—a United Drug Store—at Broad and Lehigh. The players would ask me to get them sandwiches and milkshakes. They'd usually tip me for that. Most of them were real good tippers, although some were a little tight. My two favorites were Dick Bartell and Chuck Klein."

The Paying Customers

It was always a colorful crowd that attended games at Baker Bowl.

In the early days of the park, men and boys dominated the audience. Drunks, gamblers, and rowdies were not uncommon, and at times they became downright unruly.

In 1906, they became particularly unruly, attacking the New York Giants as they were leaving the park. The fracas developed after a fight between Giants manager John McGraw and Phillies third baseman Paul Sentelle had exploded into a full-scale riot between the teams. After the two main contenders were ejected, they fought again under the stands. Later, the teams on the field nearly came to blows after the final out of the hotly contested game.

There was no clubhouse for the visiting club at that time; the teams always dressed in their downtown hotels, which were either the Ben Franklin or the Bellevue-Stratford. And the mood of the fans was ugly as the Giants left the stadium to ride back to their hotel in open carriages pulled by big black horses wearing blankets marked "New York Giants, World's Champions."

A group of angry fans tried to grab the blankets. Players snatched the coachmen's whips and swung at the crowd. Street vendors nearby were selling lemonade, and the fans plucked lemon halves from trash cans and threw them at the Giants.

Meanwhile, Giants catcher Roger Bresnahan stood in the rear carriage, kicking at the fans. Suddenly, the carriage lurched forward, and Bresnahan lost his balance and tumbled into the crowd. Apparently unaware of the catcher's predicament, the caravan moved on, leaving Bresnahan on 15th Street, surrounded by hundreds of screaming fans.

"The fall was broken by the bodies of his attackers," wrote sportswriter Jack Kofoed, who as a youth had witnessed the battle, then written about it in 1958 in an article in *Sports Illustrated*. "You never saw anybody come up so fast, slugging with both fists at every face that dared to come into sight.

"Through the mass of humanity came (John) Tight Pants Titus, still in uniform, wriggling and fighting his way. Bresnahan fell in beside him, and they forced a lane of bloody noses and bruised shins until they reached the grocery store. I opened the door. They bolted in and locked it."

Bresnahan and Phillies outfielder Titus barricaded themselves inside the store until police rescued them a half hour later. In a curious example of reverse justice, Bresnahan was fined $10 for disturbing the peace.

Fans were often more than a little involved in the action on the inside of the park, too. In 1913, a group of them gathered in the center field bleachers, waved their hats and coats, and, using mirrors, deflected the sun's rays into the hitters' faces every time the Giants came to bat.

They ignored umpire Bill Brennan's request to stop. Brennan then asked Phillies manager Red Dooin to make the same request. Dooin, who some suspected had planted his friends in the bleachers, sauntered out to the bleachers and not too forcefully asked the fans to behave. They complied briefly but in the next inning began flashing the mirrors again. This time Brennan sent the police to center field. As the troublemakers were being ejected, other fans hurled bricks at the Giants. Brennan forfeited the game to New York. (A protest filed by the Phillies was upheld, and the game was ordered resumed the next time the Giants came to town, but the Phils lost the game anyway.)

In its early days, a good season at the park would mean 200,000 to 300,000 fans. The numbers increased as the Phillies fielded a pennant contender in the mid-teens, reaching a stadium record of 515,365 in 1916. Then attendance dropped off drastically as the Phils fell back into the second division, and through the 1920s and 1930s it settled mostly into the 200,000 range or below.

"We'd draw 1,000 to 1,500 people most of the time," recalled Bucky Walters. "Sometimes there were so few fans in the park that you'd say, 'Where is everybody? They all must be down at the shore.'"

There were few promotions to attract fans in the manner of today's big league stadiums. But Horace Fogel, who presided over the club from 1909–1912, often had some gimmick. Once he released 100 pigeons with free tickets strapped to their legs in an attempt to attract fans to what he viewed—perhaps somewhat blindly—as the Phillies' pleasing ballpark.

"Philadelphia can boast of having the best ballpark in the world," said Fogel, who before he became Phillies president was sports editor of the Philadelphia *Public Ledger*. "The grounds of the Philadelphia Ball Club are a model after which other clubs have been copying. But none have as large and imposing a grandstand and as fine appointments."

Over the years, a couple was married in a lion's cage on the pitcher's mound, and a woman had a baby in one of the bathrooms.

In its best days, Baker Bowl was filled with happy fans.

In the 1930s, it cost $1.65 for a box seat, $1.10 for a seat in the grandstands, and 50 cents for a spot in the bleachers. The box seats were virtually on the playing field. None of the seats, however, was very comfortable, especially the bleachers, which were merely flat boards.

"When you sat in the upper deck," recalled Allen Lewis, "you felt you were right over the coach's box. You felt like you were right on top of the field. It was almost like you were right in the game yourself."

Fans in the upper deck, where there were usually numerous empty seats, often sat with their legs stretched out over the seats in front of them. One of their favorite diversions was throwing pennies to the kids below and watching them scramble for them. If it rained, fans would often strip to the waist and hang their wet shirts on the railings or empty seats nearby.

The Giants and Cardinals often drew respectable crowds, especially when Carl Hubbell or Dizzy Dean pitched. But for games with other teams, often as few as 500 people were in the stands.

Many of them were gamblers. Commissioner Kenesaw Mountain Landis once said that Philadelphia was the worst city in baseball for gambling. Even a sign that said "No Gambling" failed to deter the Baker Bowl bettors.

Small-time gamblers, usually numbering 200 to 300, sat in the field seats down the left field line and bet 50 to 75 cents on every pitch. Some

A big crowd of small-time gamblers sat in the left field bleachers, despite the admonishment on the wall.

had signs on which they would state their bets. Eventually, they moved over to the center field stands after kids took over the left field bleachers.

Big-time gamblers, often including center-city nightclub owner Jack Lynch, who usually attended games with three chorus girls draped on his arms, and future Philadelphia Warriors owner Eddie Gottlieb, who made his living in those days scheduling games for semipro and Negro League teams, roosted behind first base. They bet on loftier matters, such as the outcome of the game. Often, a gambler would have as many as six different bets on the outcome of the game. The odds would change after a run scored or an inning ended. Usually, the group also included local mobsters, who were accompanied by their own bevy of chorus girls.

Kids often composed another major segment of the Baker Bowl audience, particularly after Gerry Nugent made the Phillies the first club to have a Knot-Hole Gang in 1933. (The name "Knot-Hole Gang" originated at Baker Bowl when kids bored holes in a wooden gate on 15th Street and peered through a small break in the stands. They could see just a part of the playing field and the scoreboard, but it was enough to give them an idea of what was happening.) Free passes were awarded to the young fans at schools and at recreation centers.

"If you did something good at school, you would get a pass to a game from the Knot-Hole Gang," remembered nationally prominent musician Bill Doggett, who grew up not too far from Baker Bowl in North Philadelphia. "We always looked forward to getting those tickets."

If they didn't get in with a Knot-Hole Gang pass, kids would find other ways to get into the park. Sometimes, they'd badger gamblers to take them in with them. Or they'd find innovative ways of their own. "You could always get in one way or another," remembered Dutch Doyle. "It was the easiest place in the world for a kid to get into."

"I can remember just hanging around the gate until somebody gave us a ticket. Then we'd go in," said Bill Campbell, who later was a broadcaster for Phillies games.

"When we didn't have money or any other way to get in," said Anthony Pisciella, who grew up in South Philadelphia and saw his first game in 1926, "we'd wait behind the right field wall during batting practice and then get a ball and take it around to the gate. They'd let us in for free. Sometimes, we'd also carry milk or towels in to the players. Then we'd just stay in there.

"A few times," Pisciella added, "we even climbed over the right field wall to get in. We'd get out there before a game and help each other up, hanging on to pieces of the wall as we'd climb. We'd do anything to get into a game."

Fans climbing over the right field wall grasped the advertising signs along Broad Street as they went, then when they got to the top, they worked their way along until reaching the center field stands. They'd jump into the seats and hope not to be caught by a menacing Phillies guard named Firpo, a huge man who walked with a pronounced limp, had a slight speech defect, and made frightening faces as he patrolled the outfield bleachers. To be caught by Firpo was a terrifying experience for a kid.

"We were always trying to sneak into the ballpark," remembered Jack Bulman. "If we got into the bleachers, we'd try to sneak into the grandstands. It was sort of like a game within a game. They always had three or four guys watching, and we'd just try to get in any way we could."

Edgar Williams, a veteran reporter and popular longtime columnist for the Philadelphia *Inquirer*, recalled getting in to see games another way when he was a youngster growing up in Lansdowne.

"You could get a seat in the bleachers for 50 cents," he said. "I cut lawns for 25 cents, and I would hoard the money until I got enough for a subway ticket and a ticket to the game. Sometimes, I'd have a whole quarter left over for a hot dog or lemonade. That was paradise.

"We'd get there in time for batting practice. We'd go out to the bleachers and hang over the fence in center field. We'd see the players going and coming from the clubhouse. They were just 10 feet away. Sometimes, we'd go down to the pavilion in left field. The players would come over and talk to you. They'd get to know you by name, even ask you how things were going at home."

Dick Bartell was particularly friendly with the kids. He'd walk down to the left field stands before games and spend 10 or 15 minutes talking with them. Chuck Klein also visited the young fans, as did Claude Passeau, Johnny Moore, and several others.

Charles Goodwin of Philadelphia remembered as a kid either walking 14 blocks from his home at Front and Lehigh or riding the trolley to the park for eight cents, then entering the park with some of his friends. "We'd either sneak in," he said, "or wait around the center field gate. In the eighth inning, they'd open it and let you in for free. You'd stand just inside the gate and watch the rest of the game."

Getting in for free was the top priority of most kids. "They had a line drawn on the wall at the main gate," remembered Ralph Bernstein, who grew up to a 50-year career as a sportswriter with the *Associated Press*. "If you didn't come up to the line, you could get in free with a paying customer. We'd go up to strangers and say, 'Hey mister, take me in with you.' Some kids would have to slump down or bend their knees to get in under the line."

One kid who entered Baker Bowl in 1923 gained a special place in baseball history. His name was Reuben Berman. The 11-year-old youth was arrested for keeping a foul ball that he'd caught. After a night in the house of detention, he was hauled before a local judge, who, according to historian Harold Seymour, ruled that "a boy who gets a baseball in the bleachers to take home as a souvenir is acting on the natural impulse of all boys and is not guilty of larceny." Not only were the charges dropped and Berman freed, but from then on, fans in every professional baseball park were permitted to keep balls that went into the stands.

Fans were usually well dressed at games. Depending on the era, men wore either straw hats or derbies. "And the men wore neckties with stiff collars," recalled George Duross, now of Roxborough, who started watching games in 1915. "It was all very proper. Most of the fans dressed like that. The fans were very gentlemanly. They weren't troublemakers like you have now."

Joe Kline of Meclure, Pennsylvania, remembered a time when dressing well was not such a terrific idea. "All the men wore white shirts," he said, "and one time somebody in the upper deck spilled juice and it came through the floorboards and got all over everybody. On hot days, they always sold lemonade and ice water."

"I went in the grandstand one day attired in a Palm Beach suit," recalled longtime fan Grafley Stowe of Lansdale. "They had a terrific rainstorm that day, and with a leaky roof, my suit turned black in a hurry."

The sea of white shirts in the outfield bleachers on hot summer days posed a difficult background for the hitters.

Unlike today, fans got dressed up to go to a ball game at Baker Bowl.

In the bleachers, the wooden slats that made up the floor were spaced far enough apart that spectators could see down to the ground. Occasionally, fans would drop change through the openings between the boards, and kids would scramble below to search for the loose coins.

The most popular item sold in the stands was called a cold drink, which was actually a watered-down version of lemonade. "If the sale of lemonade was good, lemons would run short and water would simply be poured over the used ones," recalled Dutch Doyle from his vending days as a youth. "Because of that, we were always told to call it a cold drink instead of lemonade."

Young vendors were also instructed to collect from the stands used cups that were still intact and return them to the lemonade vat. There, they would be used again for more drinks made by Moon Kennedy, who moved inside the park once he was finished parking cars. The architect of this and other stunts to squeeze the fans' wallets was John Mallon, brother-in-law of Phils' president Gerry Nugent. Mallon ran the concessions business at Baker Bowl.

Burk's hot dogs were also sold in the stands, as were peanuts. One of the most widely known vendors was a former boxer named Kid Beebe, who sold peanuts, peanut chew, and other items out of a wicker basket that he lugged through the stands. Standing just five-foot-four, Beebe had had

637 fights and, even in his later years, could and sometimes did kayo unruly spectators who heckled him as he sold his wares.

Sometimes, Phillies games would be heavily attended by fans from other parts of the state. Groups of coal miners from upstate Pennsylvania often attended games on weekends. There were also railroad excursions from as far west in the state as Harrisburg.

Few blacks attended Phillies games at Baker Bowl. Women, however, began attending games in greater numbers after Nugent initiated Ladies Day on Friday afternoons. Women were admitted to games for the amusement tax fee of 10 cents. Players' wives were also in regular attendance, sitting together in their best attire. For them, going to games was like attending a social function, and the women wore hats, gloves, and fancy dresses.

Another common species at Baker Bowl were the hecklers, many of whom were also small-time gamblers. A large number of hecklers were men who worked as hucksters, selling food on the streets out of wagons or trucks. Their jobs were finished by two or three o'clock, allowing them the rest of the afternoons off to watch games. They showed no mercy, blistering opposing teams as well as the home team, and their insults could be heard throughout the park.

"I remember they would get on some of the Phillies unmercifully," said Duross. "They'd call Gavvy Cravath 'wooden legs' because he was slow, and they'd ride Sherry Magee because they thought he drank a lot."

There was no denying, however, that the hecklers as well as the rest of the odd conglomeration of spectators were avid Phillies fans.

"The fans were real tough," Johnny Moore remembered. "They'd give it to you if you didn't give 100 percent. The gamblers were especially tough. They'd really let you have it sometimes."

"Sometimes the fans would stomp their feet on the wooden flooring, and the noise would reverberate through the whole park," recalled Gerry Nugent, Jr., son of the former Phillies owner. "They'd do that two or three times a game." Such a practice made sitting in the upper deck preferable to many fans because they would not be subjected to the showers of dirt, rust, and debris that would rain down on them from the floor when the fans stomped their feet.

"The fans," said Bernstein, "were real baseball fans. To go to Baker Bowl, you had to be a real baseball fan because you weren't going to get a stylish seat or a whole lot to cheer about from the Phillies."

There was a clear distinction in Philadelphia between Phillies and Athletics fans. A's fans seldom ventured down Lehigh Avenue to Baker Bowl. And there were frequent arguments between the two sides.

"As kids, you had to declare yourself," said Williams. "There was no in-between. You were either a Phillies fan or an A's fan."

Gentlemen of the Press

By today's standards, press facilities at Baker Bowl were at best primitive. There was no fancy press box, no streamlined broadcasters' booth, no private press restaurant.

"The press box was actually part of the upper deck behind home plate," said Allen Lewis. "There was chicken wire on both sides. When I was a kid, I would sit on the edge and listen to the writers talk and watch them type their stories. I remember thinking how wonderful it would be to work in that place."

Writers entered the ballpark through a press gate at 15th and Huntingdon, then clamored up wooden stairs to the second deck. The press box was only about 25 feet deep. Scribes were often seen flicking their cigarette butts onto the spectators in the stands below.

The writers, especially the ones from out of town, were notorious for their pranks and for the unflattering comments they frequently penned about Baker Bowl.

Once, during a dull afternoon game in the 1930s, Chicago writer Warren Brown kept himself amused by rolling a heavy metal pipe up and down the press box floor. The pipe would clank loudly down a flight of steps, then Brown would retrieve it and do it again.

Phillies president Gerry Nugent saw what was happening and rushed from his field-level box seat to the press box. Demanding that Brown stop immediately, Nugent roared, "You fellows must remember that we have patrons and you're annoying them. Patrons who *paid* to get in," he added.

"By gosh," bellowed Brown, rushing to his typewriter. "What a story! The Phillies have *paying* patrons."

Another notorious press box comic was Red Smith, who in the 1930s covered the Phillies for the Philadelphia *Record* before going on to a memorable career in New York as a syndicated columnist.

"In most ball parks," Smith wrote, "the press is segregated in a detention pen tucked away up under the roof. In Baker Bowl, however, the press box was a section about 10 rows deep in the second deck of the grandstand directly behind home plate. There, enclosed by a fence of tall iron palings, the flowers of Philadelphia letters drowsed over scorebooks and whiled away the afternoon throwing peanuts at the head of Stan Baumgartner of the Philadelphia *Inquirer*, who sat in the front row."

According to Edgar Williams, who toiled as a youth as a press box gopher, Smith did more than write fancy prose.

"He would pour cups of water down on colleagues in front," Williams recalled. "Once in a while, water would go through the cracks and onto the people in the stands below."

Dolly Stark was an umpire, but before that he had been one of the Phillies' first broadcasters. Here he gets set to call the Phillies' Morrie Arnovich out on an attempted steal of home in a 1938 game against the Brooklyn Dodgers.

No tables were in the press box. Scribes typed their stories while seated at long boards extending the length of the enclosure.

"The press rarely came into the clubhouse either before or after a game," recalled ex-batboy Austin Aria. "They did all their talking on the field before the game."

There were no televised games at Baker Bowl, and broadcasting games on radio was in its infancy. Two stations aired Phillies games from front row seats with tables on the lower level—WIP, which had a spot on the third base side of home plate, and WCAU, which resided on the first base side of the diamond.

"We were right on top of the field," recalled Taylor Grant, who was behind the mike at Baker Bowl in 1937 and 1938. "We could hear almost everything the players said. Sometimes, their language got a little salty.

"It was tough to make a joyous event out of our chore, especially when you were uncomfortably seated and wearing the other guy's hot dog mus-

**A man with a megaphone stood behind home plate and announced
the starting batteries for both teams.**

tard on your shirt. And we had to clip batting averages and the like out of
newspapers and magazines.

"Because we were in the stands and not in the press box, we were right
among the fans. One time, I remember, a kid who wasn't too far from me
got hit in the face with a ball during batting practice. I led him down to
the office. They had no first-aid station. A nurse looked at him, and they
gave him a ball.

"Before games," Grant added, "I used to work out with the players.
They'd let me play pepper with them. I had no uniform. I just did it in
street clothes. Sometimes, I'd go back to the booth and be soaking wet
with perspiration."

Often, overzealous fans would race down to the radio locations and
shout into the microphones. Not only were the booths exposed to the
fans because they were out in the open, but they were also vulnerable
to weather conditions, including rain and hot sun. Once, Grant recalled, chief usher John Collins ran down to the broadcast area and announced over an open microphone that Grant's daughter had just been
born.

Throughout its existence, Baker Bowl never had a public address system. It always employed a man with a megaphone. He would announce

Baker Bowl was all spruced up for the 1915 World Series.

the starting batteries for each team, turning first to one side of the diamond, then to the other, and finally to the outfield to make his statement.

Francis Kennedy, one of three brothers who worked in and around the park, served as the PA announcer for many years. On those rare days when he didn't attend the game, the Phillies would find a replacement.

One substitute came on the field drunk. He slurred his words and was jeered by the fans, one of whom stuck a ball into the megaphone. Finally, Phillies president Gerry Nugent had to go onto the field and lead the man off by the arm.

The Best of Times

Without question, the high point of Baker Bowl's long and winding history occurred when the park played host to the 1915 World Series. Never before and never again would the old stadium bask in such a bright spotlight.

Unfortunately, the light shone all too briefly. It was extinguished with staggering abruptness, and by the time it went out, Baker Bowl had slid

President Woodrow Wilson became the first U.S. president to attend
a World Series when he watched the second game in 1915 at Baker
Bowl with Mrs. Edith Galt, his future wife.

back into the dark and dreary abyss that characterized most of the rest of
its glamourless existence.

The summit for the park was reached in the first game when the Phillies
and the peerless Alexander beat the opposing Boston Red Sox, 3–1, in
what turned out to be the club's only World Series victory in 97 years. For
the game, the park had been refurbished and 19,343 fans squeezed into
every available space to watch Alexander spin his magic. It attracted no
attention at the time, but Babe Ruth made his first World Series appearance in the game, grounding out to first as a ninth-inning pinch-hitter.

Another first was achieved in the second game of the Series. Woodrow
Wilson became the first U.S. President to witness a World Series game
and the only U.S. chief executive ever to see a major league game at Baker
Bowl. Wilson attended the game with his fiancée, Mrs. Edith Galt, his en-
gagement to whom he had announced just two days earlier.

Thousands of fans and other citizens mobbed the presidential motorcade as it neared the park. Wilson, an avid baseball fan, shunned free passes, purchasing his own ticket and a scorecard. As police escorted Wilson and Mrs. Galt onto the field, the crowd broke out into a loud cheer. Straining to see the couple, people who weren't inside the park climbed telephone poles and onto rooftops.

Eventually, the couple was led to a carpeted and heavily decorated box on the first base side. There, Mayor Rud Blankenburg and Phillies president William Baker greeted them. After apologizing for having delayed the start of the game, Wilson threw out the first ball to Phils pitcher Erskine Mayer at 2:10 P.M. Mayer tossed it wide on the first pitch to Red Sox batter Harry Hooper, whereupon umpire Charlie Rigler retrieved the ball from catcher Ed Burns and delivered it to the President, who stuck it in a pocket of his overcoat.

Wilson stayed for the whole game and received a rousing ovation when he departed. The game itself was a tense battle in which George (Rube) Foster held the Phillies to three hits and slammed three hits himself, including the one that drove in the winning run in the ninth inning to give the Red Sox a 2–1 victory.

An expanded crowd of 20,306 saw the game, which would be the first of seven straight World Series one-run losses for the Phillies. That crowd and a gathering of equal size in the fifth game of the Series were attributable to team president Baker's adding extra seats in front of the left field bleachers and right-center field wall in a greedy attempt to fatten the gate at the expense of seriously reducing the size of the playing field.

Not only would Baker be roundly criticized for the move, but his team would pay a heavy price in the final game for the owner's injudicious action.

After the Phillies lost the third and fourth games, both also by 2–1 scores, they returned home for the fifth game. Mayer took the mound instead of Alexander, who had pitched brilliantly in the first and third games but whose arm was too sore to take the hill in this one.

Again the Phillies lost, this time when Harry Hooper twice hit balls that bounced into the temporary seats in center field and were counted as home runs. The second one, coming in the ninth inning, made Hooper the first player in Series history to hit two or more home runs in one game and gave Boston a Series-clinching 5–4 victory.

Hooper's final home run—the first of only three that have won World Series (the others were by Bill Mazeroski of the Pittsburgh Pirates in 1960 and Joe Carter of the Toronto Blue Jays in 1993)—administered the finishing touches to a black eye that the Series had delivered to Baker Bowl in what had begun as its proudest hour.

Equally frustrating, there would not be another chance for redemption at Baker Bowl.

Sometimes in its heyday, Baker Bowl crowds were big enough to require the overflow to actually sit on the field while policemen lined the walls.

Some Other Memorable Days

Entering the World Series was the Phillies' crowning achievement during their days at Baker Bowl. But, despite their dreary performances in many of their seasons, other memorable events at the park were not wholly uncommon.

Francis (Red) Donahue pitched a no-hitter there, blanking the Boston Braves, 5–0, on July 8, 1898, before a sparse crowd of 2,636. He struck out one and walked two in what turned out to be the only no-hit game hurled by a Phillies pitcher at Baker Bowl. It was also the only shutout of the season for Donahue, who posted a 17–17 record that year.

On June 9, 1906, the park was the site of an unusual occurrence when the Phillies lost their first game by a forfeit. It happened after a heated battle with the Pittsburgh Pirates during which the ejections of catcher Red

Dooin and manager Hugh Duffy for protesting the calls of second-year umpire Bill Klem had put the Phillies in a bad mood. When rain and darkness set in, the Phils' demands to call off the game were ignored by Klem. Subsequently, the Phillies stalled, which produced a rhubarb, more ejections, and eventually a 9–0 forfeit to the Pirates.

Another memorable pitching performance was turned in at the park by Harry Coveleski in 1908 in a series of games that earned him the nickname Giant Killer. Late in the season, Coveleski beat the New York Giants three straight times. The three defeats played a major role in the Giants' losing the National League pennant to the Chicago Cubs. Coveleski beat Christy Mathewson twice at Baker Bowl, winning 6–2 on October 1 and 3–2 on October 3.

An event of another kind took place on July 10, 1911, at the park. Rookie umpire Bill Finneran called Sherry Magee out on a high third strike that prompted the Phils outfielder to flip his bat in the air as he headed toward the dugout. Finneran then ejected Magee, who rushed back to the plate and floored the umpire with a hard shot to the face. As players jumped to hold off Magee, Finneran, his face badly lacerated, arose and charged the Phillies' dugout, only to be restrained by police. The melee resulted in Magee's suspension, despite the player's claim that his action was prompted by Finneran's use of vile language when ejecting him. Magee, who later became a big league umpire himself, was reinstated on August 16.

Four years later, on July 13, 1915, Grover Cleveland Alexander gained his ninth straight victory with a six-hit, 8–0 victory over the St. Louis Cardinals. The win put the Phillies back in first place for the first time since June 17. They would not relinquish their hold on the top spot the rest of the season.

Alexander completed one of the finest pitching seasons in baseball history with another noteworthy game October 2, 1916, when he blanked the Braves, 2–0, on three hits. It was a major league record-setting 16th shutout, 33d win, and 38th complete game of the year for the great righthander.

A Phillies record was set April 30, 1919, when Joe Oeschger made the longest pitching appearance in club history, working all 20 innings in a 9–9 tie with the Brooklyn Dodgers. Oeschger, who with the Braves in 1926 matched the Dodgers' Leon Cadore by pitching a major league record 26 innings, gave up 23 hits in the game, which was called by darkness.

On April 28, 1921, in another remarkable feat, Phillies shortstop Ralph Miller and pitcher Lee Meadows both hit grand slam home runs in the same game. It was the only time in club history that two Phils hit grand slams in one game. Ironically, neither Miller nor Meadows, the winning pitcher in the Phils' 11–6 win over Boston, was noted as an accomplished hitter.

Home runs played a key role May 11, 1923, in one of the most memorable games in Baker Bowl history. It was a game in which the Phillies defeated the Cardinals, 20–14, with the teams combining for 40 hits and 79 total bases, including 10 home runs, a National League record until broken in 1966. The Phillies had six of the homers, three by Cy Williams, two by Johnny Moken, and one by Frank Parkinson. Williams, who once hit three balls over Baker Bowl's right field wall in one at-bat (two were foul), ended May with a still-standing National League record for one month of 18 home runs.

That same year Phillies' bats again exploded, this time with a club-record 12-run inning in a 17–4 victory over the Cubs. With rookie Jimmie Wilson hitting his first big league home run in the July 21 game, the Phillies sent 15 batters to the plate in a sixth-inning onslaught that produced seven hits, four walks, and an error.

Chuck Klein lashed his first major league hit—ironically, off Alexander—in a game July 31, 1928, against St. Louis at Baker Bowl. Four days later, he slammed his first major league home run in a game against Pittsburgh.

One of the more dubious events in Phillies' history happened at the park July 6, 1929, when the Cardinals set a modern National League record in the second game of a doubleheader with 28 runs. Slamming four Phils pitchers for 28 hits, St. Louis cruised to an easy 28–6 win while twice scoring 10 runs in an inning. Taylor Douthit and Chick Hafey had five hits apiece, while Jim Bottomley and winning pitcher Fred Frankhouse each had four. The Phillies won the first game, 10–6.

The shoe was on the other foot July 14, 1934, when the Phillies won by their biggest shutout margin in a home game, defeating the Cincinnati Reds, 18–0. Winning pitcher Roy (Snipe) Hansen scattered four hits en route to the first shutout of his big league career. The Phillies backed him with a 19-hit attack that ironically included no home runs. Lou Chiozza had four hits for the Phillies.

Perhaps Baker Bowl's final event of consequence occurred May 30, 1935, when Babe Ruth, playing with the Boston Braves, appeared in his final major league game. One day earlier, Ruth, making what everyone knew would be his last road trip before retiring, had been presented a floral arrangement by the Phillies. Afterward, he helped the Braves to an 8–6 victory with two fine running catches.

Now, it was a Memorial Day doubleheader, and a packed house was on hand to see the fading slugger. In the first inning of the first game, Ruth, batting third and playing left field, grounded out softly to first. In the bottom half of the inning, the Phillies had scored twice with two outs and had a man on second with Chiozza at the plate. Chiozza hit a lazy fly ball to left. Ruth rumbled in and tried to make a shoestring catch, but the ball got past him and rolled to the wall where shortstop Bill Urbanski retrieved it. One run scored before Chiozza was gunned down at the plate while trying to circle the bases.

As the inning ended, Ruth tucked his glove in his pocket, turned, and ran to the clubhouse in center field. The fans, sensing that the end of a glorious career might have arrived, rose and gave Ruth a standing ovation.

Catcher Joe Holden and trainer Leo (Red) Miller were in the Phillies' clubhouse when Ruth clattered up the stairs past Boston's first-floor clubhouse and burst through the door into the home team's locker room. "Red turned, and said,'Hello, Babe. Is there anything I can do?' He thought he might have pulled a muscle," Holden remembered. "Babe said, 'No, no, there's nothing you can do for old age. I've just had too many good days to have this happen to me.' Then I saw Red shake hands with Babe. It didn't register at the time that Babe's career was over."

A few days later, Ruth's playing career officially ended with the announcement that the Braves had given him his unconditional release. Thus ended, with an assist from Baker Bowl, the career of baseball's greatest player.

The Great Catastrophes

While there was often comedy on the field, there was occasionally catastrophe in the stands. Baker Bowl was battered by three major disasters as well as an assortment of lesser ones.

The first significant catastrophe occurred on the morning of August 6, 1894, while the Phillies were preparing for an afternoon game with the Baltimore Orioles. It was 10:40 A.M. when one of the players noticed a fire in the grandstand. Players raced to the fire and tried unsuccessfully to put it out.

Soon the fire had spread to other parts of the mostly wooden and highly incendiary stadium. "Run for your clothes," someone yelled. The players raced to the clubhouse and tried to change into their street clothes, while much of the rest of the stadium erupted in flames.

The players fought their way to the street through smoke and flames. Third baseman Tricky Charley Reilly's shirt caught fire. Even worse, pitcher George Harper, the last player to leave, was temporarily trapped inside the stadium before finally escaping by jumping out a window. Eventually, all of the players reached the street unharmed.

City fire companies responded quickly. Soon every available department in the city had rushed fire fighters and equipment to the scene as the blaze roared out of control.

"A fire gained unobserved headway in the enclosed offices and retiring rooms in the northern pavilion, finally appearing on the shingled top of one of the turrets and thence swept over the dry roofs and steeples with incredible rapidity," team president Al Reach wrote later. "Never was flame so universally destructive. Of all the magnificent buildings and fixtures, naught was left but the field, the centre fence and part of the brick enclosure wall on Huntingdon Street. Even the sod was scorched."

The fire took several hours to extinguish. By then, not only the ballpark but the nearby Omnibus Company with stables for 350 horses, several stores, and three or four houses had been destroyed. The damage was estimated to be $250,000.

The cause of the fire was never discovered. One theory suggested that it was caused by sparks from a locomotive. Another possibility was suggested by the *Evening Bulletin*: "It is by no means impossible that the notion of incendiorism may have been put in the head of some malicious scamp by the reports of a like occurrence in Chicago on the previous day," it said. Still a third and more likely reason and the one that became the generally accepted explanation was that the calamity was caused by a torch that a plumber was using to make repairs.

While the ballpark was being rebuilt by an army of workers toiling around the clock, the Phillies played their next six games at the University of Pennsylvania's University Field at 37th and Spruce Streets. They won five games before returning to their home park on August 18 with spectators sitting in temporary stands that seated 9,000.

Vowing that there would be no more fires at Philadelphia Park, Reach once again took a bold step, erecting a new ballpark using mostly steel and brick. Designed by a prominent center-city architect, John D. Allen, who had experience constructing bridges, and built by Parvin and Company of Philadelphia, the park featured a cantilever pavilion, a radical new architectural technique in stadium construction.

As it was the first time, the ballpark was hailed as the most modern in baseball and a showplace that was both the pride of Philadelphia and a tourist attraction to which visitors made special trips up Broad Street to see.

"Philadelphia can boast of having the best ball park in the world," gushed a report in the publication of the Master Plumbers' Association. "The grounds of the Philadelphia Ball Club at Broad and Huntingdon Streets are a model after which other clubs have been copying, but none have as large and imposing a grand stand, and as fine appointments."

The new building had a seating capacity of 18,800, a right field wall that was tin over brick, an uncommonly long row of racks for fans to store their bicycles, and a swimming pool in the upstairs clubhouse in center field. It contained no wood except for the floors and seats of the grandstands and featured outer brick walls on all four sides, three wide steel stairways between decks, and a series of fifteen 30-foot heavy iron girders supporting the platforms and roof of the upper deck, which extended out over the lower deck.

"This [was] only rendered possible by the adoption of the Cantilever system," Reach wrote in a letter to fans. "The novelty of the idea made it at first seem chimerical. . . . Architect Allen, however, not only gave his personal guarantee as to its practicability and safety, but has during its progress and since its completion verified his guarantee by the several tests to which any such edifice could be subjected."

Saying that "our new Pavilion, which for beauty, ornate and unique magnificence, far excels the former Pavilion," and "adds so novel and unique a structure to the many other ornamental edifices of our beloved city," Reach dedicated the new park May 2, 1895. Although there was still work to be done on the park, an overflow crowd of 20,000 packed every available space to watch elaborate pregame ceremonies, then see the Giants defeat the Phillies, 9–4.

Work was completed on the park during the season, and the configuration would remain basically untouched for nearly a decade—or until disaster struck again.

By 1903, the Phillies had been sold for $180,000 by the Reach–Rogers pair to a group led by James Potter, a Philadelphia socialite and stockbroker. Reach and Rogers, however, retained possession of the stadium, operating under the name of Philadelphia Base Ball and Amusement Company and renting it to the new owners for $10,000 a year.

On August 8, 1903, some 10,000 fans were in attendance to see the Phillies and the Boston Braves in a doubleheader. After the Braves won an exciting first game, 5–4, the teams were locked in a 3–3 tie in the second game when Joe Stanley came to bat for the Braves with two outs in the fourth inning.

Suddenly, disaster struck. As two drunks staggered down 15th Street, they were followed by a group of young girls, who were taking great pleasure in teasing them. All at once, one of the drunks turned and lurched after the girls, grabbing one of them by the hair. The girl fell, and as she did, the drunk tumbled on top of her.

Shrieks of "Help" and "Murder" filled the air. The girls' cries caught the attention of some fans in the bleachers down the left field line. They ran to an overhanging balcony to see what was happening.

The balcony, which protruded 30 feet above 15th Street, was soon filled with fans. And more kept coming. Soon, the small wooden deck, which measured 100 feet long and 23 feet wide, was overpacked with fans lured by the commotion.

Under all of the weight, the balcony suddenly broke loose and, with a roar followed by the screams of people, crashed heavily to the cement pavement below. It was 5:40 P.M.

"In the twinkling of an eye," said a report in the next day's Philadelphia *Inquirer*, "the street was piled four deep with bleeding, injured, shrieking humanity struggling amid the piling debris."

After the balcony fell, panicked fans pressed forward, forcing those now in the front off the broken deck and into the street. Some tried to hold on to broken timbers and pieces of the balcony, but they, too, eventually lost their grips and plunged into the sea of bodies below.

Fans elsewhere in the ballpark watched the tragedy in stunned horror. Then, fearing that the whole park might collapse, people began scrambling to escape. As panic set in, some people jumped 20 feet down onto the playing field. Virtually the only cool heads belonged to the players. "For God's sake, keep these people back," someone yelled from the stands. Players from both teams raced to the edges of the stands and pleaded with the fans to stay calm. In the aftermath, the players were given much of the credit for preventing further disaster.

Out on 15th Street, it was a grisly sight. "I never saw such a sight," said policeman Charles Muskert, one of the first to arrive on the scene. "People were lying everywhere, some jammed in the debris, some cut and bleeding, some struggling and kicking the others."

A policeman named Robinson described an even ghastlier scene. "Some of the people had their clothing almost torn from their bodies, while others were so besplattered with blood and mud as to be almost unrecognizable," he said.

Rescue efforts mobilized quickly. Because there weren't enough ambulances in the city to transport all of the injured and dying, police commandeered everything on wheels—private cars, trolleys, even repair wagons—passing along Broad Street. Patients were transported to nine area hospitals.

As others lay on the street, their broken bodies entangled, pickpockets and looters arrived. Police were too busy helping the victims to bother with the hoodlums.

The game was canceled, and Phillies management was distraught. Business manager Billy Shettsline was "so badly prostrated by the shock that he could scarcely tell a coherent story," the *Inquirer* reported.

The accident received front-page coverage in all of the Philadelphia newspapers. Citing the death of local politician Nicholas Moser, the *Inquirer* noted that "Mr. Moser was terribly injured. Nearly every bone in his face and body was broken, but though the bodies of others fell upon him, he never lost consciousness."

Ultimately, the death toll reached 12. The injured totaled 232. And an avalanche of lawsuits and an investigation by the city began. It was determined that timbers supporting the balcony were rotted and collapsed with the weight of nearly 400 people. The Phillies owners tried to absolve themselves of the blame. But more than 80 lawsuits were filed against the already financially troubled team and park owners Reach and Rogers. Meanwhile, as the Phillies moved to the Athletics' Columbia Park field where they played their home games for the rest of the season, a search failed to find either the drunks or the girls involved in the original incident. Six years later, the U.S. Supreme Court ruled that the fans had raced to a spot where many of them should not have been, and neither the ball club nor the ballpark's landlords were responsible for the accident, and both were absolved of all blame and financial responsibility.

Although it was the worst accident in Phillies' history, it was hardly the last. On May 14, 1927, trouble visited the Phils once again. This time it came in the form of a collapsed section of the stands as the Phillies were bombarding the World Champion St. Louis Cardinals.

Rain had started falling in the third inning. As it got heavier, hundreds of fans from the bleachers swarmed into the lower deck side of the first base grandstand, trying to squeeze in under the pavilion roof to keep dry. In the sixth inning, the Phils exploded for eight runs with Russ Wrightstone hitting a grand slam. With each run the Phillies scored, the fans cheered louder and stamped harder on the wooden grandstand floor.

Without warning in the seventh inning, two sections of the stands normally seating about 300 spectators suddenly collapsed with a loud roar under the weight of the additional fans. Each section was 20 feet wide and contained seven rows of seats.

Panic shook the stadium. Hysterical fans stampeded toward the exits. Players ran to the wall to try to calm the fans. "We did all we could," said Phils catcher Jimmie Wilson, who raced into the crowd. "But it seemed that hundreds of fans were precipitated in a cauldron and savagely fighting to be freed."

Fifty people were injured. One 50-year-old man died, although it was later determined that he had suffered a heart attack. The game was quickly called off by umpire Frank Wilson. The Phillies were leading, 12–3. "I called the game on account of the panic," Wilson said.

Owner William Baker, rushing back from a meeting in New York, was astounded at the extent of damage. He said that the Phillies had made $30,000 worth of repairs to the stands at the beginning of the season.

City officials were not impressed. "Baker Bowl is the worst constructed place I ever saw," fumed coroner Fred Schwartz, Jr. "It should be closed until thoroughly reconstructed to make it safer for a gathering of large crowds."

Again, this accident was attributed to the park's old age. A main girder had developed wet rot and was too weak to support the added weight in the stands.

Two sections of the grandstands collapsed in 1927 when fans tried to escape a rainstorm.

Once again, too, the Phillies had to find a new place to play. They wound up down the street at Shibe Park where they played their next 12 games. Meanwhile, the Phillies spent $40,000 to repair the damaged stands.

A Touch of Comedy

Humor was a commodity that was never too far from the surface at Baker Bowl. Given the sorry state of affairs at the park through most of its years, that wasn't surprising. Comedy was often the only thing that kept the spirits up.

Rotted timber underneath the stands was the cause of the 1927 collapse.

Pranks, such as the time pitcher Syl Johnson put Limburger cheese inside the cap of straitlaced infielder Irv Jeffries, were common. So were bizarre incidents. While Baker Bowl was a house of horrors in many ways, it was a lair of laughs in others.

"It's where I learned to give a hot-foot," recalled Gerry Nugent, Jr. "I also got my first taste of tobacco there. I was only seven or eight years old at the time. Pinky Whitney told me that if I wanted to be a real ballplayer, I had to chew tobacco. I didn't know you had to spit out the juice, and it made me sick."

When he worked out with the players before games, broadcaster Taylor Grant usually borrowed a player's glove. "One day they gave me a catcher's mitt that belonged to Al Todd," Grant remembered. "They knew he didn't like anybody using his glove. When he found out I was us-ing his glove, he really let me have it. He was very intimidating."

"Once when I was a batboy," Austin Aria remembered, "Bill Klem was umpiring behind the plate. It had rained and the field was muddy. The players told me, 'Every time you get a bat, walk across the plate.' Every time I did, the plate got muddy, and Klem had to walk out and wipe it off. Finally, he said to me, 'You little SOB, if you do that again, I'm going to throw you out.' The players screamed and laughed in the dugout."

Perhaps the most famous piece of comedy involving Baker Bowl was an incident during a game on a hot summer afternoon in the early 1930s with the Phillies matched against the Brooklyn Dodgers.

Brooklyn pitcher Walter (Boom Boom) Beck, who would later ply his trade with the Phillies, was getting soundly thrashed by Phils' bats. Fi-nally, after several trips to the mound, Dodgers manager Casey Stengel trudged one more time from the dugout, this time to lift his beleaguered hurler, who by then had given up three runs, three hits, three walks and thrown two wild pitches in just two-thirds of an inning.

As he did, right fielder Hack Wilson, who occasionally reported to the ballpark in less than playing condition after a night on the town, decided to lean against the wall to take a little rest. Worn out from chasing line drives, the rotund Wilson was soon fast asleep.

Meanwhile, Beck, already in a bad mood after the pounding he had taken, was annoyed even more when Stengel proposed his departure. Turning in a fit of anger, Beck hurled the ball as hard as he could against the right field fence. It hit just a few feet from Wilson's head. Awakened by the clatter, the startled Wilson, thinking the ball had been hit, jumped up, tore after the ball, scooped it up, and fired a perfect throw to second base. Gales of laughter erupted in the stands.

"Everybody on the bench just about fell down laughing," Joe Holden recalled. "Jimmie Wilson yelled to Beck that it was the best pitch he'd thrown all day."

The comic side of Stengel had been present in another incident at Baker Bowl, this one in 1921 while he was a Phillies outfielder. At the time, the Phils were as usual struggling along in the lower levels of the Na-tional League standings, and getting traded from the club was like an es-cape from purgatory.

Stengel had by now managed to get the Phillies exasperated with his pranks, which included catching fly balls with his glove behind his back, wearing his uniform backwards during batting practice, and once even let-ting a bird fly out of his cap as he caught a fly ball.

During a rain delay while the Phils idled in the Baker Bowl clubhouse, Stengel learned that he'd been swapped to the Giants. Although it was pouring rain and the field was covered with mud, the playful Casey decided to have some fun. Half dressed, he raced out of the locker room and onto the diamond where he circled the bases, sliding into each bag. By the time he slid into home, Stengel was covered with mud but grinning from ear to ear. It was his way, he explained, of celebrating his liberation from the downtrodden Phillies.

Another legendary incident at Baker Bowl involved catcher Jimmie Wilson, who later became the Phillies' manager. As the story goes, Wilson was catching in a game in which umpire Bill Klem was behind the plate. The two did not exactly get along well together.

Finally tiring of Wilson's grumbling, Klem ejected the catcher. Then he ejected manager Art Fletcher. Soon after the pair had reached the center field clubhouse, a sign appeared in one of the windows. "Catfish Klem," it said, referring to a nickname the umpire despised and showing a drawing of a catfish.

The fans roared their approval. But an irate Klem stopped the game, saying he would forfeit it unless the sign was removed. After much bickering, it was taken down and the game resumed.

Catchers and umpires were natural enemies in those days. At Baker Bowl a decade before the Klem incident, Phillies backstop Charlie (Red) Dooin, nicknamed The Scarlet Thrush and owner of a fine Irish tenor voice that carried him to a postbaseball career in vaudeville, deprecated umpires in song while squatting behind the plate. When confronted, Dooin would insist that his words of disapproval were part of a song.

Another catcher with somewhat of a problem was Bill Atwood. "He was a rookie catcher waiting in the bullpen for possible warm-up purposes when there was a call for him to run for a player at first base," recalled Ethan Allen. "Atwood leaped to his feet, ran over to first, and took his lead. The next pitch was a ground ball to third, so Atwood dashed for second and slid neatly into the bag. Regrettably for him, however, he had entered the game so abruptly that he had forgotten to remove two warm-up baseballs from his back pocket. The result was a ball-bearing slide that he remembered for a long time."

One of the most bizarre events at the then Philadelphia Park occurred in 1898 during a game with the Cincinnati Reds.

There had always been some question about why the Phillies batted so much better at home than they did on the road. Some light may have been shed on the subject after an unusual discovery by Reds infielder Tommy Corcoran, who was coaching at third base.

Pawing in the ground with his feet, Corcoran's spikes caught on something under the coaching box. At first, he thought it was a vine. But upon closer inspection, Corcoran realized it was a wire.

Corcoran pulled at the wire, and several feet came out of the ground. He halted the game and tugged some more. As he did, more wire emerged.

Then, as both teams followed, Corcoran kept yanking wire out of the ground all the way across center field. There, the wire led up the outfield wall into the Phillies' clubhouse where the puzzled party found catcher Morgan Murphy sitting with a telegraph instrument connected to the wire and a pair of opera glasses.

The surprised Murphy tried to hide his equipment but to no avail. It was too late. And the Phillies' trick was exposed.

It turned out that Murphy used the glasses to pick up the opposing catcher's signals, then relayed a signal to the third base coach. A buzzer connected to the end of the wire under the third base coaching box would be set off with one buzz for a fastball and two for a curve. By keeping his foot atop the buried buzzer, the coach knew the pitch that was coming and could then signal the information to the batter.

There was no indication how long the Phillies had been stealing signs this way. Some felt that the stunt was the work of devious manager George Stallings. Regardless, the Phillies' batting averages dropped after Corcoran's exposé.

But the humor and the unusual activities that were so much a part of the ballpark's composition continued.

Beautifully Decrepit

In its best days, Baker Bowl was generally viewed as a good place to see a baseball game. In its worst days, the park still held some magic for some, although compliments were as rare as shutouts or sellout crowds.

"I have fond memories of the place," said former pitcher Hugh Mulcahy. "We never drew too many people, but I was always treated great by the fans."

Here are the impressions of some others about Baker Bowl:

Edgar Williams, the newspaper reporter and columnist—"It was a lovely place. It was beautifully decrepit. They don't make ballparks like that anymore."

Bill Campbell, the veteran broadcaster who walked to Baker Bowl as a youth from his home in Logan—"The park had good sight lines. You could see well from almost anywhere in the park unless you were behind a pole."

Max Patkin, who also attended many games at the park as a boy living in West Philadelphia and later worked out with the Phillies before signing his first pro contract—"It wasn't the greatest place to watch a baseball game. But we didn't care. We just loved baseball and at Baker Bowl you were right on top of the action."

Baker Bowl, in this view along 15th Street, had a rustic look in later years.

Al Lopez, who once caught in more games than any other catcher in big league history and who spoke out in favor of keeping Baker Bowl when the park was about to be closed—"I definitely thought they should have kept it. It was a good park for the players."

Gerry Nugent, Jr., the owner's son—"It was a bandbox, but it was a good park to see a ball game. There was a familiarity between the fans and the players because the distance from the field to the stands was so short. I have many happy memories of the place."

Dutch Doyle, who worked at the park as a kid and who studied its history as an adult—"You always knew when you were going to a game that there was going to be some action. Everybody said, 'The fireworks start at 3:15,' and they were right. There was always something happening."

Bucky Walters, the Germantown native whose fine pitching career began with the Phillies—"I thought Baker Bowl was one of the best-located parks in baseball. It had the Reading and the Pennsy railroad stations nearby, there was the subway, and the trolley ran on Lehigh Avenue. It was real easy to get to."

A familiar view to several generations of Phillies' fans was the corner of Baker Bowl at Broad and Lehigh.

Eugene Weinert, whose father Lefty pitched for the Phillies in the 1920s—"When I first saw the park in the 1930s, it was very old. I was impressed by the amount of wood in the park. And I remember looking out at the wall in right field and thinking, 'Gee, I can hit it out of there myself."

George Duross, a longtime Phillies fan—"The park was the low man on the totem pole as far as big league ballparks went. It was an old, wooden firetrap. But it held its head high. The Phillies did the best they could with it, even though the A's always tried to jam it down their throats with how much better Shibe Park was."

Taylor Grant, who went from Phillies broadcasting to anchoring network television news in New York—"Sometimes the park would be just about empty. Often, the crowd would just be in the hundreds. The dreadful deficiencies of the place were apparent everywhere from the lousy grass and dirt to the lavatory facilities. I don't ever remember using the men's room, and I think that may be because it was just too crummy to be near."

Charles Lanz, a Philadelphian who saw his first game in the mid-1930s—"It was a cozy park and a great place to watch baseball and to hear

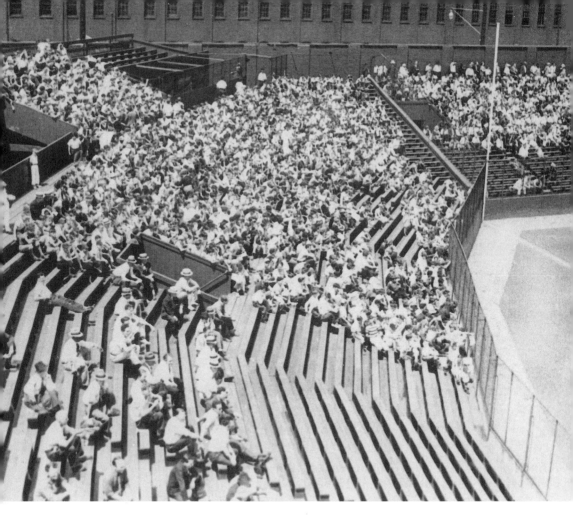

Watching a game at Baker Bowl had a special meaning for baseball fans.

baseball with the infielders and outfielders urging the pitchers to get batters out."

Dolph Camilli, the Phillies first baseman from 1934 to 1937: "One of the things I remember most about playing at Baker Bowl were the long days we put in. We couldn't draw people with single games. As a result, if it rained just a little bit in the morning, (Gerry) Nugent would call off the game, and we would play two games the next day. That meant we got more people in the park. But it also meant that we were out at the park from 9 in the morning until 6:30 at night."

Ralph Bernstein, the veteran *Associated Press* writer—"It was a musty, rustic old park. It had no class of any kind. It had no frills. But as a kid, I wasn't looking for frills. I was out to watch a game. And I liked the park. From a fan's standpoint, it was an excellent park. It was a cozy little place and a good place from which to watch a game. You could see from almost any point."

The stadium was often used as parade grounds for police and firemen's bands, as was the case here in 1913.

Not Just a Baseball Park

Throughout its existence, Baker Bowl was put to many uses, not all of them having to do with baseball.

Because of their meager finances, the Phillies always had to seek ways to produce extra income, and one of the best ways to do that was by renting the park for other sports activities as well as for nonsporting events.

The practice dated back to the days when owners Al Reach and John Rogers built a track around the perimeter of the stadium for bicycle racing. In later years, the park was used for football, boxing, wrestling, and assorted other events.

The State Police staged an annual rodeo at the park in the 1920s. Police and firemen parades were also held at Baker Bowl, as were crusades and circuses, one of which featured a diving horse that plunged from a high platform into water held in a large container near third base.

Policemen parade at Baker Bowl in the 1920s.

Probably the most prominent tenants of the park were the Philadelphia Eagles. They played there for three seasons, starting with the first year of the franchise in 1933 through the 1935 campaign. In that time, they compiled a 3–11–1 home record.

The first home game in Eagles' history was October 18, 1933, against the Portsmouth Spartans at Baker Bowl. An estimated crowd of 1,750 watched the Eagles lose, 25–0, in what was one of two night game that season. Rented, portable lights were used.

On November 12, 1933, the Eagles faced the mighty Chicago Bears featuring Red Grange and Bronko Nagurski. Always one of the leading attractions in the early days of the National Football League, the Bears drew a crowd of 17,850 to Baker Bowl in a game that ended in a 3–3 tie.

Although they averaged less than 10,000 per game, the Eagles also packed in 18,000 fans for their last game at Baker Bowl against the New York Giants.

"Back then, Bert Bell owned the Eagles," said Ralph Bernstein, who covered the team for 50 years. "He did everything—ran the team, sold tickets, was the public relations guy. They used to have standing room on the field and would put up ropes to keep the crowd back. One game, the Bears were killing the Eagles something like 60–0, and Bell was holding one end of the rope. The fans behind the rope were getting kind of unruly, and one guy finally said, 'Well, the hell with this. I'm getting out of

**The State Police staged
annual shows at Baker Bowl.**

here.' Bell said, 'What are you complaining about? I've got to stay for the whole game.'"

Football, with the field running from the left field bleachers to the first base stands, was popular at Baker Bowl well in advance of the Eagles' arrival. George Duross remembered seeing a team of Native Americans led by the great Jim Thorpe playing at Baker Bowl.

"It was around 1920," he said. "They played the Frankford Yellowjackets [forerunners of the Eagles] two or three years in a row. It was always a rough game."

College and high school football games were frequently played at Baker Bowl, too. Temple, Villanova, La Salle, and St. Joseph's all staged football games at the park in the 1930s. So did many of Philadelphia's Public and Catholic League high schools, often playing as many as four games each week there.

The high schools began playing at Baker Bowl in about 1910. The park was then the home field for both Central and Northeast High Schools. Later, the park was also the home field for Olney High. And West Philadelphia and West Catholic met there on Thanksgiving Day.

High school football games involving the city's Public and Catholic League teams were played before huge crowds at Baker Bowl.

Catholic League teams also used the stadium, often playing under temporary lights. In the 1920s, Roman Catholic and St. Joseph's Prep played their Thanksgiving game at the park, and the annual battle drew such huge crowds that the game eventually had to be moved to the roomier confines of Shibe Park.

"I played in a game [November 21] for Southern High against South Catholic in 1936," said former Philadelphia Athletics infielder Al Brancato, who caught a game-winning, third-quarter touchdown pass to give his team a 7–6 victory. "It seemed like they had 20,000 people there."

Semipro football teams often rented Baker Bowl, too. Clifton Heights and Seymour were two of the more frequent users. Manned mostly by ex-college players, they usually drew crowds of several thousand.

Boxing was also a popular attraction at Baker Bowl. With a ring set up on the infield and chairs placed around it, the park was the site of numerous bouts by local fighters as well as some significant national events.

One of the earliest bouts took place in 1904 when the great Bob Fitzsimmons, holder of the heavyweight, light-heavyweight, and middleweight championships, fought Philadelphia's Jack O'Brien to a six-round no-decision while attracting a gate of $5,000. In 1919, Benny Leonard fought Irish Patsy Kline at Baker Bowl. Primo Carnera knocked out George Godfrey in a heavyweight bout in 1930 before a sell-out crowd that brought in $180,000, the city's second-largest gate at the time.

The Wild Bull of the Pampas, Luis Firpo, fought at Baker Bowl. So did middleweight champion Mickey Walker, Jack Sharkey, and local stand-outs Tommy Loughran and Lew Tendler.

When the Phillies were on the road, baseball was still being played at Baker Bowl.

Negro League teams, especially the Hilldale Daisies from Darby, Pennsylvania, often played at the park in the 1920s and 1930s. On October 1, 1925, Hilldale faced the Kansas City Monarchs at Baker Bowl in the first game of the Negro League World Series. A sellout crowd of 18,000 saw the game.

"I often saw Negro League teams at Baker Bowl," said Gerry Nugent, Jr. "Satchel Paige pitched there. They usually drew pretty well, because it was heralded as a big event, and posters were hung all over the city. Most of the fans who came were black followers of the teams."

The biggest crowd ever to watch a baseball game at Baker Bowl came for a sandlot game on September 28, 1930. Some 23,000 were in attendance to watch Wentz-Olney meet the Eighth Ward of Lancaster in a game played for the benefit of the Strange family. The family's father had been shot to death by police after he interfered with the arrest of his son and some other boys for playing baseball in the street on Sunday. Eight children were left fatherless.

Pitchers for the opposing teams were former big league stars Chief Bender and Howard Ehmke, both of whom had enjoyed illustrious careers with the Philadelphia Athletics.

American Legion playoff games, Penn Athletic Club, and police and firemen leagues also took to the diamond at Baker Bowl. Max Patkin, who a short time later launched a more than 50-year career as the Clown Prince of Baseball, remembered one of those games.

"I was pitching for McCall Post in the American Legion state championship game in about 1937," said the Philadelphia native. "I had a big windup, and with a man on third and two outs in the 10th inning, a guy stole home and beat me, 1–0. The home plate umpire who called the guy safe was Johnny Stevens [later to become a highly respected American League umpire], who was in his first year as an umpire."

Baker Bowl was also used for donkey baseball. After the Phillies moved out, midget auto racing and ice skating became popular activities there.

The End Finally Arrives

The final years of Baker Bowl were not very happy ones. The team that played at the old park was awful. Its financial condition was even worse. And the park itself was a mirror image of its tenants—a pitifully down-trodden heap that always seemed on the verge of collapsing.

The outside of Baker Bowl, as seen here at Broad and Lehigh, had fallen into considerable disrepair.

"It was a rickety old park that was falling apart at the seams," remembered Ralph Bernstein. "It was a real firetrap. The wooden seats were always catching on fire."

Indeed, embers from passing locomotives would often fly onto the stadium roof or into the grandstands. And if it wasn't sparks that rained onto the park, it was coal dust that billowed from the trains and made Baker Bowl a dirty, grimy mess.

When fans in the upper deck stamped their feet, rust from the floor often showered the patrons on the lower level. Foul balls landing on the decaying tin roof dumped rust onto the upper deck spectators, while cigarette butts flipping indiscriminately often landed on unsuspecting fans below. A standing joke was that fans attending games at Baker Bowl had to have enough money not only for the price of admission, but also for a dry cleaning bill.

Actually, the park had begun to deteriorate long before the final years. Even by 1915, the park was showing signs of advancing age. Owner William Baker had to go to considerable expense to spruce up the place for the World Series.

In its final years, Baker Bowl drew scant crowds to Phillies games.

By the 1920s, "The Hump," as the park was somewhat derisively called, had become what Pete Sivess would later describe as "just a little dump." The stands were falling apart, and even the flagpole had been split in half after being hit by lightning.

"There was no excitement; nobody was ever there," said Huck Betts. "It wasn't much pleasure. I was always glad to get on the road because you really got tired of playing at Baker Bowl."

The park was constantly in need of repairs. Unfortunately, the Phillies rarely had the money to get the work done.

"It became a very costly ballpark to maintain because of its age," said Gerry Nugent, Jr. "The wooden flooring had to be constantly replaced. The park really became very unsafe. Once the stands collapsed in 1927, moving became a necessity."

"By then, it was just a real old-time baseball park," recalled Ed Liberatore of Abington, the longtime major league scout who had a tryout with the Phillies in 1933 at Baker Bowl. "The whole place was very small and very dingy."

For a number of years, the Phillies had been trying to leave Baker Bowl. But the team had a 99-year lease with Charles W. Murphy, former owner of the Chicago Cubs, who had taken control of the park in a complicated set of financial maneuvers.

In 1910, Mrs. William Howard Taft, wife of the President of the United States, had bought Baker Bowl and initiated the 99-year lease. Two years

A large ice rink was built at Baker Bowl in 1940.

later, Murphy put up money that enabled the Taft family of Cincinnati to finance a syndicate put together by sportswriter Horace Fogel to purchase the Phillies. In the process, Murphy gained control of the ballpark.

With an open invitation from Connie Mack to relocate to Shibe Park, the Phillies tried unsuccessfully for years to break the lease. As early as the late 1920s, it was thought that the club would soon be moving the seven blocks down Lehigh Avenue.

At one point in 1929, the recently retired baseball legend Ty Cobb and Philadelphia real estate tycoon Reymold H. Greenberg tried to purchase the Phillies and Baker Bowl. Offering $900,000, including $200,000 for the team and the rest for the property, Greenberg planned to tear down the stadium and build an office building on the site, while moving the team to Shibe Park where Cobb would run the baseball operation. After prolonged negotiations with William Baker, the deal fell apart when the Phillies' owner increased the price tag $100,000 following a Phillies' winning streak.

The Phillies were thus doomed to spend nearly another decade at the decrepit old park. In 1930, they were paying $25,000 per year in rent, plus $15,000 in taxes and $5,000 for grounds upkeep. Their financial condition couldn't have been much worse, even when the miserly Baker died that year and soon afterward the energetic Nugents took over.

"The park was so small and costly, and this along with the lack of attendance created a very difficult financial situation for my father and mother," Nugent said. (Mae Nugent, the Phillies' vice president, ran the

In the late 1940s, Baker Bowl was little else but an overgrown lot with a wall around it.

business side of the operation.) "They had no other business or background in big money to fall back on. The only other income they had was $25,000 a year for broadcast rights, starting in 1936."

When Murphy died in 1932, his will stated that the Phillies could buy out the lease for $140,000, the money payable to his 16 heirs. Lengthy negotiations followed, and eventually an agreement was reached that allowed the Phillies to abandon the park, although they still had a five-year financial commitment.

The end of the storied old relic was finally in sight. "After more than forty years in the rusty, cobwebby House of Horrors known as Baker Bowl," Red Smith wrote in the Philadelphia *Record*, "the Phillies are preparing to pull up stakes."

Years later, writing in the New York *Times*, Smith would recall that Baker Bowl in its dying days "bore a striking resemblance to a rundown men's room."

Having reached an agreement with Connie Mack to move to Shibe Park, the Phillies played their last game at Baker Bowl on June 30, 1938. Fittingly, the opponent was the Giants, the same team the Phillies faced when the ballpark opened 51½ years earlier. The Giants won the final game, 14–1, scoring nine runs in the third inning to seal the Phillies' misery.

"Baker Bowl passed out of existence as the home of the Phillies yesterday afternoon," Bill Dooly wrote in the lead of his game story in the *Record*. "Equal to the occasion, the Phillies almost passed out with it by

Even most of Baker Bowl's outer wall came down during a storm in 1950.

providing one of their inimitable travesties, a delineation in which they drolly absorbed a 14 to 1 pasting."

Stan Baumgartner, a former Phillies pitcher turned sportswriter, penned similar sentiments in the *Inquirer*: "Yesterday, they said farewell to the old orchard, packed their bags and sang Auld Lang Syne," he wrote, "and in keeping with the traditions of the Phils of recent years, took a 14–1 beating at the hands of the New York Giants."

The last out at Baker Bowl was made by Bill Atwood. Phil Weintraub of the Phillies had the last hit, a single, and the Giants' Hank Leiber hit the last home run. Mel Ott of New York scored the last run. The last winning pitcher was Slick Castleman. Claude Passeau took the loss. Phils manager Jimmie Wilson was the last to leave the clubhouse. And the Phils, of course, exited what had become the oldest ballpark in baseball in last place.

"It was a relief to be getting out of there," said Passeau some 56 years later. "It was a terrible place to play in, especially if you were a pitcher. It was a real bandbox."

For outfielder Morrie Arnovich, leaving had other advantages. Arnovich had swallowed a beetle a week earlier while chasing a fly ball at Baker Bowl and nearly choked.

"Phooey," said Morrie. "Are there any beetles at Shibe Park?"

Although trucks immediately began transporting the Phillies' property to Shibe Park, Baker Bowl remained in use. The Phillies left their two

A business with graffiti-covered walls now sits at the former site of Baker Bowl's main entrance at 15th and Huntingdon.

main groundskeepers—Tommy Lancaster and Pat Jordan—behind to maintain the playing field. That fall, 12 high school football games were played there. Other football games also took place there, along with the State Police rodeo and midget auto races. The most popular driver was Lucky Teeter, a gent with matinee-idol looks who attracted big crowds of women to the races.

The value of the building was placed at $1,500, far less than it would cost to demolish it.

In 1939, promoter Ray Fabiani leased the park for five years for boxing and wrestling matches. That same year, Father Divine and his followers held a rally there, and fire destroyed part of the bleachers. One year later, an ice rink was built. And in 1942, the clubhouse was converted into what would become a popular nightclub known as the Alpine Musical Bar, featuring groups such as the Harlem Highlanders, Three Dots and a Dash, and Daisey Mae and Her Hepcats.

A real estate syndicate with plans to convert the 200,000-square-foot block into a two-story building with stores and offices bought the park in 1944 for $150,000. The plan never materialized. Nor did subsequent plans for other uses.

Developers wanted to build a convention center on the site. The Philadelphia Board of Education wanted the property, once for a new

Central High School and once for athletic fields. The federal government had plans to build its new Mint there. The Lutheran Church sought the land for a publishing plant. In 1946, plans called for erecting a sports center and bringing in a team in the National Hockey League. And the Philadelphia Transit Company (PTC) wanted to convert the land into a bus terminal and parking lot. None ever happened.

For a while, Baker Bowl served as a used car lot. The remains of the park were hit twice more by fires, once in 1943 and once in 1950. Little was left except a low outer wall. Then also in 1950, a storm knocked down part of that outer wall, leaving a pile of broken brick and other rubble splattered across 15th Street. What remained of the ballpark was demolished shortly thereafter. In 1956, the property was sold for $400,000 to another developer with lofty ambitions that never materialized. Later, slices of the property were carved up and sold off for commercial uses.

Today, a car wash, a fast-food restaurant, and a gas station minimarket dominate the landscape of the park. There is no clue that on that same site stood a ballpark that was once the finest in the entire country.

Shibe Park/ Connie Mack Stadium

An Enduring Favorite

*F*or more than six decades, 21st and Lehigh was one of the most familiar addresses in Philadelphia.

People might have stumbled over the locations of other prominent Philadelphia landmarks—what exactly was the address of Independence Hall, the Art Museum, or the Academy of Music?—but there was never any doubt about where Shibe Park stood.

Twenty-first and Lehigh. A ballpark was there. Everybody knew it. The address was etched in the minds of virtually all Philadelphians, whether or not they were baseball fans. It was as well known as the distinctive corner tower that stood as the stadium's most prominent feature.

The address played on the hearts and minds of Philadelphians from 1909, when Shibe Park opened as the finest stadium in the land, until 1970, when it closed in a sea of nostalgia-inspired chaos as Connie Mack Stadium.

In between, the ballpark not only was the hub of the Philadelphia sports world, but was the scene of a galaxy of important events, many without precedent. Quite a few earned special places in baseball history.

Shibe Park with its distinctive tower was a Philadelphia landmark for more than six decades.

As the home of the Philadelphia Athletics for 46 seasons and of the Philadelphia Phillies for 32½ years, the park was steeped in baseball tradition. But it had many other uses. It was the home of the Philadelphia Eagles from 1940 to 1957, it was visited by three U.S. Presidents, and it played host to a far-reaching variety of other events.

In baseball, some 47 million fans watched games during the park's 62 years. Shibe Park was the site of eight World Series, seven involving the A's and one the Phillies. Two All-Star Games took place there, including the first one played at night. The first American League game played under the lights also occurred at Shibe Park.

Shibe Park was the place where the legendary Connie Mack managed, wearing street clothes on the bench and waving his scorecard to position his players; where Hall of Famers Jimmie Foxx, Eddie Collins, Mickey Cochrane, Al Simmons, Frank Baker, Lefty Grove, Eddie Plank, and Chief Bender performed much of their careers with the A's and

Some 47 million fans watched baseball games at Shibe Park/Connie Mack Stadium during its 62 years.

Richie Ashburn, Robin Roberts, and Jim Bunning with the Phillies; and where many other fine players and just as many not-so-fine ones plied their trades.

Simmons, Ferris Fain, and Ashburn each won two batting championships and Foxx and Harry Walker won one apiece while playing home games at Shibe Park. Home run titles were won or shared four times by Baker, three times by Foxx, and once each by Tilly Walker and Gus Zernial there. Foxx won the Triple Crown in 1933, ironically the same year Chuck Klein captured the same prize in the National League.

Foxx, who hit 28 balls over the left field roof during his career, hit his record 58 home runs in 1932. In 1951, a rare feat for teammates was accomplished when Fain won the batting crown and Zernial captured the home run and RBI titles. Foxx, Simmons, Dick Allen, and Del Ennis were widely known for their mammoth home runs, particularly over the left field roof.

Collins (1914), Cochrane (1928), Grove (1931), Foxx (1932, 1933), Jim Konstanty (1950), and Bobby Shantz (1952) won Most Valuable Player awards in the uniform of the home team at Shibe Park.

Jack Coombs's 31–9 record in 1910, Plank's 26–6 in 1912, Grove's 28–5 in 1930 and 31–4 in 1931, Konstanty's 22 saves and 16 wins in 1950, and the 1952 seasons of Shantz (24–7) and Roberts (28–7) were among the home teams' greatest pitching performances

A's pitchers hurled four no-hitters at Shibe Park: Bender in 1910, Joe Bush in 1916, Dick Fowler in 1945, and Bill McCahan in 1947. Phillies moundsmen never whitewashed the opposition there, but the Phils were no-hit three times (by the Los Angeles Dodgers' Sandy Koufax in 1964, the Cincinnati Reds' George Culver in 1968, and the Montreal Expos' Bill Stoneman in 1969). Ironically, the A's were no-hit at home only twice—both in the same week in 1923 by Sam Jones of the New York Yankees and Howard Ehmke of the Boston Red Sox.

The opposition also had some spectacular days at the plate at Shibe Park. The Yankees' Lou Gehrig (1932) and Pat Seerey of the Chicago White Sox (1948) both hit four home runs in one game there. Tony Lazzeri hit two grand slam home runs and drove in 11 runs in a 25–2 Yankees' victory in 1936. Babe Ruth hit a home run over the rooftops on 20th Street. And Ted Williams went 6-for-8 in a doubleheader on the last day of the 1941 season to finish the year with a .406 batting average.

Shibe Park was the home of such legends as the Athletics' famed $100,000 infield of Stuffy McInnis, Collins, Jack Barry, and Baker; the Thundering Herd led by Foxx, Simmons, and Cochrane; and the Phillies' enchanting Whiz Kids of 1950. It was also the scene of such dismal failures as an A's team that finished last seven straight times between 1915 and 1921, a Phillies team that lost more than 100 games five years in a row between 1938 and 1942, a 1961 Phillies team that lost a record 23 consecutive games, and the 1964 team that staged baseball's greatest collapse when it blew a 6½-game lead with 12 games left to play in the season.

The old park also had its share of favorite players who weren't all-time greats, but who were good, solid everyday players. Among them were Amos Strunk, Jimmy Dykes, George Earnshaw, Bing Miller, Wally Moses, Bob Johnson, Sam Chapman, Eddie Joost, Hank Majeski, Elmer Valo, Lou Brissie and Alex Kellner for the A's, and Danny Litwhiler, Ron Northey, Emil Verban, Johnny Wyrostek, Granny Hamner, Willie Jones, Andy Seminick, Curt Simmons, Tony Taylor, Chris Short, Johnny Callison, and Cookie Rojas for the Phillies.

During their tenure at Shibe Park, the A's had only three managers—after Mack's 50 years, Dykes held the reins from 1951 to 1953 and Joost was the skipper in 1954. Conversely, the Phillies in their time at the park had 12 regular managers and four interim pilots. Eddie Sawyer, who had two managerial terms totaling nearly six years, and Gene Mauch, who put in eight and one-half years at the helm, were the only long-term Phils skippers.

While the A's ownership remained in the hands of either the Shibe or Mack families, the Phillies had three separate owners in their days at the stadium. Gerald Nugent and his wife Mae were the Phillies' principal owners when the team moved into the park. Late in 1942, however, deeply in debt, owing two years' rent at Shibe Park, and effectively taken over by the National League, they were forced to sell the team to William Cox. The Nugents walked away from the sale with a paltry sum of $30,000 in their pockets. Cox held the team for less than one year. He was suspended from baseball for life for betting on his own team. The Carpenter family bought the franchise for $400,000. Bob Carpenter served as team president from 1943 to 1972, when he was succeeded by his son, Ruly, who ran the team until it was sold in 1981.

Through all of its ups and downs, Shibe Park—renamed Connie Mack Stadium in 1953—commanded a special place in the eyes of all who came in contact with it. It was a ballpark that—unlike Baker Bowl seven blocks away—was held in high esteem, generated warm feelings, and, years after it was gone, was still remembered fondly. In fact, even 25 years after it was vacated, its demise was still lamented by many fans, who probably came as close to revering the old park as was humanly possible.

The feeling was aptly captured by Ashburn, the ballplayer turned columnist and broadcaster, when he wrote in 1975 in the *Evening Bulletin*: "Connie Mack Stadium had character. It looked like a ball park. It smelled like a ball park. It had a feeling and a heartbeat, a personality that was all baseball. Players could sit in the clubhouse and see and hear the fans, and you could hear the vendors selling hots dogs and programs. It was a total baseball experience."

Indeed it was—for the players, the fans, the employees of the park, even the frequently critical Philadelphia press. No matter what was one's reason for being at the park, it was usually a pleasurable experience.

"I loved the place," said former Phillies pitcher Art Mahaffey. "Connie Mack Stadium was the greatest, bar none. It was a terrific place. Without a doubt, it was my favorite park. I can't think of another park that was better. Other parks were supposed to have atmosphere, but this one had the most. It was more intimate than any of them."

A Park for the Masses

Within a few years after they had built Columbia Park, A's owners Ben Shibe and Connie Mack realized they had made a critical mistake. Columbia Park, with its meager seating capacity, was hardly big enough to hold the large crowds that flocked to watch the A's play.

The A's needed a bigger arena, and Shibe had just the place. (Shibe owned 50 percent of the club's stock, Mack owned 25 percent, and the rest was evenly divided between Frank L. Hough, sports editor of the *Inquirer*, and Samuel H. Jones, day editor for the *Associated Press*.) It was a large lot bounded by the yet-unopened 21st Street, Lehigh Avenue, 20th Street, and Somerset Street in a then somewhat rural section of Philadelphia known as Swampoodle.

Shibe, a wealthy partner with Phillies owner Al Reach in the sporting goods business and the father-in-law of Reach's son George, had previously owned a small amount of stock in the original Athletics team that performed in the first year of the National League in 1876. At the urging of Mack, who was awarded the Philadelphia franchise by league president Ban Johnson, Shibe had become the largest stockholder in the new Athletics when the American League was launched in 1901.

Shibe's first step in the development of a new ballpark was to form in 1908 the Athletic Grounds Co., which became the park's owner. The company was authorized to issue 100 shares of capital stock worth $50 each. Shibe took 36 shares and made himself chairman. Mack, whose real name was Cornelius McGillicuddy, was awarded 26 shares and became secretary. Hough, Jones, and Shibe's son Thomas were each given 12 shares, and another Shibe son, John, got 2 shares. All were members of the board of directors.

What followed was a complex set of maneuvers in which Shibe conducted negotiations with the city to build the stadium and his contractor, Joseph M. Steele, began acquiring the seven parcels of land on the 250,120-square-foot lot. On April 13, 1908, Shibe held a ground-breaking ceremony, after which the work began to ready the land.

On December 31, 1908, Shibe officially purchased from Steele the six-acre plot of land at 21st and Lehigh for $141,918.92. At the same time, the Athletic Grounds Co. voted to establish an indebtedness of $350,000. It borrowed $150,000 from Shibe, using the money to pay him for the land he had just purchased, and floated a bond issue with Fidelity Trust Co. for $200,000. Two hundred 10-year "Gold Bonds" were sold at $1,000 each. They were payable at six percent interest semiannually ($60 per year) until January 1, 1919.

The property ran 520 feet deep along 21st and 20th Streets and was 481 feet, 3 inches wide along Lehigh Avenue and Somerset Street. Across the street at 22d and Lehigh was the rundown and soon to be vacated Philadelphia Hospital for Contagious Diseases where smallpox cases were treated and where passersby covered their faces with handkerchiefs in an attempt to ward off germs.

Many people wondered why Shibe and Mack wanted to build a stadium in such an isolated area that was so far away from center city. The area was

**Athletics and city officials gathered for a ground-breaking
ceremony for Shibe Park in 1908. Dignitaries included Tom Shibe
(*far left*), Ben Shibe (*third from left*), Connie Mack (*sixth from left*),
and John Shibe (*fourth from right*).**

a virtual wilderness with mostly vacant lots and woods. Shibe and Mack
even admitted they were taking a huge gamble.

"We wondered if we would ever fill those long rows of seats," Mack said
years later. One of the things that convinced them they would was the
presence of several nearby trolley lines that made the park accessible. And
a taxi ride from City Hall to the park was only 12 minutes.

William Weart, writing in the *Evening Telegraph*, offered his interpre-
tation for justifying the new stadium. "The Philadelphia American
League Club believed that those who live by the sweat of their brow
should have as good a chance of seeing the game as the man who never
had to roll up his sleeves to earn a dollar," he said. "They, therefore, built
for the masses as well as the classes, and Shibe Park had more room for the
poor man than for the rich one. This is as it should be, for base ball is the
people's sport."

Weart added that creating a new stadium was also important for these
reasons: "Because base ball is here to stay. Because it is now looked upon
as a business as well as a pastime. Because the game has grown beyond the
tough player and the other evils which surrounded it in the old days. A
better class of players has grown up during the past ten years."

It took two months to grade the land, with 40 workers and 50 teams of
horses carrying away 15,000 wagon-loads of dirt. Much of the sod used to
cover the playing field was imported from Columbia Park after the Athletics' season ended in 1908.

Shibe was anxious to build a stadium that was not only safe, strong, and
durable, but had visual appeal. Mindful of the problems that had plagued

When it was originally opened, Shibe Park's upper deck ran only from first to third bases.

the neighboring Phillies' ballpark, he had the William Steele and Sons Company, the designer and builder of the park, pump in more than 500 tons of steel in the structural sections of the stadium. The park became the first steel and concrete one in the nation.

Completed in less than one year, the stadium was built for $315,248.69. It was a handsome facility with an imposing domed tower highlighting the structure at the main entrance at 21st and Lehigh.

The facade of the pavilion had a French Renaissance motif. The pavilion and grandstands provided folding chairs—another innovation of the park—that seated 10,000 spectators between first and third bases. Flat two-inch-thick and eight-inch-wide pine planks that angled toward the field held an additional 13,000 in two uncovered concrete bleachers that extended to the left and right field corners.

The overall seating capacity was 23,000, but an extra 10,000 people could stand behind ropes on banked terraces in the outfield. No bleachers were in the outfield, and a 12-foot-high wall extended all the way around the outfield from the right field corner to the left field corner. The distance was 515 feet from home plate to center field, 378 feet down the left field line, and 340 feet to the wall at the right field corner.

Sixteen turnstiles were in the park. Behind them was a 14-foot-wide promenade leading to the right and left field bleachers. A "grand stairway" at the main entrance led to the pavilion. For exiting, 14 large gates opened onto the street level at various parts of the park.

On duty in the attractively furnished rest rooms were matrons for the women and attendants for the men. Water fountains were located around the park. A garage for up to 200 cars was beneath the right field bleachers. Additional parking spaces were provided under the left field stands. Stores and restaurants, called "a valuable asset to the businessmen of the section," lined the Lehigh Avenue and 21st Street sides of the stadium's first floor.

An early view of Shibe Park looking along Lehigh Avenue toward the main entrance at 21st Street. Originally, stores and a restaurant lined the Lehigh Avenue side of the park at street level.

The Athletics' locker room was located behind third base under the grandstands. It consisted of four rooms with entry through a reception area and lounge, which was furnished with heavy oak chairs and a pinochle table. Thirty steel lockers were available to players and coaches in the carpeted clubhouse. There were three showers, plus a small trainer's room. A tunnel led from the clubhouse under the stands to the dugout, which was a concrete basin containing a wooden bench and built slightly below ground level.

The visitors' clubhouse was basically the same, except it had 20 lockers and two showers. It was located on the first base side of the stadium.

Executive offices were located in the tower. Mack's office, furnished ornately with thick oak desks, leather-upholstered chairs, and green burlap wall pads, much of which were covered with photographs and engravings, was at the top level of the tower. It was reached by a runway, called the Bridge of Hope, which led across from the upper pavilion. Situated below that office and decorated in much the same way as Mack's was the office of business manager John Shibe. Other offices flanked Mack's on either side.

A press box was also on a level with the upper pavilion and located directly behind home plate. In it were 18 desks, each seating two writers and one telegraph operator, arranged in three rows.

The Athletics, incorporated in 1901 as the American Baseball Club of Philadelphia, paid no rent for the use of the stadium. Initially, the Athletics' debt included merely paying repairs and taxes.

Big crowds flocked to Shibe Park in 1909 to see what was then considered the finest stadium in the nation.

The Big Day Arrives

Excitement filled the air as April 12, 1909, the day scheduled for the opening of Shibe Park, finally arrived. The whole city, then with a population of about 1.5 million, had anxiously awaited the unveiling of what was being breathlessly proclaimed as the finest park in the nation.

Named for the principal owner of the Athletics, Shibe Park was certain to be filled to capacity for the grand opening. Spectators began forming lines for tickets at 7:00 A.M., five hours before the gates opened and eight hours before the 3:00 P.M. starting time.

A man named George McFadden from South Philadelphia bought the first ticket. After leaving his Stanley Street house at 6:00 A.M., he had been huddled against the window since his arrival at 7:00 A.M. As the purchase was being made—McFadden shortly afterward turned down an offer of $35 for the ticket—a vintage form of gridlock was occurring on Lehigh Avenue. Cars jammed the street, their paths blocked by other cars and the huge throng that had gathered for the game.

It was the largest crowd ever to watch a baseball game up to that point. Eventually, a crowd of 30,162 paid its way into the game. Close to another 5,000 got in with free passes. Several thousand crowded onto the rooftops

**Players from the Athletics paraded behind a band to help celebrate
the opening of Shibe Park.**

on 20th Street, and police estimated that another 30,000 stood outside
the park. When the gates closed, angry fans who didn't get in tried to
storm the gates and pelted the ticket windows with rocks before police
moved in to break up the vandalism.

Mayor John Reyburn, escorted to a box seat by Shibe and calling the
park "a pride to the city," threw out the first ball. Also present were many
other city officials, assorted celebrities, and baseball dignitaries, including American League president Ban Johnson and a number of Phillies
players.

"Shibe Park is the greatest place of its character in the world," gushed
Johnson. Others called the new structure "magnificent" and "immense."

George Wright, the old shortstop of the original Cincinnati Reds and
brother of Harry Wright, threw up his arms in amazement as he surveyed
the park. "It is the most remarkable sight I have ever witnessed," he said.
"In my days, we never played to such crowds and on such grounds. Why,
I would have stage fright if I had to face such an assemblage."

Connie Mack directed his team from a small wooden dugout during the Athletics' early years at Shibe Park.

The giddiness was fueled by a report in the *Evening Telegraph*. "Shibe Park," it said, "is an enduring monument to the national past-time: baseball—the greatest game ever intended for all classes of people, for all ages and for women as well as men."

At 1:00 P.M., the First Regiment Band, led by Samuel H. Kendle, began a concert that would later also include selections by the Third Regiment Band under the direction of Edwin Brinton. Then at 2:30 P.M., Frederick Yockel led the crowd in singing "America." Then the Athletics and visiting Boston Red Sox marched to the center field flagpole where Old Glory was raised as the bands played "The Star-Spangled Banner."

The game itself began with the A's getting off to a 1–0 lead in the first inning. With their ace lefthander Eddie Plank on the mound, the A's went on to an 8–1 victory. Plank scattered six hits while striking out eight and walking four. The A's, pummeling losing pitcher Frank Arellanes, clubbed 13 hits, four by right fielder Danny Murphy. Third baseman Simon Nicholls laced three hits and scored four runs, while making his major league debut was an 18-year-old shortstop named Stuffy McInnis, who would become one of baseball's finest first basemen.

The game, however, was marred by tragedy. A's starting catcher Maurice (Doc) Powers had eaten a cheese sandwich before the game. Although the 38-year-old defensive standout, later called one of his greatest catchers by Mack, played the whole game, the sandwich failed to digest properly. In the clubhouse afterward, Powers, a practicing physician himself, was stricken and rushed by ambulance to Northwest General Hospital. Despite three operations, his condition worsened, and the enormously likable Powers died of intestinal complications two weeks later.

Powers's problem was not immediately known to the spectators, so the euphoria produced by the new ballpark continued unabated following the end of the game and into the next day.

"It was a great day for Philadelphia in the baseball world, it was a great day for the fans, a most profitable one for the owners of Shibe Park and a grand start for the Athletics," reported the *Evening Bulletin*. "The attendance will probably go on record as the largest in the history of baseball."

At the end of the season, the total attendance in the park's first year was 674,915, a total the A's did not equal again until 1925. Shibe Park made such a strong impression, not only locally but in other cities, that within the next five years 10 more new stadiums made of steel and concrete were built. Braves Field in Boston, Comiskey Park in Chicago, Ebbets Field in Brooklyn, Fenway Park in Boston, Forbes Field in Pittsburgh, League Park in Cleveland, and Wrigley Field in Chicago arose on new sites, and Crosley Field in Cincinnati, Navin Field in Detroit, and the Polo Grounds in New York replaced existing fields at the same locations. Clearly, the era of wooden ballparks had come to an end.

Some Things Changed

In the first few years following its maiden season in 1909, Shibe Park had no need for change. The sparkling new park was the envy of major league baseball, and its owners merely had to settle back and watch the fans click through the turnstiles.

Their expenses were meager. In 1910, for instance, the Athletic Grounds Co., which owned the park, spent $87.40 for plumbing, $59.78 for lumber, and $37.75 for the installation of telephones.

The company added Connie Mack's sons, Roy and Earle, to its board of directors in 1912, replacing newspapermen Frank Hough and Sam Jones. Then in 1913, a new company, American Baseball Club of Philadelphia, was incorporated. In what was essentially a book transfer, it bought out the company that owned the A's (also named American Baseball Club of Philadelphia and incorporated in 1901) as well as the Athletic Grounds Co., which comprised the same stockholders who owned the ball club.

In its early days, Shibe Park had a pavilion with adjoining grandstands and standing room in right field.

The purchase price for all real estate and personal property was $150,000, with $5,000 being disbursed in cash and $145,000 in stock.

With the team and the park now all under one roof, so to speak, a major step was taken later in 1913 to make the first alteration in Shibe Park. The Steele Co. was commissioned to build an addition to the stands. The plan called for putting a roof over the uncovered bleachers in left and right fields and adding bleachers across the outfield from left field to the flagpole in center.

Only minor changes occurred thereafter until 1925 when another significant addition took place. This time, upper decks were added to the bleacher sections extending from first base to right field and from third base to left field. At a cost of $400,000, the extended decks added some 10,000 seats to the park, bringing its total capacity to 33,500.

Another addition occurred in 1928 when a mezzanine—from which Connie Mack watched games after he retired as the A's manager—with 750 box seats was built between the upper and lower decks. One year later, 3,500 more seats were added to the grandstand.

In the 1930s, two more major alterations were made to the park. Both were highly controversial.

The first occurred in 1935. Mack had long been disenchanted with the way fans sat on rooftops along 20th Street and got a free view of his team's games. From a rooftop, fans could peer over the 12-foot right field wall and see the entire field and also get a suntan in the process. It was a practice they'd been following since the park was opened in 1909.

"You could put up to 80 people on a roof of a house," recalled Bill Brendley, who lived from 1915 until the mid-1940s on 20th Street behind right field. "Plus, you could seat about 18 more people in the bay window of the front bedroom."

Most people had steps that would lead up the outside of their houses to the roofs. A few put up ladders in their bathrooms so that fans could climb to the roofs through skylights in the ceilings. Some homeowners sold hot dogs and sodas. Many fans would bring their own.

"There were bleachers that extended from one end of the block to the other," Brendley added. "Sometimes, you'd get a couple thousand people up there. You'd charge 35 cents during the regular season. We got $5.50 per person during the World Series."

Fans outside the park could watch the game while standing in trees or atop buggies in 1910.

Tiring of this practice, Mack had 22 feet added to the existing 12-foot wall. Called the "spite wall" by the 20th Street fans, it ran from the right field grandstands to dead center field and effectively blocked the views of the rooftop squatters. Neighborhood residents took the team to court in an attempt to have the wall removed, but the A's, represented by a rising young lawyer named Richardson Dilworth, won the case.

Mack raised the ire of the fans again in 1939 when he announced plans to install lights for night baseball. Twenty-five residents of 20th Street appeared at City Hall to protest the plan. The lights and the night-time crowd noises would disturb their sleep, they claimed. Furthermore, the possibility of getting plunked with a baseball would prevent them from sitting on their porches at night. Worst of all, fans from the upper deck would be able to look directly into their bedrooms, an invasion of privacy the residents found intolerable.

The protests were ignored. And shortly afterward, the lights were installed at a cost of $115,000.

"It was a real problem," Brendley said. "The neighborhood was upset. The lights lit up everything in the house. You couldn't sleep. You had to pull the shades down. And the noise was terrible."

The original installation included two free-standing towers, each one

Crowds lined the right field wall, either standing or sitting in a few rows of bleachers, during the early years of Shibe Park.

147 feet high, and six towers on the pavilion roofs. Each tower had eight banks of lights. The eight towers contained 780 lights altogether, each light giving off 1,500 watts. That gave the stadium some 1.2 million watts of electricity and more than two billion candlepower, enough to light a highway running from Philadelphia to Cleveland.

In 1947, Mack wanted to tear down the right field wall and erect bleachers seating 18,000 in its place. His petition to the city to allow the addition was denied. As an alternative, Mack added 2,500 more box seats along the first and third base lines. All the seats were pointed toward home plate.

On February 13, 1953, Shibe Park underwent another alteration. This one was a name change. The park was renamed Connie Mack Stadium. Such a plan had been in the works for many years, but Connie Mack, because of his admiration for Ben Shibe, had resisted all attempts to change the name. Finally, with Mack in failing health and vacationing in Florida, the change was accomplished by the A's board of directors.

When the A's moved to Kansas City after the 1954 season, the park was purchased reluctantly by Phillies owner Bob Carpenter. The price tag was $1,657,000. "We need a ballpark as much as we need a hole in the head," said Carpenter.

Rooftop viewing on the houses along 20th Street was a popular way to watch a game, as was the case here in 1926, before the wall was raised in 1935.

One year later, the center field fence was moved in from 468 to 447 feet, and for the first time, the portable batting cage was stored behind a gate in dead center. In 1968 the fence would be moved in even more to a distance of 410 feet from home plate.

The last major changes in the park occurred in 1956 when the antiquated scoreboard on the right field wall, which had been there since 1941, was replaced and 24 more box seats with six chairs per box were added. That required moving the dugouts closer to the playing field. The new 50-foot-high scoreboard, which had been in Yankee Stadium, was purchased for $175,000 by the Phillies after the New York club bought a new one. Dismantled and trucked to Philadelphia, it towered above the right field wall. A Ballantine beer sign reached 10 feet above the top of the scoreboard, and a Longines clock extended even higher to 75 feet.

A scoreboard was purchased from the New York Yankees and installed at Connie Mack Stadium in 1956.

Idiosyncrasies

As one of the longest-standing ballparks in major league baseball history, not only was Shibe Park/Connie Mack Stadium the home of countless events and unusual situations, but it also had many subtleties and nuances. It was truly a unique park.

"It was a typical old ballpark," recalled Hall of Fame pitcher Robin Roberts. "When I joined the Phillies, it looked like the best stadium in the world. It was a real major league park, and I was always happy to play there. From my standpoint, it was beautiful.

"When the wind was blowing out, the ball really jumped out of the park," said Roberts, who during his streak of six straight seasons of 20 or more wins captured his 20th victory twice at the stadium—in 1954 and 1955. "A lot of people thought it was a small park, but it was bigger than three or four of the other stadiums in the league."

One of the most appealing aspects of the park for fans of five decades ago was that for 16½ years, there was always a game there. Few other parks could make that claim, but at Shibe Park from mid-1938 until the end of 1954, either the Phillies or the A's were always playing. And although each team had its loyalists, many fans avidly followed both clubs and felt fortunate that on any given day, there was baseball at the park.

Sometimes, the dugouts at Shibe Park flooded after heavy rainstorms. It happened in 1952, and batboys Vic (*left*) and Joe Iannucci had to swim through five feet of water.

The existence of two teams in the same city also fostered one of the most popular attractions of the season—the annual City Series. Although played at various times during some years, it was most often held at the beginning of the season. The number of games each year also varied—in 1912, the teams met 12 times in games both before and after the season— but most often in the latter years of the series, two or three games took place. Overall, 101 games were played at Shibe Park, with the Athletics winning 53 and the Phillies 48.

"Everything at the park was centered on baseball and the game," said Eddie Collins, Jr., who began attending games at the park with his Hall of Fame father in the 1920s and who later became an outfielder with the A's and a front-office executive with the Phillies. "It was good for the players and it was good for the fans. I can remember sitting on the third base line with my family, and you could see everything. It was a good place to watch a game."

The stadium was also the place where an entire set of baseball cards was photographed. Every card in the 320-card 1955 Bowman set shows Connie Mack Stadium in the background. Bowman, in its last year of producing its own cards, was a Philadelphia-based company located at 10th and Somerset.

"Shibe Park was a fine place to play ball," recalled former Phillies manager Eddie Sawyer. "The infield was very good, the lights were good, the fans were close to the action, and it was a good park for both hitters and pitchers.

Huge crowds often surrounded the park, attempting to purchase tickets. These fans were trying to see a 1952 game in which Bobby Shantz would beat the Boston Red Sox.

"There weren't many things wrong with the park," Sawyer added. "About the only problem were the dugouts. They were so deep you could hardly see the outfield or the bullpen. You had to come out of the dugout to see well."

At its peak, Connie Mack Stadium had a seating capacity of 33,608. But on numerous occasions, it exceeded that figure as standing room space behind the grandstands was sold.

The park's largest baseball crowd totaled 41,660 (40,952 paid) for a Phillies–Dodgers doubleheader on May 11, 1947. Many were there to see Brooklyn's exciting rookie Jackie Robinson, who one month earlier had become the first black major leaguer in the 20th century. In the twin-bill, Dutch Leonard and Schoolboy Rowe pitched the Phillies to 7–3 and 5–4 victories over the pennant-bound Dodgers. On September 19, 1946, the Phillies drew 40,007, their second largest crowd, for a night game against the Cincinnati Reds.

The Athletics' high point in attendance was reached August 13, 1931, when they attracted 38,800 for a doubleheader against the Washington Senators. Their next-highest crowd was the 37,684 who came to see a July 15, 1948, doubleheader with the Cleveland Indians.

Connie Mack visited the Elephant Room in 1951 with former pitcher Chief Bender (*left*).

The Phillies' season-high in attendance was reached in the ill-fated season of 1964 when they attracted 1,425,891. Second-highest was the Whiz Kids' year of 1950 when they drew 1,217,035. The Phils' lowest for a full season at the park was 207,177 in 1940 when the club was in the midst of losing more than 100 games five years in a row.

The Athletics hit their high point in season attendance in 1948 when 945,076 spectators watched the team make its last serious bid for the pennant in Philadelphia. The 1915 club, playing in the first year after Connie Mack had broken up his dynasty and stumbling to a 109-loss season, attracted a team low of 146,223.

Typically, opening day attendances were high, although neither the A's nor the Phillies of the Shibe Park/Connie Mack Stadium era engaged in the kind of pageantry that's common at current stadiums. A Phils record of 37,667 saw the no-frills opener on April 16, 1957, against the Dodgers. The Athletics' best opening day gathering was 32,825 on April 20, 1927, in a game with the New York Yankees.

Interestingly, local boys who grew up to become major leaguers were among those who labored to join the crowds at the ballpark.

"A lot of times, a couple of us would just hitchhike to the park," recalled Marcus Hook native Mickey Vernon. "We'd pack a bag of sandwiches and

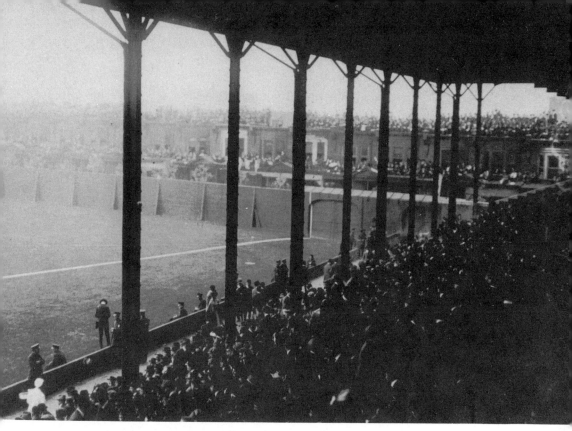

Obstructed views, caused by the many pillars holding up the upper deck, were always one of the park's most irritating features.

leave around nine in the morning to go watch a doubleheader. It took a couple of hours to get there, and most of the time we just sat in the bleachers, but we all thought it was well worth it."

Lee Elia grew up in Olney. "It was not unusual for a bunch of us to take the subway down to Lehigh Avenue and then walk up to 21st Street," said the former Phillies manager and coach. "We paid 50 cents to sit in the bleachers. When the guard wasn't looking, we'd hop the fence and go down to the grandstand."

In the Athletics' final years at the park, fans could also visit the Elephant Room under the right field stands. There, they could gaze at huge photos of A's teams and players, trophies the team had won, and other forms of memorabilia. Opened in 1951, the room was closed after the A's left town in 1954.

The A's also featured mascots in their early years. Lou Van Zandt, whose hunched back players rubbed for good luck before games, served basically as a batboy for the first championship teams at Shibe Park. Later, Hughie McLoon, another hunchback, took over. He was reportedly killed by gangsters in 1928.

The park was known for its obstructed views, its boobirds, its curfews, its absence of beer, and its delicious hot dogs. "The hot dogs," said South

Philadelphia native Al Brancato, who grew up to become an infielder with the A's, "were as good as you could get anywhere. They were the best."

Beer was introduced at the park in 1961 after a long and tedious battle with the state. Over the protests of religious groups, the sale of beer had been urged since Prohibition ended in the 1930s. Many legislative hearings and court cases followed until a license was finally granted.

Advertisements also came late to the park. Only a few ads were ever in evidence until the Phillies introduced billboards on the left field roof and signs on the outfield walls in the 1950s. Huge Philco, Cadillac, and Coca-Cola billboards were among the most prominent over the years on the left field roof. Alpo dog food in left field and Mertz Tours in right were long-term decorators of the lower outfield walls.

Curfews and a ban on Sunday baseball had a substantial effect on games for many years. The A's had tried for years to have the ban lifted, often threatening to move to Camden and even playing a Sunday game in 1926 against the Chicago White Sox in an act of defiance. Yet, the first official Sunday game—a City Series match between the A's and Phillies—was not held until 1934 following a referendum on November 7, 1933, in which Pennsylvania's electorate had voted to permit games on the Sabbath.

For many years thereafter, though, Sunday games were still affected by laws that prohibited the start of a game before 2 P.M. Again defying the law, Connie Mack regularly began Athletics' Sunday doubleheaders at 1:30 P.M. He reasoned that the fine for violating the law was so minimal that it was worth paying, and for years, Mack dispatched one of his aides every Monday morning to City Hall with the money to cover the infraction.

Laws also governed when a game had to be finished. The curfews changed slightly over the years, but by 1950 the rule was solidified: teams were prevented from starting an inning after 6:50 P.M. and could not play at all after 7 P.M. Originally, both leagues considered it a complete game at the point of stoppage if five innings had been played. The National League changed the rule in 1950, calling it a suspended game that had to be finished at a later date.

The bullpens underwent changes, too. Located down the lines in the far corners of foul territory, the home team originally used the left field bullpen, while the visiting team warmed up in right field. After becoming manager of the Phillies, Gene Mauch switched bullpens, not only so he could see his pitchers warming up from his spot in the third base dugout, but because his bullpen coach could wave a white towel when a ball was going to hit the wall. "I saw countless times when balls were hit off that high wall in right and the player on first didn't know whether the ball was off the wall or not," Mauch said. "He'd hesitate, and we would end up with guys on second and third."

According to former pitcher Dallas Green, the bullpen served other useful purposes, too. "I probably wouldn't want Gene Mauch to hear this," he said, "but we used to sleep in the bullpen during games. You could get in the back of the bullpen, and nobody could see you. We'd take little naps until we were called."

The A's were one of the first major league baseball teams to install a loudspeaker system when they did it in 1930. It served well in later years when the booming voice of Dave Zinkoff handled the public address, announcing at the park in the late 1940s before he went on to a legendary career with the Philadelphia Warriors and 76ers. Sherry O'Brien and Pete Byron were two other distinguished handlers of the PA mike during the post–World War II years at the stadium.

The park also had its share of zany incidents. Who can forget the time in 1953 when ex-Phillies pitcher Russ Meyer, then of the Brooklyn Dodgers, flipped a resin bag in the air in disgust after he was thrown out of game following a walk to Richie Ashburn, and the bag landed squarely on his head? Or the bunts that A's first baseman Ferris Fain charged at breakneck speed? Or reliever Jim Konstanty's warm-up tosses to undertaker-friend Andy Skinner, who had a special knack for being able to diagnose the hurler's problems?

Then there was the time left field ballboy Jackie Donnelly, who would fight fans for foul balls, not once but twice scooped up balls hit by Del Ennis only to find out they were still in play. After Donnelly's second defensive gem, New York Giants left fielder Bobby Thomson told the embarrassed gloveman that he'd talk to the commissioner about getting Jackie credited with an assist.

A Wall of Its Own

Shibe Park and Baker Bowl had practically nothing in common except that they both housed major league baseball teams and were located seven blocks apart in the same section of North Philadelphia.

Isn't it ironic, then, that the two dominant ballparks in Philadelphia baseball history both had the unusual characteristic of having a high, solid right field wall? In each case, the wall ran from the right field corner to dead-center field and was the most conspicuous feature of the ballpark's interior.

Because it was much farther from home plate and was not a flimsy barrier over which cheap home runs flew, Shibe Park's right field wall did not

The right field wall was not a particularly inviting target, especially to lefthanded hitters.

share the same kind of scorn as Baker Bowl's widely condemned wall. But it did have its detractors, especially among lefthanded line drive hitters who were regularly deprived of home runs on shots that would have fallen safely in the stands at many other stadiums.

Hard-hitting outfielder Johnny Callison, who learned to pull the ball after being traded to Philadelphia, slammed 185 home runs while playing with the Phillies, but he probably would have hit many more had the wall been a normal height. "It cost me a lot of home runs," he said. "I got a lot of doubles and triples instead."

Originally just 12 feet high, the wall was heightened to 34 feet when Connie Mack built the "spite wall" in 1935. From that point forward, the wall stayed 34 feet high for the remainder of the stadium's days.

"Guys like me just couldn't hit home runs there because of that wall," said slugging A's outfielder Elmer Valo. "It was just too high."

Former two-time batting champion Mickey Vernon saw many of his line drives crash into the wall during his 20-year career in the big leagues as a visiting player at Shibe Park. "You had to get the ball up in the air and hit it well to get it over the fence," he said. "A line drive would just hit the wall for a double."

The wall's distance from home plate varied slightly over the years. It was originally 340 feet. It became 331 in 1934 when the wall was moved closer to the plate. In the mid-1950s, the Phillies installed a 12-foot-high wooden fence in front of the concrete wall in an attempt to keep players from getting badly injured while running into the wall. The distance from home plate to the base of the wall became 329 feet, but the top of the concrete wall remained 331 feet away.

When he hit the first home run at Shibe Park on May 29, 1909, Frank (Home Run) Baker smacked the ball over the 12-foot-high wall. Many more four-baggers followed while the wall was at its lowest level.

Although the ball was in play if it hit the wall, after night baseball started at Shibe Park, there was a slightly different rule if a ball hit a light tower or a sound amplifier that extended above the wall. Balls striking either of those were in play if they landed back on the field and were home runs if they caromed out of the park. In the National League, the rule was eventually changed to allow balls hitting above a yellow line at the top of the wall, even if they hit a light tower, to be declared home runs.

Once in a game with the A's, the New York Yankees' Charley Keller hit a towering drive that struck three-quarters of the way up one of the light towers in right-center and bounced back onto the playing field. Keller had to settle for a double.

Numerous drives of note went over the wall, including one by Ted Williams that landed in a backyard on 20th Street and others by Mickey Mantle, Stan Musial, and Willie McCovey. The most famous was undoubtedly the shot that Babe Ruth pumped. It not only cleared the rooftops of the houses on 20th Street, but landed with a resounding thud on Opal Street, one block east of the wall.

Bill Nicholson also hit a legendary home run over the wall while playing with the Phillies in 1951. It landed on a roof at 2728 N. Opal Street, bounced across the street, and came through a kitchen window at 2727 N. Opal, just as the occupant was about to devour a slice of apple pie.

Houses and people beyond the right field wall were always in danger of being hit during batting practice and games. Once, a passerby was hit in the face with a ball and knocked unconscious. When he returned to his senses, he appeared, wobbly and with a bloody face, at the right field gate seeking some kind of restitution. He was given a job at the ballpark.

"Some people took their windows out during summer games," recalled 20th Street resident Bill Brendley. "If a window was broken, a man who worked for the A's would appear within 15 minutes and install a new window. The A's always had a guy wearing a red cap walking around outside the park. Before the spite wall went up, he would try to keep people from climbing over the low wall to get into the game."

In the 1930s during day games, a man named Charles Evers perched on a porch roof on 20th Street and supplied fans below with a running play-by-play.

Although balls were often pulled over the wall in straightaway right by lefthanded batters, hitting them over the scoreboard and beyond in center field was a rare feat, accomplished by only a few of the game's top long-distance clouters. Jimmie Foxx and Dick Allen were two of the best at doing that. Negro League star Josh Gibson was also said to have hit a ball over the roof at the point where it ends in dead-center field.

"It was a tough park for me to hit in because center field was so deep and because of the way they would pitch me," said Allen, who hit some of the longest drives in the stadium's history, including quite a few over the roof atop the left field stands. "So I always tried to keep the ball on the right side of second base. If they made a mistake and played around pitching me inside, then I could reach that billboard on the roof in left. If they pitched me outside, I'd go to right."

While going to right, Allen hit two prodigious clouts at what had become Connie Mack Stadium. One, hit in 1967, cleared the wall in center field between the flagpole and the scoreboard, the only ball ever to leave the park at that point. Another cleared the top of the scoreboard in right-center. (Allen also once hit a 529-foot drive over the roof in left-center.)

"I never knew where they went," Allen said. "I left home plate on a dead run with my head down. I was never one of those guys to stand around home plate and take a look at where the ball was going."

Probably, Foxx didn't see his legendary shot, which went out between the flagpole and the grandstands, go over the center field wall, either. But Brendley and his friends did.

"There must have been a dozen of us standing on the corner of 20th and Somerset," he recalled. "Foxx hit the ball over the wall, and it landed right in the center of the intersection. They said later it carried over 500 feet. The ball bounced up against the brick wall of an A & P store. It's a good thing it didn't hit the plate glass window in the store. It bounced back off the bricks and 10 or 12 of us all piled up on top of each other trying to get the ball."

While many balls over the years clattered off or sailed majestically over the wall, the wall was also a party to some unusual hits, too. Once, in the 1940s, Dale Mitchell of the Cleveland Indians slammed a line drive off the top of the head of A's pitcher Alex Kellner. The ball landed against the right field wall with Mitchell winding up with a triple (and Kellner staying in the game). Another time, the Indians' Hank Edwards socked a titanic drive high off a light tower in right-center. The ball bounced back onto the field, and Edwards hustled around the bases with an inside-the-park home run.

For outfielders, playing the wall was always a bit tricky. Callison, the Phillies right fielder through most of the 1960s, said he usually got 10 to 15 feet in front of the wall as he prepared to field a ball as it ricocheted off the corrugated tin barrier. "You'd have to get back, then run like hell to grab it," he said. "The fence had ripples in it, and you could never get too close.

"You never knew what to expect when a ball hit off that wall," Callison added. "You just had to give it room. The ball could wind up in the bullpen, in center field, or back at second base. Sometimes, it would drop straight down. Other times, it would angle off the wall like a rocket. It was the toughest wall in the league to play."

"The only way to play it was to surround the ball as it came off the wall," Rich Ashburn said. "I stayed on one side and the right fielder stood on the other side. You very seldom got a straight bounce because the wall was corrugated. And you could play the wall exactly the way you were supposed to play it, and you'd still mess up the play sometimes."

Valo, who patrolled right field from 1940 to 1954 with the A's and later briefly during two stints with the Phillies, also affirmed the difficulties of playing the wall. "The ball could go right, left, or straight down," he said. "If it hit the scoreboard, it would bounce toward center field. There were little protrusions on the wall, and if it hit them, the ball would bounce toward right field.

"The center fielder, whether it was Sam Chapman, Dave Philley, or Richie Ashburn, would always come over and help," he added. "And I would always try to figure out how the wind was blowing. That would help, too. The only time I had trouble was when the ball was hit real high, and the wind was blowing off the (Delaware) river."

Del Ennis, the former Phillies slugger of the 1940s and 1950s, cited one other trouble with playing right field. "It was the sun field," he said. "You always had some trouble with playing out there during the day. Also, the ball seemed to carry well to right."

The wall had one other peculiarity, according to Bill Virdon, the gifted center fielder of the St. Louis Cardinals and Pittsburgh Pirates.

"The thing that really comes to mind about it was the scoreboard in right-center," he said. "It had wooden nails that held different signs projecting from it. You could impale yourself on them if you weren't careful.

"One thing we did all the time when we came into the park was go around and check it. We'd look and see what was on the wall because there was no uniform system in those days about keeping the fences clean and padded. So you'd go looking for things like nails and hooks. You were liable to find practically anything."

A Player's Park

Rare was the player who didn't enjoy performing at Shibe Park. For numerous reasons, players from both the home teams and the visiting clubs viewed it as one of the better parks in baseball.

The field was always in immaculate condition, according to many of the players who performed there.

That was true, even in the early days of the stadium. "It was a very nice park," said outfielder Whitey Witt, who broke in with the A's in 1916 before going on to a fine career with the New York Yankees and living to the ripe old age of 92. "It wasn't the biggest park in the world, but it was nicely kept. People used to bring their chairs and sit in right field to watch the games, FOC. That's free of charge."

"Shibe Park was a great park," added Rich Ashburn. "The playing field was always immaculate, just like a carpet. It was also a good hitter's park. I came from playing on cow pastures where we played on skinned infields and used cow chips for bases. So I never complained about Shibe Park. To me, Shibe Park was as good as any park in the league. I loved the place."

"Everything there was first-class," recalled Bill Werber, the fiery third baseman who played with the A's in 1937–38 and with visiting teams both before and after that. "The lockers were of adequate size, the training room facilities were good, the toilet facilities and showers were of quality and convenience. The entire facility was maintained immaculately. It compared favorably with all the others."

For hitters, the park was especially favorable. Through the years, it was known as a hitter's park with many features that supported the fine art of placing bat on ball.

"The background was very good. You could see very well at the plate, except when the sun was out," said Del Ennis. "The fences weren't very far away, either. The ball carried well. It was just a great park to play in."

A's outfielder Sam Chapman agreed. "It was a very good park," he said. "It was laid out nicely. It was small enough that you could get a home run in it, but big enough that you couldn't hit one out all the time. It was a good hitters' park."

Joe Hauser, who turned 96 in 1995, played at Shibe Park as a first baseman with the Athletics in the 1920s. Afterward, he went on to a legendary career in the minor leagues, during which he became the only man ever to hit 60 or more home runs in two different seasons. He has fond recollections of Shibe Park.

"I liked the park very much," Hauser said. "When I played at Shibe Park, the fences weren't too high, and I hit many a ball into the houses behind right field. Sometimes, the balls would land on the roofs of the houses, and there were always fans sitting up there watching the game. It was just a good park; always in good shape, the grass was never too high, it had a good background for the hitter. I really liked playing there."

The park was equally appealing to visiting players, many of whom anxiously took aim at the left field stands. One of them was seven-time National League home run king Ralph Kiner of the Pittsburgh Pirates.

"It was a great hitter's park, and I always enjoyed playing there because the ball carried so well," said the Hall of Fame slugger. "It was a big thrill hitting home runs over the roof in left field. That wasn't easy to do, but you could do it, and when you did, everybody was amazed by it.

"The only bad thing I can remember about the place was when I came up in 1946, they had some lockers in the visiting clubhouse, but if you were a rookie or not much of a player on the team, you had to hang your clothes on a nail."

Most players appreciated the intimacy of the park that was created by the proximity of the playing field to the stands.

Said Maje McDonnell, who joined the Phillies as a batting practice pitcher in 1947, became a coach, and is still working in the club's front office: "You were very close to the action. That made it very intimate. There was a good relationship between the players and the fans because the foul lines weren't far from the stands."

"Shibe Park was really a very personal park," added former A's pitcher Lou Brissie. "Everything was close. But I liked to pitch in it. If I had one complaint about it, it was that the ball carried too well."

Although not every pitcher relished the assignment of taking the mound at Shibe Park, there were some benefits. For one thing, "the mound was very good to pitch from, probably one of the best in the league," according to Bobby Shantz, the diminutive A's pitcher, a favorite of the hometown fans during his years in Philadelphia.

"What made it really good," said ex-Phillies hurler Art Mahaffey, "is that there wasn't much foul territory, and when you were warming up in

The playing conditions and the field's nearness to the fans were two of the park's chief assets.

front of the stands, as we did back when I was pitching, or even throwing from the mound, you felt like you were throwing the ball 200 miles an hour because the sound of the ball popping into the catcher's mitt echoed through the park.

"There were catchers in the league who would try different gloves until they got one that popped real loud when the ball hit it. That made the pitcher think he was throwing harder than he really was. Even guys who couldn't throw hard thought they were throwing 120 miles an hour. It was a total psychological advantage. And I loved pitching there, even though the outfield walls were pretty close."

Larry Jackson, who pitched for the Phillies from 1966 to 1968, liked the park for another reason. "I liked the park because of its uniqueness," he said. "It was a good ball park to pitch in, although that tin was awful close in right. But you had to hit the ball hard to get it out in left. And if you could keep it low and away from lefthanded hitters, they didn't rattle that tin too much in right."

The playing surface also added to the popularity of the park. It was always well kept in the days of Connie Mack's stewardship, but it became in even better shape when the A's and later the Eagles moved out and there was more time to devote to the maintenance of the field.

This regular crew of groundskeepers took care of the playing field at Shibe Park. The Phillies found the conditions to be much better than those at Baker Bowl.

"Everything was so green," said ex-shortstop Al Brancato. "It was one of the best infields in the league. They always had good groundskeepers, and they kept the grass cut and manicured. You got true hops in the infield."

"The playing conditions after the ground crew got done were phenomenal," Dick Allen claimed. "The ground crew was probably the best in baseball. Some of those guys were there 30, 40 years, and they never got much credit. But they kept the playing conditions far better than any park in the league."

Although experts at their trade, some of Shibe Park's groundskeepers were legendary drinkers. Once, one tripped over first base and fell flat on his face as he prepared to drag the infield midway through a game. Another time, a groundskeeper who likewise had tipped a few too many stumbled and fell under the tarpaulin as it was being spread over the infield during a rainstorm. It took his co-workers several minutes before they discovered that the lump under the tarp was one of their fellow groundskeepers.

The park's outfield was always kept in excellent condition. There were times, however, when groundskeepers tampered with it to benefit a home team player. Such was the case in 1942 when Phillies left fielder Danny Litwhiler was on the way to becoming the first major league outfielder to register a perfect 1.000 fielding percentage for the season.

"The head groundskeeper was a man named Bill McCalley," Litwhiler said. "He had that job for about 25 years. In 1942, during the last two weeks of the season when I was going for the record, I told him to let the grass grow a little higher in left field. He said, 'I'll do what I can,' and then he lowered the blade of the mower in right and center fields but raised it when he got to left field. One day, Joe Medwick passed me. He was playing left field for the Dodgers. He said, 'Hey, Litwhiler. How in the world do you keep from tripping out there? The grass is so long.'

"The left field wall was slanted, and about three or four feet from the ground was a ledge," Litwhiler added. "You couldn't jump over the wall, but you could put your foot on the ledge and boost yourself up to catch a ball."

Groundskeepers also manicured the third base line during Richie Ashburn's tenure so that his bunted balls would stay in play as they dribbled down the line.

"Groundskeeping was a special talent back then," remembered former Phillies president Ruly Carpenter. "It's a lost art now with the artificial turf, but the guys we had at Connie Mack Stadium had been working on the grounds for years, and they really knew what to do."

But there was nothing they could do about the wind. "At times, pop-ups were tough because of the wind currents," said Mickey Vernon. "One time, I saw Lou Gehrig pop up. The ball looked like it was going to land on the roof. The third baseman drifted over to the stands to try to catch it, but the wind blew the ball back over the field. The ball landed behind third base, and Gehrig, who was running all the way, wound up with a triple."

Sometimes, playing at Shibe Park could be hazardous even without the wind. On sunny days, the white shirts in the center field bleachers bothered the hitters. In the late afternoon of day games, half the field would be in the sunlight and half would be in the shadows, making it hard to hit hard-throwing pitchers like Bob Feller, Ewell Blackwell, and Virgil Trucks. And the nearness of the stands meant that players often ran into the walls, too.

Elmer Valo, who did that on occasion with sickening results, encountered yet another annoyance. "You could see the ball pretty good coming out of the pitcher's hand," he said, "but once in a while, gamblers sat in the center field bleachers and shined mirrors in the batter's eyes. They finally got them to stop it, but it was real dangerous until they did."

A player's first visit to Shibe Park often left a lasting impression. In the days before mass-produced franchises and the omnipresent television, many young players had never seen the insides of a big league ballpark until they performed in one.

"I remember my first day in 1943," said former Phillies catcher Andy Seminick. "I was just awed by the park. Its size, the fact that it was en-

Shibe Park was a plain and simple stadium with no advertisements on the roofs or walls when the Phillies arrived.

closed. It was just a big ballpark, and I was used to playing in little, open minor league parks. I was very impressed."

Pitcher Edgar Smith, who began his 10-year big league career with the A's in 1936, had a similar experience. "I had never been to Shibe Park before I signed with the A's," he said. "When I first walked in, I couldn't believe it. I just folded my arms and looked around. It was just amazing."

"It was a very nice ballpark," added 1930s Detroit Tigers shortstop Billy Rogell. "I don't know why, but it always reminded me a little of Wrigley Field. It was a good park to play in; you could see the ball well and the infield was very good. I always enjoyed coming to Shibe Park and playing against the A's."

Nostalgia played a part in Allen's appreciation of the park. "The biggest thing to me was just being able to stand on the same grounds where all the greats played, from Babe Ruth all the way up," he said. "It was a really big thing to me to hold down one of those positions on the field."

"It was just a baseball park," Brancato said. "It wasn't a stadium like they have today. It had atmosphere. The field was great. When you played there, you felt like you were playing baseball."

The Phillies Arrive

"I'm sure the Phillies will play better at Shibe Park, and I look for a real spurt once they have gotten to know the field," said Connie Mack as he welcomed his new tenant to Shibe Park.

After a prolonged round of negotiations to escape their contract with the Murphy Estate that bound them to Baker Bowl, the Phillies finally succeeded in getting away in 1938. They had been trying to leave the decrepit old park at Broad and Lehigh for nearly 10 years.

Mack had been wooing the Phillies since the late 1920s, even going so far as to prepare offices and a clubhouse for them at the grounds on which his Athletics had played since 1909.

"I think the change will benefit both clubs," he said, "and will make for better baseball in Philadelphia."

How he figured that would happen was not quite clear. Nevertheless, he and a coterie of A's officials met with Nugent and his cohorts at the Phils' center-city office in the Packard Building. There, they signed the papers that made the Phillies' move to Shibe Park official.

"The Phillies have leased Shibe Park for a sufficient length of time," Nugent announced. "I am satisfied that the Phillies will play much better baseball in their new home."

Several questions remained, however. Would the aging Chuck Klein be able to cover the larger expanse of territory in right field at Shibe Park? Would the Phillies' home run production be curtailed? Would the club really play any better? Would it draw any better?

"I'm sure the opposition will continue to hit as hard, but there might be relief in the fact that some of the balls that might strike the fence (at Baker Bowl) will be caught," wrote Al Horwits in the *Public Ledger*.

"Definitely, the attendance will improve, which is more than we can say for the ball club. Certainly, it can't be any worse, either in attendance or performance. Besides a couple of 25,000 crowds, the Phils could use a couple of good ball players."

The Phillies were not exactly strangers to Shibe Park. Along with having played there in City Series games over the previous 30 years, they had performed in 12 regular-season games at Shibe Park in 1927 after they were forced to vacate Baker Bowl when some stands collapsed.

Playing there on a regular basis, though, would be a vastly different experience.

"It was a big difference because it was a big park," recalled pitcher Claude Passeau. "We finally got into a big league park."

The Phillies made their Shibe Park debut on July 4, 1938, in a double-header with the Boston Bees. A disappointing crowd of 12,000 showed up. Before the game, Nugent and his wife Mae, the Phillies' vice president, were presented a bouquet of flowers by the A's. A band played before the game and between innings.

The Phillies lost the first game, 10–5, but came back to win the nightcap, 10–2. Passeau, the losing pitcher in the final game at Baker Bowl, went all the way to get the win.

"It's a swell place to pitch in," he said at the time. "Jimmie Wilson told me to use a knee-high fast one as much as I wanted to. In Baker Bowl, that toss was usually good for a smack against the right field wall by lefthanded hitters. Today, when I let the number one go, I had no fear."

The hitters were happy, too. "The park was made for me," chortled Morrie Arnovich, who had three hits in the second game.

There was mixed reaction among the fielders. "I felt five years younger and 100 percent safer," said third baseman Pinky Whitney. "I never knew when a ground ball was going to bounce off a pebble and go for a hit or hit me in the chin at Baker Bowl."

Conversely, right fielder Tuck Stainback lost two fly balls in the sun. And center fielder Hersh Martin played a scoreboard carom so badly that Arnovich had to race over from left field to retrieve the ball in right-center.

"I didn't really have to alter the way I pitched," recalled Passeau many years later. "We had a terrible club. We usually gave the other team four to six outs per inning. I just kept pitching the way I always did."

In retrospect, pitcher Hugh Mulcahy appreciated the change. "We thought that Shibe Park was a much better ballpark, all the way around," he said. "We were glad to leave Baker Bowl. Shibe Park held more people, but I don't know if we drew many more when we got there."

Catcher Bill Atwood thought the move was a good one, too. "Just about everybody was happy to move to Shibe Park," he said. "The pitchers, especially, were happy. Of course, the lefthanded hitters hated to leave Baker Bowl. But Shibe Park was a much better ballpark than Baker Bowl, although Baker Bowl had a good background for the hitters."

Although batting averages soon thereafter began to dip, the new park was a strong tonic for the morale of the club. But it had no effect on the team's overall performance. The Phillies went on to produce five straight eighth-place finishes and seven in the next eight years. Included in those dismal years were five of the seven losingest teams in Phillies' history.

The World Series

Baseball's most spectacular event, the World Series, was no stranger to Shibe Park. During the life of the park, the fall classic was held there eight times. Only Yankee Stadium and the Polo Grounds in New York and Sportsman's Park in St. Louis had more World Series.

In seven of those World Series, the Athletics were the participants. And some of baseball's most memorable moments occurred.

With fans filling the stands and crowding the rooftops on 20th Street, the A's won American League pennants and advanced to the World Series in 1910, 1911, 1913, 1914, 1929, 1930, and 1931. They won the Series in five of those years.

The World Series also visited Shibe Park in 1950 when the Phillies captured the National League pennant with a heavy concentration of hustling, young players who were called the Whiz Kids.

Probably the most unforgettable event in Shibe Park's World Series history happened in 1929 when the A's staged their famous 10-run seventh inning in the fourth game. Behind, 8–0, the A's roared to a 10–8 victory in a game that virtually broke the backs of the visiting Chicago Cubs.

"At the World Series games back then," Bill Brendley recalled, "fans lined up two and three deep along the wall before the first game. They had blankets. Vendors sold hot dogs for 10 cents, sodas for 5 cents. To be eligible to get a ticket, you had to show 50 rainchecks from regular-season games. During the season when each game was over, I used to go around and pick up all the rainchecks I could find. Most people just threw them away. I'd get 10 to 15 rainchecks a game. Then I'd give them to people in the neighborhood so they could use them to get World Series tickets."

The A's had made their first trip to the Series at Shibe Park in 1910. After entering an earlier World Series at Columbia Park in 1905 (the A's also won the pennant in 1902, but there was no World Series), the A's met the Cubs in what shaped up as a potentially spectacular match. The Cubs had captured 104 victories while winning the National League pennant by 13 games, and the A's cruised home in the American League with a 14½-game lead and 102 wins. Both teams featured strong hitting and outstanding pitching.

The youthful A's, led by 23-year-old Eddie Collins and 24-year-old Frank Baker, used only two pitchers to dispose of the Cubs in five games. With Eddie Plank nursing an ailing arm, 23-game winner Chief Bender and 31-game winner Jack Coombs were all that the A's used in the entire Series. Bender won the opener at Shibe Park, 4–1, with a three-hitter, and Coombs came back with a 9–3 win the next day as the A's exploded against Mordecai (Three-Fingered) Brown with a six-run seventh. After Coombs won the third game and Bender lost the fourth, both at Chicago, the A's clinched the Series at home on October 23 with a 7–2 win as Coombs again bested Brown before a crowd of 27,374. Collins had three hits in the final game to end the Series with a .429 average. Baker hit .409.

The A's were back in the Series in 1911, this time in a rematch of the 1905 pitching classic with the New York Giants. Hoping to intimidate the opposition, John McGraw's Giants wore black uniforms and boosted the pitching of Christy Mathewson and Rube Marquard and a running offense that set a modern major league record with 347 stolen bases. They

As spectators lined the outfield walls, Eddie Collins dashed to second base with a double in the 1910 World Series.

had a 99–54 record, winning the pennant by 7½ games, while the A's carried a 101–50 mark and a 13½-game cushion into the Series.

On their way to another Series victory, the A's lost the opener in New York, then moved to Shibe Park where Baker's two-run homer in the sixth broke a 1–1 tie and gave Plank and the A's a 3–1 win over Marquard. Back in New York for the third game, Baker hit a ninth-inning home run to give the A's a 1–1 tie, and the A's won, 3–2, in 11 innings as Coombs pitched a three-hitter to beat Mathewson. Six straight days of rain followed before Game Four was played at Shibe Park. This time, Bender beat Mathewson, 4–2, with Baker, Danny Murphy, and Jack Barry each hitting two doubles. After losing Game Five in New York, the A's returned to Shibe Park to win the sixth and deciding game, scoring seven runs in the

Before a game in the 1911 World Series, the area around the main
entrance of Shibe Park was filled with dapper-looking fans rushing
to buy tickets.

seventh to coast to a 13–2 victory for Bender. Baker's long-distance clout-
ing in the Series earned for him the nickname of Home Run, which stuck
with him for the rest of his career.

After a year's absence from the Series, the A's returned to the spotlight
in 1913, again against the Giants. A 96–57 record had given the A's
the American League flag by 6½ games, while the Giants with a 101–51
mark finished in front with a 12½-game cushion. All year the A's had
been without the services of Coombs, who was sidelined with typhoid
fever, but had put in his place rookie Joe Bush, who became a 20-game
winner.

Bender beat the Giants in the opener at New York, but the Giants
bounced back with a win the next day at Shibe Park as Bucknell graduate
Mathewson outpitched Plank, his old college rival from Gettysburg, to win
3–0 in 10 innings. Bush followed with a victory at the Polo Grounds. Then
the A's won again at Shibe Park, 6–5, as catcher Wally Schang drove in
three runs to give Bender the win, despite a three-run homer by Fred
Merkle. Plank evened the score with Mathewson by hurling a 3–1 triumph
in Game Five at New York to give the A's their third world championship.
Baker finished the Series with a .450 average, and Collins hit .421.

With bleachers erected on the rooftops of houses and crowds milling around 20th Street, fans got set to watch a game in the 1929 World Series.

The A's, who had become the dominant team of the era, were back in the Series in 1914, but this time with a disappointing result. Despite raids by the new Federal League, resulting in the loss of key outfielder Murphy, the A's had rumbled to the American League pennant with a 99–53 record and an 8½-game lead. Conversely, their Series opponents, the Boston Braves, had been in last place in the National League on July 18 but had exploded in the second half to win the flag by 10½ games with a 94–59 record.

The Miracle Braves, as they became known, swept the powerful A's in four games, winning the first two at Shibe Park. With a large contingent of Braves fans known as the Royal Rooters and led by Boston mayor John F. (Honey Fitz) Fitzgerald, grandfather of John F. Kennedy, in the stands, manager George Stallings' club beat the A's, 7–1, behind the five-hit pitching of veteran Dick Rudolph in the first game. In Game Two, Bill James beat the 39-year-old Plank with a two-hit, 1–0 decision. The underdog Braves went on to win the next two games at Fenway Park (borrowed from the Red Sox because it was a more attractive facility), holding the mighty Athletics' offense to a .172 batting average. Experiencing financial problems and so stunned by the rude disaster, Connie Mack began dismantling his team during the winter.

An A's World Series team did not surface again until 1929. But what a team it was. The A's roared through the American League with a 104–46 record, finishing 18 games ahead of the powerful New York Yankees. Outfielder Al Simmons led the league with 157 RBI while hitting .365 with 34 home runs, first baseman Jimmie Foxx hit .354 with 33 homers and 117 RBI, and catcher Mickey Cochrane went .331–7–95. It was as powerful as any Athletics' team in history, and to boot, it had a pair of 20-game winners, Lefty Grove and George Earnshaw, on the mound.

With the Cubs, owners of a 98–54 record and a 10½-game lead in the National League, providing the opposition, it was expected to be a fiercely battled Series. But the crafty Mack had a surprise up his sleeve for the opener at Chicago's Wrigley Field. He had 35-year-old Howard Ehmke start on the mound, and the fading veteran responded with a then-Series record 13 strikeout, 3–1 victory.

After the A's won again in the second game in Chicago, they returned home and dropped a 3–1 decision in Game Three, despite a 10-strikeout, six-hit complete game by Earnshaw. Then in Game Four, history was made.

Trailing 8–0 in the bottom of the seventh, the A's sent 15 batters to the plate in a batting rampage that produced a Series-record 10 runs in the inning. Simmons led off with a home run onto the roof in left field. Singles by Foxx, Bing Miller, Jimmie Dykes, and Joe Boley followed. Before the inning was over, Mule Haas had hit a line drive that went for an inside-the-park three-run homer when Hack Wilson let it sail past him, Dykes had hit a two-run double, and the A's had routed four Cubs pitchers with Simmons, Foxx, and Dykes all collecting two hits in the inning.

The shell-shocked Cubs lost, 10–8, with reliever Eddie Rommel getting the win for the A's. The next day it was all over as the A's rallied with three runs in the bottom of the ninth to capture the championship with a 3–2 victory. A two-run homer by Haas over the right field wall was followed by doubles against the scoreboard by Simmons and Miller. Rube Walberg got the win in relief of Ehmke, who this time lasted just three innings.

The first four games of the Series were marked by heavy razzing between the two teams. So fierce was the bench-jockeying that before the fifth game, Commissioner Kenesaw Landis called rival managers Mack and Joe McCarthy together. "If the vulgarities continue," Landis told them, "I'll fine the culprits a full Series share." When Mack passed the word to his players, Cochrane went out on the field and shouted to the rival Cubs, "After the game, we'll serve tea in the clubhouse." Mack cringed, fearful that Landis would learn about Cochrane's wisecrack. But when Landis entered the Athletic's clubhouse following the fifth game's final out, he headed straight to the catcher and shook his hand. "Now, where's the tea?" Landis said.

There was no tea then or the following year as the powerful and relentless Athletics went back to the Series after roaring home with a 102–52 record, eight games into first. The A's faced the St. Louis Cardinals, no slouches themselves. The Cards had compiled a .314 team batting average with every man in the starting lineup hitting over .300 as they hammered their way to a 92–62 finish, two games ahead of the Cubs.

By Series end, though, the A's had collected their fifth world championship. In the opener at Shibe Park, Grove beat Burleigh Grimes, 5–2, with Simmons and Cochrane each hitting home runs and the A's getting only five hits, all for extra bases. The A's won again before the home fans in Game Two as Cochrane's home run and an RBI double by Foxx gave the A's a two-run lead in the first and Earnshaw all the runs he needed in coasting to a 6–1 decision with a six-hitter. The A's then lost two out of three games in St. Louis before returning to Shibe Park to win the Series with a 7–1 victory in Game Six behind the five-hit pitching of Earnshaw and home runs by Simmons and Dykes. Earnshaw wound up as the Series pitching star, yielding just two runs and 13 hits in 25 innings, while Simmons hit .364.

That, however, was the Athletics' final championship, although they went to the Series again in 1931. This time the Cardinals, who romped away with the National League pennant with a 101–53 record and a 13-game lead, won the Series in seven games as Pepper Martin stole the show. The A's had finished the season with a 107–45 record and a 13½-game lead.

The teams divided the first two games at St. Louis. Back at Shibe Park for the third game, Grimes, a 38-year-old spitballer, pitched a no-hitter for seven innings before finishing with a two-hitter and a 5–2 win. Earnshaw, a 20-game winner for the third straight year, answered with a two-hitter of his own and a 3–0 victory in Game Four with Foxx homering. In the final game of the Series at Shibe Park, St. Louis won Game Five with Martin driving in four runs and scoring three to back Wild Bill Hallahan as he beat veteran Waite Hoyt, 5–1. The A's then tied the Series in St. Louis before Earnshaw lost Game Seven to Grimes, 4–2. Martin, nicknamed the Wild Horse of the Osage, finished with a .500 batting average, which included a record 12 hits and five stolen bases.

Along with Martin's brilliant performance, the Series was marked by the appearance of President Herbert Hoover, who attended Game Three at Shibe Park. Hoover had also attended Series games at Shibe Park in both 1929 and 1930.

Hoover's appearance in 1931, however, was greeted by boos, which became louder as he moved across the field with his wife to a private box. The United States at the time not only was immersed in a depression, but under the Volstead Act of 1920 was also in the midst of the Prohibition era. As Hoover moved into his box, the booing changed to a chant. "We want beer. We want beer," the fans screamed.

When Hoover left the game in the eighth inning, according to *Baseball, The Presidents Game*, by William Mead and Paul Dickson, the public address announcer pleaded for silence. But as the President walked past the Athletics' dugout, the booing and chanting erupted again. "We want beer. We want beer."

"It is a shocking manifestation of bad manners and lack of respect," Joe Williams wrote the next day in the New York *World-Telegram and Sun*. "This must be the first time a president has been booed in public, and at a ball game, of all places." Connie Mack was equally dismayed, claiming to be thoroughly embarrassed by the episode.

It would be 19 years before Shibe Park got another chance to play host to a World Series. This time, though, the home team was the Phillies, making just their second postseason appearance in 67 years.

The Phillies had captured the attention of the entire city, if not the country, with their colorful and daring style of play. Nicknamed the Fightin' Phils and the Whiz Kids, they had blown a 9½-game lead in late August, then won the pennant on the final day of the season when Dick Sisler hit a three-run home run in the 10th inning to give the gritty Robin Roberts a 4–1 victory over the Brooklyn Dodgers at Ebbets Field.

The Phils, a mixture of youth and grizzled veterans who had finished the season with a 91–63 record and a slim two-game lead, were matched against a powerful New York Yankees team. Managed by Casey Stengel, a former Phillies player, the Yanks had romped to the American League title with a 98–56 record, finishing first by three games, and were in the midst of a streak in which they would capture five consecutive world championships.

The Phillies were badly overmatched. But that didn't matter to their fans. People began lining up for general admission tickets at Shibe Park the day before the first game. By 7:00 A.M. the morning of the game, the line was five blocks long. It didn't move until the gates were open at noon, by which time the line was considerably longer. Unfortunately, because of a blunder in the Phillies' office that resulted in some 600 bags of mail not being opened, some 2,000 reserved seats went unsold.

Reminiscent of the 1929 Series opener when Connie Mack made Howard Ehmke his surprise starter, Phillies manager Eddie Sawyer stunned everyone but himself by selecting reliever Jim Konstanty as his starting pitcher. Konstanty, who had saved 22 games and won another 16 for the

In the clubhouse after the 1950 season, Phillies players met to vote
on the distribution of World Series shares. Captain Granny Hamner
(white shirt and tie, holding paper) led the discussion.

Phillies in 1950 while working in a record 74 games strictly out of the
bullpen, hadn't started a game since 1948. But he was the best—perhaps
the only—choice on a weary staff whose members were simply too worn
out from the just-completed season to pitch.

"The Yanks are a free-swinging team," Sawyer said. "Konstanty throws
the kind of stuff that will stop a free-swinging team."

Sawyer's strategy nearly worked. Konstanty allowed just four hits in
eight innings, but his opponent Vic Raschi was even better, scattering two
hits. The Yanks won, 1–0, on a double by Bobby Brown and fly balls by
Hank Bauer and Jerry Coleman in the fourth inning.

Another outstanding pitching duel dominated the second game at
Shibe Park. In this one, Allie Reynolds bested Roberts, 2–1, with Joe
DiMaggio's leadoff home run in the 10th inning making the difference.

The Phillies then traveled to New York where the Yankees completed
a sweep by winning the next two games. With another one-run loss in the
third game, the Phillies extended their Series streak, carried over from
1915, to seven straight one-run losses. The Phillies wound up hitting just
.203 in the brief Series. The Yankees weren't much better, batting .222.

There would be no more World Series at Shibe Park, although the
Phillies came close again in the infamous year of 1964.

The Phillies take the field for the first game of the 1950 World Series at Shibe Park.

The line of fans attempting to buy one-dollar bleacher tickets for the opening game of the 1950 World Series reached for six blocks along Somerset Street.

All-Star Games

Shibe Park was the scene of two All-Star Games, both of particular distinction.

The first one, played in 1943, was the first All-Star Game played at night. With the A's serving as the host team, the American League captured its eighth victory in 11 games with a 5–3 verdict before a crowd of 31,938.

The National League jumped out to a 1–0 lead in the first inning against American League starter Dutch Leonard. The lead was soon erased when Bobby Doerr hit a three-run home run in the second inning off National League starter Mort Cooper.

Doubles by Ken Keltner and Dick Wakefield added another run off Cooper in the third before Johnny Vander Meer came on in relief to strike out Rudy York and Chet Laabs. Vander Meer went on to fan six in two and two-thirds innings.

The batting hero for the National League was outfielder Vince DiMaggio. Entering the game in the fourth inning, he hit a pinch-hit single. Later, he added a triple and home run.

Before a packed house, Robin Roberts works from the mound in the second game of the Series with the New York Yankees.

Leonard was the winning pitcher, while Cooper took the loss.

The only local players in the game were the Athletics' Dick Siebert, who started at first base, and the Phillies' Babe Dahlgren, a substitute first baseman.

The game was delayed at one point for 65 minutes as city officials practiced a blackout and all lights were turned off at the park.

Six members of the New York Yankees made the American League team, but manager Joe McCarthy didn't use any of them. Apparently resentful of earlier criticism that he favored his own players, the Yanks' pilot decided to show his detractors that he could win without playing any of his own men.

The second All-Star Game was played at Shibe Park in 1952 and was the first All-Star Game halted by rain. Some 32,785 were in attendance as the National League won its third-straight midsummer classic with a 3–2 triumph in five innings.

The game was noteworthy because A's pitcher Bobby Shantz struck out three straight batters—Whitey Lockman, Jackie Robinson, and Stan Musial—in the fifth inning. Rain deprived the little lefthander of the chance to go after Carl Hubbell's record five-straight strikeouts, achieved in the 1934 All-Star Game.

Some 33 years later, Shantz still had vivid recollections of his feat. "I only threw 13 pitches," he said. "I had a real good curveball that day. The one I threw to strike out Robinson must have dropped two feet into the dirt. Even to this day, Musial says the one I struck him out on was outside."

Rain had fallen intermittently throughout the morning. It turned into a downpour before gametime, and both teams were forced to forgo pregame warm-ups. The start of the game was delayed 20 minutes while officials waited in vain for a break in the weather.

Along with Shantz, the game had a heavy Philadelphia flavor as the Phillies' Curt Simmons was the starting pitcher for the National League. Simmons' start came in the midst of a string of five All-Star Game starts by teammate Robin Roberts.

Simmons gave up just one hit and struck out three in three innings of work. Robinson gave him a 1–0 lead with a home run off Vic Raschi in the first inning. The American League came back with two runs off Bob Rush in the fourth on a pinch-hit double by Minnie Minoso, a walk, and RBI singles by Eddie Robinson and Bobby Avila.

Hank Sauer regained the lead for the Nationals and provided the winning margin with a two-run home run off Bob Lemon in the bottom of the fourth inning. The blow made Rush the winning pitcher. An inning later, heavy rain forced termination of the game.

Only one other Philadelphia player participated in the game. The Phillies' Granny Hamner was the NL's starting shortstop.

Great Games by the Visitors

Some of the most memorable events in Shibe Park history were achieved by visiting players. Hall of Famers Ted Williams, Ty Cobb, Babe Ruth, Lou Gehrig, Jackie Robinson, and various others all performed special feats at the park.

Williams's final day of the season in 1941 when he became the last player to hit .400 was undoubtedly the premier accomplishment at Shibe Park by a visiting player.

The Boston Red Sox left fielder entered the September 28 finale with a batting average of .39955. Rounded off, the average would have been .400, but Williams refused manager Joe Cronin's offer to sit out the Sunday doubleheader with the A's. "If I'm going to be a .400 hitter, I want to have more than my toenails on the line," he said.

After walking the streets of Philadelphia far into the night in an effort to clear his head and settle his jumpy nerves, Williams proceeded to go

6-for-8 in the twin bill to finish the season with a .406 average. In the first game, he slammed four hits in five trips to the plate, including a home run off Dick Fowler over the right field wall, to lead the Red Sox to a 12–11 victory. In the second game, he had two hits in three at-bats, one a double that broke an amplifier atop the wall in right. The A's won, 7–1.

Overall, Williams finished the day with 10 total bases while facing four pitchers and becoming the first big league player since Bill Terry in 1930 to hit .400. Williams's feat earned a spot in baseball history as one of the game's greatest hitting accomplishments.

Another brilliant piece of work with the bat was performed by Babe Ruth over a two-day period in 1930. Playing in successive doubleheaders at Shibe Park, Ruth—who had slammed his first hit as a New York Yankee at Shibe Park in 1920—blasted Athletics' pitching for six home runs.

In a May 21 twinbill, Ruth clouted home runs in the first, third, and eighth innings of the first game, the first time he hit three homers during a regular-season game. Although his six RBI in that game were not enough to prevent a 15–7 win by the A's (the defending world champion A's also won the second game, 4–1), Ruth came back to power the Yankees to 10–1 and 20–13 victories the next day. He hit two home runs in the opener and another in the nightcap in a game in which Lou Gehrig hit three home runs and drove in eight runs.

Gehrig had a moment of glory at Shibe Park all to himself on June 3, 1932, when he blasted four home runs in a game won by the Yankees, 20–13. Touching A's pitcher George Earnshaw the first three times up and Roy Mahaffey the fourth, Gehrig homered in the first, fourth, fifth, and seventh innings, becoming the first 20th-century player to hit four home runs in one game. After grounding out in the eighth, he barely missed a fifth home run in the ninth inning when he crushed a drive to deep center. Al Simmons, playing center field, leaped high against the wall to rob Gehrig of what might have been an unmatched fifth home run. The Yankees first baseman, who had six RBI in the game, had considerable offensive support from Ruth, who homered in the ninth inning, and from Tony Lazzeri, who hit for the cycle, his home run being a grand slam.

Lazzeri had a bigger game May 24, 1936, at Shibe Park, just one day after he'd hit three home runs in a doubleheader against the A's. This time, he again smacked three home runs, including two grand slams, and collected an American League record 11 RBI in a 25–2 Yankees' rout of the A's. In becoming the first major leaguer to hit two grand slams in one game, Lazzeri cleared the bases in the second and fifth innings, hit a solo homer in the seventh, and slammed a two-run triple in the eighth that just missed going over the left field wall.

An incident of another kind occurred in 1909 in Shibe Park's first year of operation. It was one of many at the park that involved Ty Cobb.

Following a 1908 spiking of Frank Baker, Cobb was hated by A's fans and even by the club's manager Connie Mack, who campaigned to get the Detroit Tigers outfielder banned from baseball. Fueling the fans' hatred, early in the 1909 season, Cobb beat and stabbed a black employee of a Cleveland hotel. When Cobb arrived in Philadelphia a few days later, A's fans were ready for him.

Cobb received numerous death threats. Before the game, the Aldine Hotel, where he was staying in center-city Philadelphia, was surrounded by an angry mob of several thousand. A 12-man police motorcycle escort was needed to transport him to Shibe Park. During the game, A's owner Ben Shibe had guards circulating through the stands with megaphones, asking the bugs (fans) to stay calm. No incidents occurred during the game, but afterward, fans stormed the field and surrounded Cobb. Ultimately, he was led safely off the field by a group of sympathetic Masons.

Cobb had another big outburst at Shibe Park in 1912 when he collected 14 hits in 19 at-bats in two straight doubleheaders. The hitting spree included seven straight hits—four singles, two doubles, and a triple. Another time, the Georgia Peach leaped over a rope in right-center to snare a line drive and crashed down on a spectator, breaking the fan's straw hat. The next inning, Cobb gave a five-dollar bill to the fan for the purchase of a new hat.

In 1915, Cobb was up to his old tricks, spiking A's catcher Jack Lapp on a play at the plate. As Lapp lay hurt, Cobb spit on him, inciting some 20 fans to attempt to rush onto the field after him. They were stopped by police. Outside the park afterward, an angry crowd stormed after Cobb, who escaped their wrath by climbing onto a passing trolley. While managing the Tigers in the 1920s, Cobb also punched a Shibe Park groundskeeper who was using a telephone that he wanted. And, of course, he finished his playing career with the A's in 1928.

In later years, Shibe Park was still the scene of noteworthy accomplishments by visiting players. With the Boston Red Sox scoring 35 runs, third baseman Jim Tabor slammed three home runs, including two grand slams in the second game of a July 4, 1939, doubleheader, to finish the twinbill with four homers, 11 RBI, and seven runs scored. Chicago White Sox outfielder Pat Seerey hit four home runs in an ll-inning, 12–11 victory over the Athletics in the first game of a July 18, 1948, doubleheader at Shibe Park. In becoming only the fifth major league player to hit four home runs in one game, Seerey bashed homers in the fourth, fifth, and sixth innings before his llth-inning four-bagger won the game for Chicago. He had seven RBI.

In 1956, while closing in on a record eight home runs in eight straight games, Pittsburgh Pirates first baseman Dale Long hit the seventh homer of the streak at Connie Mack Stadium. It came against Phillies reliever Ben Flowers on an 0–2 count in Long's last time at bat in the eighth inning. Long's teammates carried him off the field after he'd crossed the plate.

Jackie Robinson had many outstanding games at Shibe Park, including one in 1949 in which his two-run, ninth-inning home run off Jim Konstanty gave the Brooklyn Dodgers a 7–5 victory over the Phillies. But Robinson's most memorable Shibe Park performance was certainly the one in the final regular-season game of 1951 when his heroics allowed the Dodgers to tie the New York Giants for first place. In a hard-fought skirmish September 30, Brooklyn had battled back to tie the Phillies, 8–8, sending the game into extra innings. In the 12th inning, second baseman Robinson, knocking himself out on the play, made a sensational diving catch of a line drive by Eddie Waitkus that kept the Phillies from scoring the winning run. Then in the 14th, Robinson laced a home run off Robin Roberts, pitching in relief, to give the Dodgers a dramatic 9–8 victory.

Another Dodger, Sandy Koufax, also distinguished himself at what was by then Connie Mack Stadium. In 1964, he pitched his third no-hitter, a one-walk, 12-strikeout masterpiece against the Phillies at the stadium. Two years later, on October 12, 1966, he hurled the last regular-season game of his career at the park. The game was doubly significant because Koufax's 10-strikeout, seven-hit, 6–3 victory gave his Los Angeles club the National League pennant. It was the 27th win of the season for the soon-to-be-retired Koufax.

Bob Feller won his 20th game of the season in 1941 at Shibe Park. Willie Mays made his major league debut there, going 0-for-5 in 1951. And Ernie Banks often pounded on the door of Phillies' offices on his way into the park, screaming "Let's play two."

Other Memorable Games

Owing in part to its long existence, but also to its many colorful and excellent teams and players, Shibe Park/Connie Mack Stadium was the site of some of the most memorable games in baseball history. Other than Yankee Stadium in New York, probably no other ballpark had more major events.

The All-Star and World Series games, as well as the first and last games at the park, are covered elsewhere in this book. What follows are descriptions of some other significant games.

May 29, 1909 – Frank Baker hit the first home at Shibe Park with a drive over the right field wall in the first game of a doubleheader with the Boston Red Sox.

May 12, 1910 – Using a blazing fastball, Chief Bender fired Shibe Park's first no-hitter, beating the Cleveland Naps, 4–0. In winning his fifth game without a defeat, Bender struck out four and walked one.

May 18, 1912 – With the team refusing to play in protest of the suspension of Ty Cobb, who three days earlier had leaped into the stands in New York to pummel a heckler, the Detroit Tigers were forced to field a makeshift team of Philadelphia-area college and sandlot players rounded up by manager Hugh Jennings. Failure to play would have cost the Tigers a $5,000 per game fine. The A's trounced baseball's first replacement team, 24–2, slamming 26 hits (but no home runs) off Aloysius Travers. Travers, the manager of his college baseball team, never pitched either before or after his one major league outing. The future priest pitched the entire game, earning $25 for his efforts (the other players received $10 each).

September 27, 1912 – In the longest major league game to date, the Washington Senators defeated the A's, 5–4, in 19 innings. Losing pitcher Eddie Plank went the distance, allowing 12 hits. Walter Johnson got the win in relief, working the last 10 innings. The winning run crossed on a throwing error by Eddie Collins.

May 9, 1916 – Pitchers for the Athletics and Detroit Tigers walked a combined record of 30 batters in a 16–2 win for the Bengals. Three A's hurlers combined to walk 18. Amazingly, the game was played in two and one-half hours.

August 26, 1916 – One day after he had been knocked out of the box in the third inning, Joe Bush came back to pitch a no-hitter against the Cleveland Indians. In winning, 5–0, the hard-throwing Bush walked lead-off batter Jack Graney but allowed no one else to reach base while striking out seven.

September 28, 1916 – Setting a record that lasted for 77 years, A's pitcher Jack Nabors lost his 19th-straight game, bowing to the Washington Senators, 4–1. At the time, the loss sent the hapless A's reeling to a 33–115 record, 54½ games out of first place.

September 29, 1920 – Babe Ruth, passed over by Connie Mack six years earlier when the A's had a chance to purchase the budding star from the Baltimore Orioles, climaxed a stunning season with his 54th home run of the year. The total far surpassed Ruth's own record of 29 set the previous year. Ruth's home run helped the New York Yankees to a 7–3 win in the first game of a doubleheader.

Home run balls occasionally flew over the billboards atop the left and left-center field roof. The most notable practitioners were Dick Allen and Jimmie Foxx.

September 4, 1923 – Aided by a fine running catcher by center fielder Whitey Witt, New York Yankees pitcher Sam Jones tossed the first no-hitter by a visiting player at Shibe Park, beating the A's, 2–0. Jones walked one and struck out none.

September 7, 1923 – The punchless A's were no-hit for the second time in less than one week as Howard Ehmke of the Boston Red Sox beat them, 4–0. For Ehmke, who struck out one and walked one, it was his sixth victory over the A's that season.

June 15, 1925 – The A's staged one of the great comebacks in baseball history when they overcame a 15–4 eighth-inning deficit with a 13-run explosion that carried them to a 17–15 win over the Cleveland Indians. The winning margin came on a titanic three-run homer by Al Simmons onto the left field roof that concluded an inning featuring nine hits and four walks, including a two-run triple by Jimmy Dykes. Reliever Tom Glass got the win.

February 9, 1927 – In a special ceremony at Shibe Park, former A's nemesis Ty Cobb, once the most hated man in Philadelphia, signed a contract to play with the Athletics. The ex-Detroit Tigers star would be paid $60,000.

July 21, 1928 – Jimmie Foxx became the first player ever to hit a drive clear over the roof atop the double deck at Shibe Park. His shot was estimated to have traveled 450 feet in the fifth inning of the first game of a doubleheader with the St. Louis Browns. The A's won both games, 8–2 and 7–3, with every player in the lineup hitting safely in both games.

May 25, 1931 – After Lefty Grove struck out Babe Ruth and Lou Gehrig in the ninth inning, with the tying run on base in a 4–2 Athletics' victory, the home team came back in the second game of the doubleheader to run their winning streak to 17 straight games. Delighting a capacity crowd of 32,000, the A's erupted with nine runs in the first inning. A two-run triple by Mickey Cochrane and a three-run triple by Joe Boley sparked the club to a 16–4 rout.

June 8, 1931 – On his way to a brilliant 31–4 season, Lefty Grove launched a 16-game winning streak with a 7–3 decision over the Detroit Tigers. Grove's streak would tie an American League record before it ended August 23 at St. Louis.

August 29, 1934 – The 16-game winning streak of Detroit Tigers pitcher Schoolboy Rowe came to an end as the A's coasted to an easy 13–5 victory. Detroit shortstop Billy Rogell's two-run single had given the Tigers an early lead, but five-run innings in the fifth and seventh with Pinky Higgins swatting a two-run homer gave the A's the win.

May 23, 1936 – In the start of an explosive three-game series, the New York Yankees slammed 30 hits, scored 27 runs, and collected 61 total bases in 12–6 and 15–1 doubleheader wins over the A's. With Tony Lazzeri leading the way, the Yanks returned the next day to complete the carnage with 19 hits and a 25–2 victory.

June 12, 1938 – Bob Johnson set an A's record and tied an American League mark with eight RBI in an 8–3 victory over the St. Louis Browns. Johnson hit a grand slam home run in the first inning, an RBI single in the third, and a three-run homer in the eighth.

May 16, 1939 – The first American League night game was played at Shibe Park. AL president Will Harridge was among the 15,109 in attendance, declaring the lights were wonderful. "I could see details of a baseball game as well as I could if it had been daylight," he said. The Cleveland Indians spoiled the occasion for the A's, scoring five runs in the 10th inning to take an 8–3 verdict. Hal Trosky of Cleveland and Frankie Hayes of the A's hit home runs, and Jeff Heath poled a two-run double in the 10th to help get the win for John Humphries.

June 2, 1939 – In their first home night game, the Phillies lost to the Pittsburgh Pirates, 5–2, before a small crowd of 9,858 who sat most of the game through a driving rain. Kirby Higbe, acquired a few days earlier in a trade for Claude Passeau, took the loss, walking eight.

June 29, 1939 – With Joe DiMaggio, Babe Dahlgren, and Joe Gordon each hitting three home runs, the New York Yankees blasted 13 homers in a doubleheader in a record-setting outburst. The Yanks hit eight homers in a 23–2 win in the first game before winning the nightcap, 10–0.

September 24, 1940 – Although he was now playing with the Boston Red Sox, beloved former A's star Jimmie Foxx hit the 500th home run of his career in a 16–8 win over his former team in the first game of a doubleheader. Foxx's homer was the middle of three consecutive home runs hit in the sixth inning off A's pitcher George Caster. Ted Williams and Joe Cronin had the others. In the same inning Jim Tabor also had a home run for the Red Sox.

May 17, 1941 – Commissioner Kenesaw Mountain Landis, actor George M. Cohan, and Philadelphia mayor Robert Lamberton were among the many dignitaries on hand to help the city honor Connie Mack with a tribute to the Grand Old Man of Baseball. A ceremony at City Hall was followed by a parade to Shibe Park where more festivities took place, including a band concert and a specially written song by Cohan.

July 7, 1943 – Dick Barrett pitched all 14 innings to get his first big league shutout with a 1–0 victory over the Cincinnati Reds. Barrett gave up nine hits. Pinky May's pinch-hit single scored Coaker Triplett with the winning run.

July 18, 1943 – In an incredible display of ineptitude, the Phillies and New York Giants left a record-tying 30 runners on base in a 10–6 victory by the Giants. The Phils knocked out New York starter Carl Hubbell in the fourth inning and collected 15 hits and four walks. The Giants, who stranded 17 runners, rapped 19 hits against three Phillies pitchers.

July 21, 1945 – The longest game ever played at Shibe Park resulted in a 1–1 tie when the A's and the Detroit Tigers fought 24 innings before the battle was canceled by darkness. Underhanded hurler Russ Christopher pitched 13 innings for the A's, and Les Mueller worked 19⅔ innings for

Detroit. Promising third baseman George Kell failed to hit safely in 10 trips to the plate for the A's.

August 19, 1945 – In the only big league start of his career, Jimmie Foxx gained his only big league victory as he pitched the Phillies to a 4–1 triumph over the Cincinnati Reds. Foxx allowed one hit over the first six innings but tired and was lifted with two outs in the seventh.

September 9, 1945 – Just three weeks after he was discharged from the Canadian army, Dick Fowler won his only game of the season by pitching a no-hitter against the St. Louis Browns. The 1–0 victory was played in 1 hour, 15 minutes, the fastest no-hit game in modern times. Fowler registered six strikeouts and walked four. The A's scored the winning run in the bottom of the ninth on a triple by Hal Peck and single by Irv Hall.

August 11, 1946 – Frank McCormick's bloop double off Hugh Casey in the eighth inning drove in the winning run as the Phillies defeated the Brooklyn Dodgers, 7–6, in the first game of a doubleheader. The Dodgers had beaten the Phillies 18 straight times dating back to 1944.

May 11, 1947 – With spectators lining up at the gates starting at 5:00 A.M., the biggest crowd ever to see a baseball game at Shibe Park watched as the Phillies defeated the Brooklyn Dodgers, 7–3 and 5–4, behind the stellar pitching of Dutch Leonard and Schoolboy Rowe. The main reason for the 41,660 (40,952 paid) crowd was the appearance of Jackie Robinson, who was playing in Philadelphia as a major leaguer for the first time that weekend. In an earlier series in Brooklyn, Robinson had been viciously taunted by Phils manager Ben Chapman and some of his players. Chapman was ejected from the second game after arguing too strenuously that Robinson had stepped into a pitch while trying to bunt and should not be awarded first base. The twin-bill ended when Harry Walker made a diving catch of a line drive by Pee Wee Reese. Some 1,000 fans poured onto the field to help the stunned Walker get up.

September 3, 1947 – Bill McCahan pitched the A's last no-hitter, beating the Washington Senators, 3–0. While striking out two and walking none, McCahan was prevented from hurling a perfect game by a second-inning error by Ferris Fain. Elmer Valo helped out with a brilliant running catch in right-center of a drive by Mickey Vernon. Sam Chapman also made several fine catches.

July 16, 1948 – With thousands turned away at the gate, 37,684 made it inside for a doubleheader pitting the first-place A's and the Cleveland In-

Schoolboy Rowe, Del Ennis, Andy Seminick, and Willie Jones (*left to right*) tied a major league record when they combined to hit five home runs in one inning in a 12–3 victory over the Cincinnati Reds at Shibe Park in 1949. Seminick hit two homers in the (eighth) inning and three in the game.

dians. The Indians, who would eventually emerge with the pennant in a torrid four-team race, won both games, 6–1 and 8–5, to knock the A's out of first.

June 2, 1949 – The Phillies tied a major league record with five home runs in one inning as they rallied with 10 runs in the eighth to defeat the Cincinnati Reds, 12–3. After Del Ennis and Andy Seminick hit back-to-back homers off ex-teammate Ken Raffensberger, Willie Jones, Schoolboy Rowe, and Seminick again homered.

April 18, 1950 – Wearing their flashy new red pin-striped uniforms for the first time, the Phillies opened what would be their most successful season in 35 years with a 9–1 victory over the powerful Brooklyn Dodgers. Robin Roberts handily defeated Don Newcombe.

July 25, 1950 – After Bubba Church beat the Chicago Cubs, 7–0, in the opener, the Phillies went into first place to stay as Robin Roberts won the second game, 1–0.

July 27, 1950 – Del Ennis drove in seven runs in the seventh and eighth innings with a grand slam home run and a three-run double in a huge display of power as the Phillies defeated the Chicago Cubs, 13–3.

September 15, 1950 – In their longest game at Shibe Park, the Phillies beat the Cincinnati Reds, 8–7, in 19 innings. Del Ennis and Eddie Waitkus had five hits apiece.

October 18, 1950 – At a press conference at Shibe Park, the venerable Connie Mack announced that he was retiring as manager of the A's after holding the post for 50 years, the longest in baseball history. He managed the A's in 7,466 games, compiling a 3,582–3,814–70 record. Mack, 88, would be replaced by his former third baseman Jimmy Dykes.

April 17, 1951 – The first American League opening game ever held at Shibe Park resulted in the A's bowing to the Washington Senators, 5–1.

April 16, 1953 – Connie Ryan became the only modern Phillies player to slug six hits in one game when he drilled four singles and two doubles in a game against the Pittsburgh Pirates. The Phils lost anyway, 14–12, although the teams combined for 15 runs in one inning.

July 7, 1953 – Robin Roberts's streak of 28 consecutive complete games came to an end when he was lifted in the eighth inning of a game with the Brooklyn Dodgers. Trailing, 5–4, at the time, the Phillies rallied to win, 6–5.

May 13, 1954 – After giving up a leadoff home run to Bobby Adams, Robin Roberts retired the next 27 batters in order in an 8–1 victory over the Cincinnati Reds.

September 19, 1954 – Although it was not fully realized at the time, the A's played their last game in Philadelphia with a scant crowd of 1,715 in attendance. Gil McDougald's three-run homer in the eighth inning gave the New York Yankees a 4–2 win. Pete Suder had two of the Athletics' seven hits. Johnny Sain got the win, with Jim Konstanty working the last inning in relief for the Yankees. Ed Burtschy took the loss. The A's, who drew just 305,362 for the season, were sold that winter to businessman Arnold Johnson for $2 million and moved to Kansas City.

In 1963 the Whiz Kids returned to the scene of their 1950 triumphs to stage a reunion before a sellout throng.

September 26, 1954 – Richie Ashburn played in a Phillies' record 730th consecutive game as the season ended with a 3–2 loss in 11 innings to the New York Giants. The streak began June 7, 1950, and ended in 1955 when Ashburn was prevented from appearing in the home opener because of an injury. In an exhibition game a few days earlier in Wilmington, Delware, he had collided with Del Ennis while chasing a fly ball hit by Mickey Mantle.

April 12, 1955 – In a rousing home opener against the New York Giants, Robin Roberts pitched a no-hitter for eight innings en route to a 4–2 victory. The no-hitter ended in the ninth on a hit by Alvin Dark. Several batters later, Monte Irvin drilled a two-run double.

April 23, 1961 – Art Mahaffey tied a National League record held by Dizzy Dean. In the second game of a doubleheader, he had 17 strikeouts

in a 6–0 victory over the Chicago Cubs. Mahaffey allowed four hits and walked one.

July 29, 1961 – One of the most dubious streaks ever compiled was launched when the Phillies dropped a 4–3 verdict to the San Francisco Giants. Orlando Cepeda hit a first-inning grand slam. The streak would go on for 23 straight games, an all-time major league record. Don Ferrarese took the loss, his first of three during the streak.

September 21, 1964 – With Frank Robinson at bat, Chico Ruiz incredibly stole home for the only run of the game as the Cincinnati Reds defeated the Phillies and Art Mahaffey, 1–0. The loss, coming when the first-place Phils had a 6½-game lead with 12 games left to play, started Gene Mauch's club on a downward spiral. It didn't end until the team had lost 10 straight and fallen out of first in the greatest collapse baseball had ever seen.

There was always a considerable amount of activity outside the park before games. Parking, however, was always hard to find.

May 29, 1965 – Dick Allen hit one of the longest home runs in baseball history when he smashed a first-inning shot over the left field roof off Larry Jackson to begin a 4–2 Phils' win over the Chicago Cubs. Phillies publicity director Larry Shenk and sports columnist Sandy Grady found where the ball had landed and, by calculating distances, concluded that the ball had traveled 529 feet.

June 30, 1967 – Cookie Rojas pitched a scoreless ninth inning in a 12–3 loss to the San Francisco Giants. Since joining the Phillies in 1963, Rojas had played all nine positions, the only Phils player ever to do that.

August 16, 1969 – Rick Wise concluded a streak of four straight complete-game shutouts by Phillies pitchers with a four-hit, 7–0 win over the Houston Astros. Wise and Dick Allen hit home runs. Jerry Johnson, Woodie Fryman, and Grant Jackson had preceded Wise in the streak.

Around the Edges

There was always a lot happening outside the park on game days. Depending on the size of the crowd, the intensity of the activity varied, but it was never quiet when the A's or Phillies were playing.

Vendors' shouts of "Peanuts" and "Getchur scorecard lineup" along with the piercing whistles of the traffic cops punctuated the air. Buses, trolleys, and automobiles choked surrounding streets. And fans scurried to the ticket windows to buy seats that even as late as the 1960s cost a mere $1.30 for general admission.

Kilroy's, a bar that became Quinn's Tavern in 1942, did a landslide business at 20th and Lehigh with patrons standing four and five deep at the bar. So did Peg and Dave's Luncheonette at 20th and Somerset. Often, players stopped there for a sandwich on their way to the game. During games, players in the right field bullpen often slipped out the gate and over to "Quinnies" for a quick brew when the action became dull. Over the years, many of them bent their elbows there after the game, too.

During much of the park's existence, players lived in the area. Lefty Grove, for instance, rented a place on Lehigh Avenue. Al Simmons had a home at 2745 N. 20th Street, and during one of his celebrated holdouts, he spent his days sitting on the porch until Connie Mack sent an A's employee over to negotiate a settlement on opening day.

Many A's and Phillies players of later years also lived in the area. Some single players lived two to a room at Mom Keyborn's rooming house on 23d Street. Others lived in the Lorraine and Majestic hotels on Broad Street.

"My first year with the Phillies [in 1940], I lived two blocks away from the park in a home with several other players," recalled outfielder Danny Litwhiler. "You'd walk to the park each day, and the kids would follow you along. Normally, you'd take one or two of them in the gate with you. After I got married, I lived about 10 blocks away in an apartment."

Tom Ferrick, who pitched with the A's in 1941, after which he played for four other American League teams, was another neighborhood resident. "I lived right up the street in a room with a couple of other players," he said. "I walked to work. When I first signed with the A's, I came to Shibe Park my first day with my gloves, shoes, and a sweatsuit in a brown bag. They wouldn't let me in. They thought I was a neighborhood kid. They didn't know I was a player."

Players who didn't live in the neighborhood often used public transportation to get to the ballpark. One of them was pitcher Dallas Green, who grew up to become manager of the Phillies' only World Championship team.

"I used to take the train all the time from Wilmington [his hometown] to North Philadelphia Station," Green said. "I'd walk to the ballpark from the station. After the game, I'd walk back and catch the latest train that stopped. It came from Boston and would get me back to Wilmington around midnight. But if the game went late, and I missed it, I'd have to get over to 30th Street Station and catch a milk train home.

"Riding the train back and forth to the ballpark was really no big deal," Green added. "After a game, I hustled to get out, and I'd just walk along with the crowd to the train station. At that time, train stations were safe."

Parking was always at a premium. Because they arrived early, players who drove to games had the first crack at the lot at 21st and Lehigh. It held only about 300 cars. A few small lots were located within the first few blocks north of Somerset Street. If a fan couldn't get into one of those lots, street parking, sometimes many blocks away, was the only other option.

If you parked on the street, you had to contend with the youthful hustlers who as early as the 1920s demanded "a quarter to watch your car." Most fans, mindful that a flat tire might be forthcoming if they didn't pay up, readily acquiesced.

"There were all kinds of rackets going on around the park," recalled Jimmy Cochrane, a neighborhood resident who worked at Shibe Park starting in the 1930s. "Sometimes you'd give a guy a buck, and he'd take your car and park it somewhere else. Parking was ruled by 'The Big Seven,' a group of local guys. The cops backed them up and were paid a couple bucks a game." One cop was said to have boasted that he could make an extra $125 a night when there was a big crowd.

Newspaper writers parked their cars on 22d Street. A policeman on duty there had the names on a list and checked them off as the writers pulled into their spots.

Once a game began, the streets became quiet, except for the neighborhood kids who congregated outside of the right field wall in the hopes of landing baseballs that flew out of the park. For many years, a man named George Brand was in charge of the press gate, but he also collected balls that kids had caught. When they showed up with a ball, he would let the youthful retrievers into the park, then pocket some of the balls himself, using them later with the semipro team that he managed in Lancaster.

"If anyone got a ball that Babe Ruth hit out, you could bring it over to him when he came out after the game," recalled Bill Brendley. "He'd give you 50 cents for each ball."

Although somewhat rural at first, the surrounding neighborhood became one of mostly row houses and businesses. A number of factories operated in the area. Across from Shibe Park on Lehigh Avenue was Reyburn Park. Next to it was Dobbins Vocational High School, which was opened in 1938.

"Reyburn Park was kept as nice as some golf courses," said Cochrane. "Going there was like going out to the country. When they built Dobbins, it ruined the park."

In the early days of Shibe Park, the A's gave away scorecards for free. Later, both the A's and the Phillies affixed a price to the small but always appealing little booklets, which were printed right on the premises. Yearbooks were first issued by both teams in 1949 and for the Phillies have continued ever since. And in 1964, the Phillies' new public relations director, Larry Shenk, created what is thought to be the first baseball media guide. He mimeographed 300 copies, on the covers of which his wife Julie had hand-colored a Phillies' "P".

Getting autographs was a favorite postgame activity of youthful fans. "In 1929," remembered Brendley, "I bought a new baseball and took it around to the main gate. Just inside, I saw Mickey Cochrane. I yelled, 'Hey, Mickey, how about getting the ball signed for me?' He said, 'Sure, kid,' and took the ball in the clubhouse with him. A few minutes later, he came back with it, and the whole team, including Connie Mack, had signed it."

Home team players exited the stadium through a door near the corner of 21st and Lehigh. While attempting to cross the street to the parking lot, they'd be surrounded by autograph hounds, who'd besiege them all the way to their cars.

Visiting players usually came to the park by cab or subway and trolley until Joe McCarthy began the practice in the 1940s of chartering buses for players. Eventually, the use of charter buses was adopted by all visiting teams. The players, who piled into a bus that waited on Lehigh Avenue near the main entrance to the park, were fair game for autograph seekers as they sat waiting for the rest of the team to arrive. Often, the star players left the park clandestinely through a gate in right field, avoiding both autograph seekers and the more mundane form of transportation offered by the bus.

If a collector of signatures was especially diligent and it was getaway day for the visiting team, he could race the seven blocks to North Philadelphia Station. There, he would find players idling on the platform, awaiting the train that would take them to the next city. With nothing better to do, the players were usually willing signers.

Inside Jobs

There was something about working at Shibe Park that appealed to an awful lot of people. During the park's 62 years, thousands had full- or part-time jobs, many holding their positions for years on end.

Groundkeepers, including men such as Ted Forr (*left*), were highly regarded by many of the players.

"It was like home. Everybody knew each other. It was like one big family," Bill Hoopes explained. He should know. He worked at the park from 1942 until it closed, and for most of that time he was a supervisor of ushers in the upper deck. In those days, ushers were called "blue caps" for obvious reasons.

Hoopes, who still works at Veterans Stadium, had plenty of company, not only in his feelings for the park, but in longevity. Some of them were named Mack, as in Connie and sons Roy, Earle, and Connie, Jr. Among many others, there were park superintendent Andy Clark; left field ballboy Jackie Donnelly; batboy, then equipment manager Kenny Bush; front office executives Tom Hudson and Frank Sullivan; groundskeeper Ted Forr; clubhousemen Yitz Crompton of the A's and Unk Russell, Ace Kessler, and Ted Kessler of the Phillies; and the versatile Pat Cassidy, who performed numerous duties over the years.

"It was just a great place to work," recalled Charlie McCormack, who performed a number of jobs at the park starting in 1944. "It was fun, and you got to see the players and talk to them. Some lasting friendships were made."

For many of the players who performed at the park, the feeling of kinship with the park personnel was reciprocal. "I loved the people who worked around the park," said Dick Allen. "They made the stadium for me. A lot of times, they said I was late getting to the clubhouse, but I was

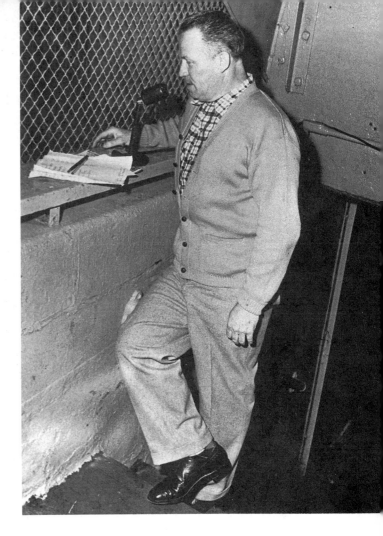

Pete Byron served as a longtime public address announcer at Shibe Park.

really walking around the ballpark, saying hello to the people who worked there. They were some of my best friends."

In the final decades of its life, the stadium had a full-time ground crew of 10 to 12 men. Most came from the neighborhood, including Jack Kelleher, who lived on Somerset Street.

"The park was always kept in top shape," said Kelleher, who still works for the Phillies. "They'd hire 20 guys to paint during the off-season. The ground crew, when it wasn't mowing or sprinkling the field, would paint, too. The park always looked nice."

Seymour Steinberg remembered when he started as a vendor in 1954 at Connie Mack Stadium and the park was full of people selling everything from pennants, hats, bats, and yearbooks to food. A hot dog cost 45 cents, a Dixie cup with ice cream was 30 cents, and a soda was 25 cents. In his first year, he worked both A's and Phillies games, 154 games altogether.

"I used to love those Sunday doubleheaders," he said. "I'd sell hot dogs as the main course in the first game and ice cream for dessert in the second game. We got a 15 percent commission on everything we sold. We'd

The Phillies' clubhouse in 1966 was still anything but spacious.

have a lot of repeats during a game because the price was low. People buy less today, but you make more because the price is so much higher.

"I always worked downstairs," Steinberg added. "You had territories, like home to first or home to third. Everybody liked what they were doing. Saturdays were always good days because there were always a lot of kids at the game."

Steinberg, who still sells at Veterans Stadium, laments the passing of earlier days at Connie Mack Stadium. "Back then, vendors were part of the ballpark," he said. "They worked longer. Today, you don't see them after the sixth inning. Years ago, they worked until the game was over. Vendors like that are a dying breed. They took their jobs seriously. Most were family men who were working two jobs to make ends meet."

Shibe Park had some legendary and colorful vendors. Charley Frank sold hot dogs and was so good at it that he had his own group of fans and signed autographs. His favorite cry was a loud "Dogeo!"

A man named Joe Angel was credited with selling more than one million hot dogs in 13 years at Shibe Park. He also sold Coca-Cola, calling it Coke on the rocks and bellowing to his would-be customers, "Give your tongue a sleigh ride."

"Connie Mack owned the concessions," recalled Maje McDonnell. "He had them bring in fresh food every day. That's why the food always tasted so good. After every game, he sent the leftovers to St. Joseph's Home for Boys at 16th and Allegheny."

Tom Hudson sold tickets, beginning in 1951 when he and Hugh Doherty established for the Phillies the first sales department in sports. "We flew a blue flag on game days," he said. "I saw a lot of great moments at the park. I was not all that enamored with Connie Mack Stadium itself. It had poles and obstructed seats and parking problems and other problems. But there was the glamour of going to the park every day that really had an appeal."

After the A's moved out of the park following the end of the 1954 season, the Phillies took over the American League team's offices and clubhouse. Previously, the Phils had used a makeshift office that Mack had built in anticipation of their arrival—although their main office remained in center city at the Packard Building—and a clubhouse that was located under the stands down the left field line passed a break behind third base.

"It wasn't much," remembered catcher Andy Seminick. "It was all open, and you could look up and see the stands above. It was very small."

When they moved into the Athletics' clubhouse, the quarters were slightly larger, but not a lot. Having been substantially altered from its early days, the clubhouse contained a main locker room, a little manager's office, an equipment room, and a loft where the trainer tried to work his magic.

"You had to go up steps to get to the trainer's room," recalled Frank Wiechec, Jr., whose father, Frank Wiechec, was the highly respected trainer of the Phillies from 1948 until the mid-1960s. "It wasn't very big, maybe 20 by 15 feet. It had a whirlpool, a diathermy machine, two rubbing tables, and a cabinet for the supplies. That was about it. It was just a one-man operation then. My dad would work on two or three players at a time. Sometimes when Eddie Sawyer would come out and talk to the players in the clubhouse, my dad would run me up there to get me out of the way."

Above the clubhouse was one of three separate offices used by the Phillies in later years. Reached by a flight of stairs near the break in the third base stands, it was the workplace for team owner Bob Carpenter, the general manager, and the farm director.

A few feet away from the employee entrance near the press gate at 21st and Lehigh another flight of stairs led to other Phillies' offices where the public relations director and traveling secretary worked. From there, a walkway led to other offices for sales and promotions people. The team's financial department worked in yet a third set of offices in the tower where Connie Mack once ran the A's.

Before the Yankee Stadium scoreboard was brought to Philadelphia in 1956, operators of the previous scoreboard had to hang the numbers from a small gangplank inside the facility.

"If I wanted to see [general manager] John Quinn," recalled public relations director Shenk, who joined the Phillies in the fall of 1963, "I had to go down one flight of stairs, across the third base side of the concourse, and up another flight of stairs. The offices weren't connected. It was a tough place to communicate. You had to do it mostly by phone because we were so spread out."

Mack's old office in the tower had been a legend almost from the time the park opened. Sedate but handsomely furnished, it was approached with an appropriate degree of reverence by visitors.

"You opened the door and there was Connie Mack sitting in a big leather chair facing right toward you," recalled Tom Ferrick. "It wasn't very big."

Ralph Bernstein, who covered sports for the *Associated Press* for 50 years starting in 1943, remembered the off-season bash that took place in the office. "The first week in December was Mack's birthday," he said. "It was a big media event. They'd have a big cake, and all the writers would go to congratulate him and write about the grand old man on his birthday."

The umpires' dressing room stood across a corridor from the Athletics'—and later the Phillies'—locker room. It was small and somewhat dingy.

"After games, the umpires used to come up the same stairway from the home team dugout as the manager and players," remembered Jimmy Higgins, who served as custodian of the umpires' room at both Shibe Park and Veterans Stadium. "I would hear them arguing all the way up the steps. Sometimes, it used to get pretty heated by the time they got to the room. The funny thing was, the next day they always acted like nothing happened. The night before, you were sure they were ready to kill each other.

"A few times, I also remember fans getting through to the room, banging on the door and yelling for the umpire," Higgins added. "Normally, that corridor was blocked off after a game, and fans couldn't get through. It got scary a couple of times, but nothing ever happened."

As Tough As There Is

If one word could be used to describe the fans who came to Shibe Park, it would have to be "avid." Unlike modern fans who often seem to have merely a casual interest in baseball, the fans of the old A's and Phillies rooted long and hard for their teams.

The fans of Shibe Park were also extremely knowledgeable. And they were tough. They were about as tough as any fans anywhere.

"Even though they were tough, they didn't bother you if you hustled," said former Phillies first baseman Bill White who went on to become president of the National League. "If you gave the fans their money's worth, they appreciated it."

Powerful A's outfielder Gus Zernial had his troubles with the fans, as did numerous other top-level players who performed in Philadelphia. "But they were good fans," he said. "They used to give me a hard time, but often I would egg them on. I talked to them a lot when I was out in left field. Sometimes, I'd get them all riled up."

When that happened, the fans were quick to unleash a chorus of boos. Booing, in fact, was a trait for which Shibe Park fans were famous. Fans didn't boo at Baker Bowl. But, as the original booers in Philadelphia, the Shibe Park patrons built the practice nearly to an art form.

"They were all wolves," said longtime National League umpire Shag Crawford. "And they never changed. From the first game I worked until the last, they always gave the umpires a hard time."

Once in the early 1940s, fans were so acrimonious in their criticism of the Phillies that coach Hans Lobert, Chuck Klein, Mickey Livingston,

In the early days of Shibe Park, most fans rode to games on trolleys.

and Ed Murphy charged up to the second deck to confront a heckler. After threatening to render him serious physical damage, the group was persuaded to return to the sanctity of the dugout.

In 1949, fans caused the Phillies to lose a game by forfeit when they littered the field with debris in protest of an umpire's decision. Umpire George Barr had ruled that a drive by Joe Lafata of the New York Giants had been trapped by center fielder Richie Ashburn. Ashburn and others argued vehemently. "It was the most stupid decision I have ever seen," said manager Eddie Sawyer. Fans booed and threw bottles, cans, papers, and anything else they could get their hands on onto the field for 15 minutes. A tomato hit umpire Al Barlick and a bottle grazed umpire Lee Ballanfant. When the mob refused to calm down, a 9–0 forfeit win was awarded to the Giants.

"Philadelphia had some of the toughest fans in the world," said 1940s Phillies first baseman Tony Lupien. "A couple of guys used to sit up in the second deck right over first base. They never let up on me from the beginning of the season to the end. And there was always a flock on [Ron] Northey out in right field and another on [Jimmy] Wasdell in left. You could hear them all over the park. They'd wait until it got nice and quiet, and wham . . . they'd let you have it.

Groundskeepers had a wheelbarrow load of debris to remove from the field in 1949 when fans protested an umpire's call that went against Richie Ashburn and the Phillies.

"Phillies fans," Lupien added, "are just about as tough as they come because they're very knowledgeable. They're as knowledgeable about baseball as any."

They could also be malicious. It was not uncommon for fans to throw beer cans or other instruments of derision onto the field if they didn't like an umpire's decision or the performance of either a visiting or hometown player.

"The fans were very tough, especially the ones in the upper deck in left field," recalled outfielder Ralph Kiner. "They would shoot staples at you during a game. You'd get hit in the back. It happened a lot. It was tough playing out there with those fans doing that all the time."

As tough as they often were, Shibe Park fans also had their soft spots. Not only were they extremely forgiving, but they showered the players they liked with warmth and affection.

Al Brancato, an A's infielder before and after World War II, remembered the fans knitting sweaters for the players. And Hugh Mulcahy said fans used to send cakes to the clubhouse on Ladies Day. "The fans weren't as rowdy then as they are now," said Brancato. "It was a much nicer atmosphere."

"Maybe it was because I was a little guy," said Bobby Shantz, "and they liked to root for the underdog. But the fans were great to me. They treated me wonderfully. To me, they were really good fans."

Following World War II, there was an outbreak of fan clubs in Philadelphia, some numbering several hundred members and all idolizing the players for whom they were formed. At one point in the early 1950s, one dozen Phillies players had fans clubs. Most club members were teenage and young adult women.

The largest club backed catcher Andy Seminick. It had 350 to 400 members, according to its founder and president Anne Zeisler, and it charged 50 cents a year in dues. The group even had special days at the park on which they honored Seminick, showering him with gifts rounded up from local merchants.

"It was a great fan club," remembered Andy Seminick. "They came to games, had a newsletter; they gave out pictures of me; they did all kinds of things. I think the fans back then were much closer to the players than they are today. You had better relationships with them, one reason being you were so close to them on the field."

Added Art Mahaffey: "Connie Mack Stadium was just a very intimate place. The fans were really close to you. They'd talk to you when you were warming up, ask you how you were doing. It was all very friendly."

Many fans have fond memories of their trips to the ballpark and the things they did once they got there. One of them is Ernie Montella, a resident of Warminster, who as a youth often spent one and one-half hours traveling from his native Marcus Hook to Shibe Park.

"Sometimes, I'd shine shoes all Saturday night at bars so I could earn $20 to get to a doubleheader on Sunday," he said. "On Sundays, I'd leave the house at 7:00 A.M., get the train to center city, ride the subway to Broad and Lehigh, then walk seven blocks to Shibe Park. I'd get there two hours before the players did. Why? I didn't want to miss anything. You had to see the players come in, didn't you? You'd be standing there, and somebody would say, 'Here comes [Eddie] Joost.' 'Here comes [Hank] Majeski.' Everybody ran after them to try and get an autograph.

"I'd pack four or five sandwiches. After all the players arrived, I'd go upstairs and watch batting practice. When I'd walk up the steps and see that fabulous green all around, it was all worth it. I was in awe. I can still remember my first game, walking in and seeing all that grass. It was like going to heaven.

"Sometimes, if the game got dull. I'd walk from deep center field all the way around the park to right field along the corridor in the upper deck. When I got a little older, I always bought a first-row seat near the dugout. It cost $3.75. I'll never forget sitting there one time and seeing Joe DiMaggio in the on-deck circle. He had a hole in his stocking. I couldn't believe it."

Trips to Shibe Park seem to evoke happy recollections and warm feelings of nostalgia among fans who went there years ago. Some, such as Jim Ring, an Abington resident whose grandfather Jimmy pitched for the Phillies in the 1920s, raise the memories of their trips almost to a religious level.

"Going to the stadium was like a cultural experience," said Ring, who grew up in Frankford. "The ballpark was the center of kids' lives, even though we didn't live near the stadium. It was like going to church. We tried to scrape enough money together to sit in the bleachers. The players were our heroes. We just loved the game and going to the park."

Bob Schmierer of Maple Glen had similar feelings when he went to Shibe Park as a youth. "I can picture walking into the place for my first game in 1949 like it was yesterday," he said. "It was a baseball park, not a multipurpose stadium. It was fun. It had grass. Dirt basepaths. Even the way the ball sounded when it was hit was different from what you hear today.

"The players were people with whom you could identify," he added. "And you could point to where things happened. You could point to a spot where Gehrig almost hit his fifth home run in one game; where Jackie Robinson hit the home run in the 14th inning in 1951. It was exciting. There was nothing like it then, and there certainly isn't now."

George Duross began going to games at Shibe Park much earlier, back at a time when holiday doubleheaders meant having one game in the morning, clearing out the park, and holding another game in the afternoon. But he shares the same passion as the fans who came later.

"I'd get a thrill when I'd walk in. There was just something about the place that excited me," he said. "I worshipped the Athletics, and I thought the Phillies were intruding when they came to Shibe Park.

"I remember when Ty Cobb came to town. We hated him because he had spiked Home Run Baker. And I remember when Jimmie Foxx used to drive up with a chauffeur. He lived in Huntingdon Valley then, and he was living like a king. Of course, when the crash (of 1929) came, he had to get rid of the chauffeur."

Loyal fans weren't always from just the Philadelphia area. Many trekked to the park from upstate Pennsylvania and from the central regions of the state. To accommodate those fans, the Phillies in 1951 began running special Pennsylvania Railroad excursions to the park. The trips continued for the rest of the life of the stadium.

Some excursions originated in Harrisburg, making three stops along the way. Others began in Newark, Delaware, with a stop in Wilmington. And still more came from either Atlantic City, Trenton, Reading, Allentown, or Lancaster.

"We averaged 800 to 1,000 people a trip," said Tom Hudson, a Phillies executive who was one of the people running the trips and is still with the club. "We usually ran the trips on weekends and Friday nights."

The trips were promoted on the air during Phillies broadcasts. Sometimes, the efforts were particularly successful. One excursion attracted more than 8,000 people. Five whole trains had to be used.

Tragedy occurred in June 1962 when a train full of fans from Harrisburg went into the Susquehanna River after it derailed on a bad section of track and slid down an embankment. Three cars plunged into the river, 22 passengers were killed, and 75 were hurt.

"I was one of the few people to walk off the train with his shoes on and still intact," recalled Hudson. "I was scared to death. It was the only accident we ever had, thank God."

Over the years, the park had some legendary hecklers, many of whom had loud, booming voices that they used to hurl insults at both the home and visiting players and the umpires. Once, American League umpire Billy Evans kayoed two hecklers outside his dressing room.

The Ziegler brothers were two of the most prominent. They were among a group of hucksters who sold food out of wagons while going street to street and who came to the ballpark neary every day. In those days, afternoon games began at 3:00 P.M. The Ziegler brothers, who came from a family of hecklers whose last name was Kessler, sat in the lower deck, one on the first base side and one behind third base. In loud voices that echoed throughout the park, they carried on conversations about the players, using less than flattering terms.

Another well-known heckler was Harry Donnelly. He booed and bothered players so vigorously that in 1927 Connie Mack pressed charges against the 26-year-old fan, claiming that he ruined the morale of the A's players, made them nervous, and caused them to make errors. One player, Bill Lamar, Mack testified, was so "wrecked" by Donnelly's "awful loud speaker" that the A's had to release him. Donnelly was charged with disturbing the peace and ordered to stay away from Shibe Park.

"There were also always two rather obese women who used to be at just about every game," said Gerry Nugent, Jr., the son of the former Phillies owner. "They really bellowed a lot. Their lament was always, 'We wuz robbed.'"

The most famous Shibe Park heckler was Pete Adelis, a 260-pound department store employee. He first perched in the upper deck at the bend along the left field foul line before moving to a spot behind first base. Known as The Foghorn and Leather Lungs because of his deep, resonant voice, Adelis heckled players, managers, and umpires with such vehemence that in 1948 umpire Larry Goetz stopped a game for 15 minutes in a futile effort to find someone with authority to eject the loudmouthed fan. Adelis was eventually barred from Shibe Park and was later said to have been hired by Cleveland Indian's manager Lou Boudreau to heckle the rival New York Yankees.

Shibe Park also had its share of gamblers. Initially, they sat as a group in the lower bleachers but later moved to the upper deck. Under pressure

Ladies Day was inaugurated in 1936 by Connie Mack, and it became
a regular feature for the next two decades. This group of avid
rooters came to the park for a game in 1939.

from Commissioner Kenesaw Mountain Landis, the groups began dispersing in the 1940s. Many arrests occurred in the 1940s and 1950s before the gamblers faded away.

"When they were at their peak, they'd bet on almost anything," recalled baseball historian Ed (Dutch) Doyle. "But no money ever changed hands. The idea was to have as many bets as you could so you couldn't lose. Every time a run scored, the odds would change. Al Simmons was the only player who would be even money in the late innings."

Ladies Day games and Knot-Hole crowds were regular occurrences from the 1930s on. Connie Mack inaugurated Ladies Days in 1936, and it became a regular feature of the park on Thursday afternoons. The Knot-Hole Gang also poured into the park for Saturday games, as did other huge groups of young fans such as the Cub Scouts, who packed into the center field bleachers.

"In those days, a lot more kids went by themselves to games," said vendor Seymour Steinberg. "We always sold well to the bleacher crowd on Saturdays because there were so many kids."

"Overall, the fans weren't as wild as they are today," said Charlie McCormack, who served as a ticket taker, supervisor of ushers, and press box supervisor at Connie Mack Stadium. "People were just interested in the ball game. They would sit there and just be entranced by the game itself. They concentrated on the game."

Even when the game was over, a fan, especially a young one, still had

For just 88 cents, a young fan could get not only a ticket to a game, but also a free bat, as was the case in this 1967 promotion.

things to do. "We would run onto the field after the game," Montella remembered. "There'd be 19 kids at home plate, all imagining they were swinging a bat. You'd swing and run to first. Then you'd slide into second, slide into third, and finally slide into home. You'd have dirt all over your pants, and you'd go home a mess. But I'm proud of that. I'd do it again today, and I'm 60 years old.

"But you weren't done yet. You didn't go right home. You had to get autographs down at the main entrance. Finally, about 6:30 or 7:00, you'd leave. You'd get home exhausted, but you'd know you'd had a great day."

The Fourth Estate

To cover baseball during much of Shibe Park's existence, a member of the press could not be afraid of heights. That's because the press box afforded the highest seat in the stadium, tucked under the roof above the upper deck grandstand.

It was high, very high, perhaps the highest press box in baseball. And only those who weren't acrophobics dared climb to such a lofty perch to cast an eye on the proceedings far below.

"It was so high," proclaimed By Saam, the Hall of Fame announcer who broadcast games at the park from 1938 until it closed in 1970, "that sometimes we had to make some guesses on certain pitches. We did the best we could, although normally we could see pretty clearly."

In the early days of the park, Philadelphia had seven daily newspapers. Some of the biggest names in the city's literary community—Jimmie Isaminger, George Graham, Stony McLinn, Tiny Maxwell, Sig Grauley, and a host of others—vied for spots in the original press box and scoops in the clubhouse.

The first press box was located amid the grandstands in the park's upper deck. It was relocated to the top of the second level in 1928 and remained there for the rest of the stadium's days. Filled to capacity, which it rarely was, the press box could seat about 40.

"When I came up to visit the Athletics in 1941," recalled pitcher Lou Brissie, "they took me to Shibe Park, and we saw Sugar Ray Robinson fight. We sat up in the press box. It was not only the first fight I ever saw, it was the highest I'd ever been."

In the later years of the park, when the number of Philadelphia dailies had been reduced to three, usually just five local writers—those from each of the three dailies and the two wire services—plus a few visiting writers and telegraph operators required space in the press box. That was before the proliferation of columnists and suburban dailies that deemed it necessary to cover big league baseball.

Hall of Fame writer Allen Lewis began covering baseball in the late-1940s and served as the beat writer for the Phillies at the *Inquirer* from 1957 until 1979. He remembers the days of covering games at Connie Mack Stadium when the press box was vastly different from the luxurious facilities that the media enjoy today.

"You got there by going through a press gate at 21st and Lehigh, and then bulling your way through the crowd and getting on an elevator that took you up to the press box level. You'd get out and walk across a little catwalk to the press box.

"It was high," he added. "Maybe you didn't see ground balls too well. But there was no problem. You could see the whole playing field quite well."

Publicity director Larry Shenk, now a veteran of more than 30 years on the job, remembered going to the press box carrying a handful of sheets with statistics and notes he'd typed. It was unlike today when such material is kept on a computer and printed in numerous pages for the large press contingent. It wasn't easy getting to the press box, either.

"If you were going to the press box, you made sure you only had to make

When they broadcast games at Shibe Park in the early 1940s, Taylor Grant (*foreground*) and Byrum Saam (wearing hat) were stuck in a tiny open-air booth hanging out from the second deck.

one trip," he said. "You weren't about to go up and down several times.

"My first couple of years there, the hours between four and eight seemed like eternity," he added. "Sometimes, I'd go out in the outfield and shag flies during batting practice."

Eating in the press box was a spartan-like procedure. Through many of the years, a hot plate was used for cooking hot dogs and hamburgers. And a small refrigerator held sodas and sometimes sandwiches brought from home by the writers. Eventually, a small kitchenette was installed for dispensing sandwiches.

"About the sixth inning, they'd come around with slices of ice cream," remembered Charlie McCormack, who served for a while as the press box custodian. "There weren't too many slices needed, because there weren't too many people there. Along with the writers, there were usually three or four telegraph operators from Western Union. They transmitted the writers' stories. There was only one phone in the place for all the writers to use."

Art Cassidy, who began working in the press box in 1963 and still works in the one at the Vet, also recalled minimal facilities. "There was only one pencil sharpener," he said. "We didn't have the paperwork or the sophisticated equipment that we have today. It was actually kind of a very antique press box."

Bob Carpenter, his general manager, and later Ruly Carpenter sat in the press level in a special box on the third base side. Organist Dorothy Langdon, who performed at the park for many years at both A's and Phillies games, was also situated on the press level on the first base side. There were also seats on the first base side for about 50 special guests of the club.

Of course, two radio booths were also located on the press level, although when games were first broadcast from Shibe Park in the late 1920s, play-by-play was aired from a spot behind home plate at field level. In 1936 when live broadcasts became a regular feature of home games, the radio men, at the time Bill Dwyer and former umpire Dolly Stark, were moved to a small balcony that protruded from the bottom of the upper deck on the third base side of the diamond.

"Everything about the press box was small," recalled Ralph Bernstein. "Some of the writers got very possessive. I remember Frank Yeutter, who covered the A's for the *Evening Bulletin*. He wore a big handlebar mustache and had been a major in World War II. He was a character in his own right. He tried to be very dignified. He took over a corner of the press box, and he made it very clear that nobody was to sit in his corner.

"The elevator was built to take Connie Mack up to his office in the tower," Bernstein added. "If four people got on, it was a crowd."

One time, a Phillies executive who had a warm relationship with the bottle got on the elevator with two writers. Feeling the effects of a few too many rounds of barley, he staggered to the back of the elevator as it started down. Suddenly, lurching forward, he pressed the red emergency button that stopped the elevator between floors. When the door opened, he tried to walk out but succeeded only in smacking into the cinder-block wall. As he bounced back toward the rear of the elevator, he was heard to say, "That damned door never did work."

Often, the whole elevator didn't, either. It was known to break down at least two or three times a season, usually stranding cursing sportswriters inside.

Although the writers and broadcasters enjoyed what few amenities existed in the press box, other members of the media had to cope with even less comfortable working conditions.

"In the 1960s," recalled former *Evening Bulletin* photographer Mike Maicher, "you worked from a little balcony that hung out from the upper deck on the first base side of the field. You had to climb out over a railing to get there. You used long-range lenses. We always had machine-gun cameras, too.

"I can remember also crouching in the aisles in the grandstands to

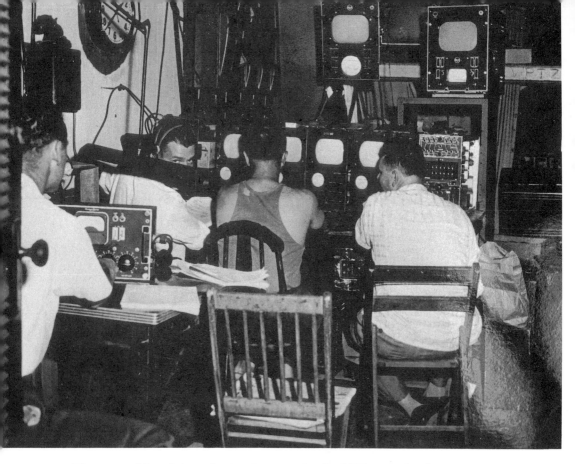

The control booth for televised games in the 1950s was far less complex than the sophisticated TV facilities of today.

shoot. Sometimes, I'd also get a stool and sit in a box seat beside the dugout. Of course, we often went into the clubhouse afterward to get a picture of somebody who'd starred in the game."

For American League games, photographers were allowed on the playing field until 1954. The National League barred photographers from the field in 1955.

"Before then, a lot of guys were hit with balls, some not by accident," remembered Sam Psorasi, who made pictures for many years for the *Daily News*. "Sometimes, a player would let a ball get past him when they were warming up just so it would hit a photographer. It was like a sport with them. If they could hit you, it was a feather in their cap. I got hit many times.

"Being on the field had advantages, though," Psorasi added. "Sometimes, you'd be standing at first base, and the coach would say, 'Do you need a picture? I'll have him [the runner] slide back into the bag for you.'"

When television came along, with games at Shibe Park first aired in 1947, working space also had to be found for the crew. Cameramen worked from the balcony protruding from the third base stands and later from the photographers box on the first base side. There was also a camera behind home plate, and in the early days of televised games, the broadcasters also worked in a cage there, reaching it by climbing down a ladder from the second deck.

"At home plate, there wasn't much room," said Don Paine, a cameraman at the stadium for WFIL-TV in the 1950s and 1960s. "My back was right up against the screen. You worked in this little cage that hung down from the upper deck. To get to it, you had to climb down a ladder. Cameras had to be lowered down the ladder, too. When the big color cameras came along, it took four guys to get the camera in there.

"The lens of the camera pointed out through an opening about 18 inches wide in the cage. A foul ball could go through there and knock the camera out. One time, a cameraman got knocked out when a ball hit him right in the head. When you were working behind home plate, you put your life in jeopardy. Once, I tried to keep a ball that came in during batting practice. Benny Bengough, who was coaching with the Phillies, looked up and yelled, 'Throw that ball back, kid.'"

In the early days of television games, live commercials were aired from a spot behind the stands in the upper deck. Company spokemen such as Gary Gears for Tastykake and Bob Graham for Atlantic Refining made the pitches.

Paine also remembered working the camera for a show called "Grandstand Manager," hosted by veteran sportswriter Bill Duncan. It was done between games of doubleheaders and after single games from a spot in the first base photo balcony.

"One time, Duncan was interviewing Phillies outfielder Wes Covington," Paine recalled. "He said, 'Wes, you used to be a good ballplayer. What happened to you?' I'll never forget that."

A Park for Many Occasions

While the A's and Phillies were the primary occupants of Shibe Park, they were hardly the only ones. Beginning in its early years, the stadium had many other users, not all of them involved with sports.

Presidents and presidential candidates used the park. Musicians used it. And most of all, boxers and football players used it.

The outside organization that used the park the most was the Philadelphia Eagles of the National Football League. Shibe Park was the Eagles' home field from 1940 to 1942 and from 1944 to 1957. (In 1943, the team performed as an amalgamation of the Eagles and Pittsburgh Steelers called the Steagles.)

In one of the most memorable football games at Shibe Park, the Eagles defeated the Chicago Cardinals, 7–0, in heavy snow to win the 1948 National Football League championship.

One of the three most famous games in Eagles history was played at Shibe Park. It happened in 1948 when the Eagles beat the Chicago Cardinals, 7–0, to win the championship of the National Football League in a raging snowstorm before 28,864 shivering spectators. Steve VanBuren scored the game's only touchdown while rushing for 98 yards on the snow-covered field.

It had snowed heavily the night before the game, and it continued to snow throughout the hard-fought contest. Huge snowbanks, formed when workers had tried to clear the playing surface, lined the edges of the field.

VanBuren, living in Lansdowne at the time, almost didn't make the game. Thinking it would not be played, he was still at home as game time approached.

"I didn't think there was any way they could play," said the Hall of Fame running back some 47 years later. "I couldn't even get my car out of the drive. Then Greasy Neale [the Eagles head coach and a one-time Phillies outfielder] called wondering where I was. He told me they were going to play.

"I ran out of the house and got a trolley to 69th Street. Then I got the el down Market Street, and finally a subway up Broad Street. I walked the

Steve Van Buren plowed through snow and the Cardinals' line to score the only touchdown in the December 19, 1948 NFL title game.

last seven blocks to the stadium. I got there about one-half hour before the start of the game, which had been delayed about one hour."

Once the game got under way, the greatest running back in Eagles history dominated the game, although it was snowing so hard that players could barely see where they were going.

"It was so bad, I couldn't even see the Cardinals safety man," VanBuren recalled. "And you couldn't see when you were out of bounds because the lines on the field were covered. It was tough trying to figure out first downs, too.

"At least, the footing was okay. The ground wasn't frozen. It wasn't nearly as bad as the game in Chicago [in 1947 when the Eagles lost to the Cardinals in the NFL title game]. When I scored the touchdown, a hole opened up and I just stumbled across. There were some pretty good blocks on that play."

VanBuren was the best of a long line of fine players who performed for the Eagles at Shibe Park. Davey O'Brien, Frank Reagan, Pete Pihos, Al Wistert, Bucko Kilroy, Tommy Thompson, and Chuck Bednarik were among the great names in the Eagles' colorful history who also performed at the stadium before the club moved to Franklin Field.

In their 17 seasons at Shibe Park, the Eagles compiled a 57–35–6 record. Their biggest crowd was 40,059 for a game in 1946 against the New York Giants. They drew 38,114 in 1945 for a 28–14 victory over Bob

During World War II, bond drives, which included parades and demonstrations of military equipment, were held at Shibe Park.

Waterfield and the Cleveland Rams. In their last year at Shibe Park, however, the Eagles drew a mere 130,000.

The football field ran from left field to the first base area. Temporary bleachers holding an extra 4,000 to 5,000 extended across the front of the right field wall. In the 1950s, the Eagles, using white footballs, played many of their home games on Saturday nights.

The first big football game played at Shibe Park was on December 12, 1925. In it, a professional team called the Pottsville Maroons defeated a team composed largely of members of the 1924 Notre Dame University team, including the legendary Four Horsemen, 9–6, before a crowd of 10,000. After then-Villanova head coach Harry Stuhldreher had quarterbacked the Horsemen to a 7–0 lead, former Lafayette All-American Charlie Berry, drop-kicked a 30-yard field goal late in the fourth quarter for the winning margin. That same year Berry was a rookie catcher with the A's in what would be the start of an 11-year playing career in baseball. (Later he would become an American League umpire.)

In another big game at Shibe Park in 1926, the Frankford Yellowjackets, forerunners of the Eagles, defeated the Chicago Bears, 7–6, for the NFL championship.

For a while in the 1940s, Villanova University's football team played its home games at Shibe Park. In the 1930s, Howard and Lincoln universities also played at the park in their annual Thanksgiving Day games. The

President Franklin D. Roosevelt (waving from car) held a campaign rally at Shibe Park in 1944.

two squared off in the afternoon, and Roman Catholic and St. Joseph's high schools tangled in the morning.

High school football was extremely popular at Shibe Park. In fact, the largest football crowd in the stadium's history was the 43,000 who came November 10, 1946, for a high school game in which West Catholic defeated Roman Catholic, 12–7.

Boxing was also a frequent feature at the stadium, going back to its early days. The first fight was held in 1914 when Philadelphia's Jack O'Brien lost to 42-year-old Bob Fitzsimmons. Three years later, Benny Leonard successfully defended his lightweight title by defeating Johnny Kilbane.

In other memorable fights, Tommy Loughran battled Jack Delaney in 1925 in the rain, Sugar Ray Robinson downed Sammy Angott in a non-title bout in 1941, Gil Turner beat Ike Williams in a bruising match in 1951, and Kid Gavilan fought Joey Giardello in a tough middleweight fight in 1953.

Softball wizard Eddie Feiner, with his legendary barnstorming team called The King and His Court, struck out opposing batters pitching blindfolded, behind his back, and from second base in exhibition games at Shibe Park.

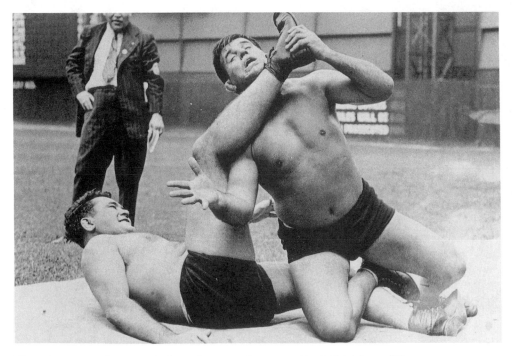

Wrestling matches, including this one between Jack Smith and Jim Atlas in 1945, also took place at Shibe Park, mostly during baseball's off-season.

Negro League teams also played there. Two Philadelphia teams, the Hilldale Daisies and later the Philadelphia Stars, were booked into Shibe Park by Eddie Gottlieb, who scheduled Negro League games before becoming the owner of the Philadelphia Warriors.

"We usually drew quite well," said outfielder Gene Benson, one of the top players for the Stars. "Most of the fans who saw us were our followers, but we also attracted a lot of white fans who wanted to see us play. Our park [at 44th and Parkside] only held five to six thousand, so playing at Shibe Park gave us a chance to play in front of a lot more people. The players didn't make anything extra, though. Our owners split the money with Connie Mack.

"Our games at Shibe Park were generally on Monday nights," Benson added. "In the 1940s, we played there at least 20 times a year. It was much nicer than what we played on. We dressed in the A's locker room."

At the peak of the Negro League's existence, most of its top players appeared at Shibe Park. Satchel Paige pitched there, Josh Gibson caught there, Buck Leonard hit there, Judy Johnson stopped hard smashes at third there, and Cool Papa Bell flew around the bases there.

In 1920, the Atlantic City Bacharachs, led by ace pitcher Dick Redding, defeated Babe Ruth's all-stars, 9–4, at Shibe Park. That same year, another all-star team put together by Ruth was trounced by Hilldale, 5–0, at Shibe Park.

By the mid-1960s, the Phillies could only attract minuscule crowds to Connie Mack Stadium.

Hilldale won the National Negro League championship in 1923 when it defeated Rube Foster and the American Giants of Chicago, three games to one, in a series at Shibe Park.

In another big game, a Negro League all-star team defeated Dizzy Dean and a team of major league all-stars, 7–1, in the first game of a double-header on October 12, 1935, at Shibe Park. The second game, with the Pittsburgh Pirates' Bill Swift pitching for the big leaguers, ended in a scoreless tie after five innings.

Baseball clown Max Patkin made one of his first appearances in a major league arena in 1946 at Shibe Park. At the time, he was doing a three-inning routine as a first coach with the Cleveland Indians.

"The crowd responded great," he recalled. "I was really surprised because usually there was no nonsense once the game started. But the crowd loved my act. I guess the fans had never seen anything like that before.

"In 1951 when I was working for the St. Louis Browns," Patkin added, "Ferris Fain was at first base for the A's. He'd just come back after breaking his ankle kicking the bag. I did an imitation of him, kicking the bag, and falling down, grabbing my ankle. The fans thought it was hilarious."

College and high school baseball games were also held at Shibe Park. The city championship game for Philadelphia's Catholic and Public League high schools was a fixture at the park for many years.

In the 1960s, jazz concerts were popular at the stadium. They featured some of the great names in the business, including Count Basie, Dave Brubeck, Maynard Ferguson, and Nat (Cannonball) Adderly.

Presidents and would-be presidents also appeared at Shibe Park. Although Herbert Hoover was the only standing President ever to see a baseball game at the park (see section on the World Series), Franklin D. Roosevelt held a campaign rally there on October 27, 1944. With 40,000 in

Long before the final out, fans began to carry out rows of seats and other souvenirs at the last game at Connie Mack Stadium.

attendance, Roosevelt made what was one of his few public appearances during his race that year against Thomas E. Dewey.

Wendall Wilkie led a campaign rally at Shibe Park in 1940 when he was the Republican nominee for president. Progressive Party candidate Henry Wallace accepted his party's nomination for the presidency in a rousing speech in 1948 at Shibe Park. And, while running for president the first time, Richard Nixon held a fund-raiser called Baseball with Dick on July 1, 1960, before a Phillies 10–6 loss to the Los Angeles Dodgers.

Circuses, wrestling matches, soccer games, and religious rallies were also held at the stadium. It was a rare date during the spring and summer that something wasn't going on.

Farewell to a Ballpark

The end of major league baseball at Connie Mack Stadium did not come gracefully. It came sluggishly and painfully, like a disease slowly spreading through its victim.

During much of its final decade, Connie Mack Stadium underwent a

As players raced for safety at the end of the final game, fans poured onto the field in a wild attempt to grab anything that wasn't nailed down.

slow death. The park became increasingly obsolete, and the surrounding neighborhood became increasingly dangerous.

The area of businesses and working-class residents had been slowly deteriorating since the late 1950s. Businesses and better-off residents began fleeing to the suburbs, while those who remained were joined by an influx of even poorer neighbors.

Crime became a particular problem, not only in the surrounding area, but even inside the ballpark.

"In the 1960s," said Harry Graeff, a security guard at the park in that period, "we had a lot of robberies, especially in bathrooms. Boys stayed inside the bathrooms and jumped people when they came in. And women lost their pocketbooks after leaving them under their seats in the stands. We had gate-crashers, fights, and people stealing things from the concession stands. We'd put them out on the street, and they'd come back. It wasn't safe parking your car on the street and walking to the park.

"We even had a murder in the stands one night," added Graeff, who with 15 to 20 other security guards roamed the upper deck during games. "It happened in the top deck on the first base side. Two guys were arguing with somebody, and then all of a sudden a guy comes rolling down the steps. Somebody had stabbed him. I don't think they ever found the killer."

City police patrolled the stands. Once, there was a rape. "I had a phone, and if I had any trouble, I'd get right on the phone and the police would be there in seconds," recalled Bill Hoopes, the upper deck supervisor of ushers.

When writers left the park after finishing their game stories late at night, police escorted them to their cars. One writer, though, had a problem before he even got to his car.

A major fire in 1971 destroyed much of Connie Mack Stadium.

"Harry Hoffman was covering the game for the Atlantic City *Press*," remembered Ralph Bernstein. "He was down in the lobby at street level late one night dictating his story on a phone when a guy came up to him with a knife. Harry said to the guy on the other end of the line, 'Hold on a minute. I've got a guy with a knife at my throat.' And the guy at the other end said, 'Tell him you're on deadline.' At that point, the guy with the knife panicked and ran away."

In the summer of 1964, much of the area near the ballpark went up in flames as rioters took to the streets, looting and burning in a week-long demonstration that was one of many that swept the nation that year. Although the Phillies set an attendance record that year of 1,425,891— a total that was fully attributable to the team's ill-fated run for the pennant—Shibe Park was never again the same. By 1969, with hundreds of police officers ringing the area on game days, the total attendance had plunged to 590,205.

"By the last year, it was really bad," said Graeff. "Gangs roamed the

The stadium was a mass of burned debris following the 1971 fire.

streets. It got so bad that people didn't drive to games unless four or five of them came in one car."

Phillies owner Bob Carpenter had long envisioned his team in a modern stadium, and by 1970 that dream was soon to become a reality. The aging Connie Mack Stadium, at the time the oldest park in major league baseball, was about to be replaced by a brand new stadium in South Philadelphia.

"Things had really gone to hell in and around the ballpark," recalled Ruly Carpenter, who three years later would take over from his father as team president. "The handwriting was on the wall. Dad had bought some land in Cherry Hill as a possible site for a stadium, but he was also negotiating with the city for a new park in Philadelphia. Either way, he had to get out of Connie Mack Stadium."

On October 1, 1970, one day after just 1,186 fans had attended a game, the Phillies played for the last time at Connie Mack Stadium, facing their former manager Gene Mauch and the Montreal Expos. A gala farewell was planned for the occasion. It never materialized.

What the fire didn't get, the wrecking ball did as a demolition crew took down the remains of Connie Mack Stadium in 1976.

"We planned to give away slats from seats [that were used for repairs] to the first 5,000 paying customers," recalled Bill Giles, then the club's vice president and the man in charge of planning the closing festivities. "But by the fourth inning, people were using them as hammers to remove everything they could from the stadium. I never expected those slats to be used as weapons."

From the fourth inning on, the steady sound of hammering could be heard in the stands as many of the season's largest crowd of 31,822 fans prospected for souvenirs. Others used wrenches, screwdrivers, and whatever else they brought to tear away seats and other parts of the park.

"People brought toolboxes with them," Giles said. "During the game, they were taking chairs apart, taking the concession stands apart. They were even walking out with stuff from the restrooms. I saw one guy going down the street with a urinal.

"Periodically, we'd raffle off things from the clubhouse like caps and shirts. We had certificates that people filled out as they came into the park, and we would call out the names of the winners between innings. I'll never forget, one lady didn't pick up a locker stool of Tony Taylor's that we were giving away. When I called her the next day and told her she'd won Tony Taylor's stool, she said, 'What the hell do I want with that? You can keep the damn thing.'"

After the debris was cleared, the site where Connie Mack Stadium stood existed for a number of years as a large empty lot.

By the late innings, bedlam had set in, and the fans were getting so unruly they were out of control. The park's infirmary was overloaded with fans requiring treatment for injuries incurred while trying to pilfer pieces of the stadium. And the game was frequently delayed by spectators running onto the field to scoop up dirt or grass or into the dugouts to snatch hats, bats, balls, or gloves or to shake hands with the players. Public address announcer Art Wolfe's repeated requests for order were ignored.

"I made an announcement several times, but they kept running out on the field," remembered Wolfe. "With almost every batter, somebody ran out on the field. Finally, I announced that if they wouldn't stay off the field, the Phillies would have to forfeit the game. John Quinn [the Phillies' general manager] called and said, 'What the hell are you doing?' An umpire had told me to make an announcement to keep people off the field, but I guess I carried it a step farther.

"But it was really crazy. People had come to the park with the idea of taking something home with them. And they were determined to do it. The noise was tremendous."

The game was tied at 1–1 after nine innings. After the ninth, Mauch

A church now stands at 21st and Lehigh where the main entrance to Connie Mack Stadium was once one of the city's classic landmarks.

and Phillies manager Frank Lucchesi got together behind home plate with the umpires and agreed that if a run wasn't scored in the 10th inning, the game would be stopped.

"You could just feel the tension in the air," recalled Giles. "The fans were really getting rowdy."

In the bottom of the 10th, Tim McCarver singled, stole second base, and scored on a single by Oscar Gamble to give the Phillies a 2–1 victory. As McCarver crossed the plate, and organist Paul Richardson played "Auld Lang Syne" as loud as he could, thousands of fans poured onto the field.

Lucchesi also charged onto the field to give Gamble a hug. Surrounded by fans, Gamble brushed off the skipper's attempt to celebrate. "Run, man, run like hell," Gamble yelled. "We'll be happy later."

Giles's plans called for a helicopter to swoop down onto the field, pick up home plate, and carry it away to its new home at Veterans Stadium. "But there was such a mob on the field with people tearing up the turf and the fences that we couldn't get the helicopter down," Giles said. "So we just dug up the plate later and took it down to the Vet."

The last winning pitcher at the park was reliever Dick Selma. The last loser was Howie Reed. The last word on the park was delivered by Bob Carpenter. "Progress," he said. "I guess that's what you'd have to call it. But damn, I hate to leave this place."

After the Phillies departed, the old park virtually fell apart. Much of it was destroyed by a fire in 1971. Some 1,500 seats were removed and

The church property covers the full block that used to be the site of Connie Mack Stadium, but the row houses on 20th Street and the corner bar still exist.

shipped to Duncan Park in Spartanburg, South Carolina, where a Phillies farm team played. Liens and mounting back taxes plagued owner Jerry Wolman, who had bought the stadium as an investment in 1964 while he was owner of the Philadelphia Eagles. Ultimately, the city ordered the demolition of the park in 1976, and the site was sold to a developer.

Different plans that called for using the lot for a hospital, an industrial park, and a supermarket surfaced. None materialized, and the site existed as a rat-infested lot overgrown with weeds and littered with debris.

Although residents finally succeeded in convincing the city to clean up the lot, it remained vacant until 1990 when the Deliverance Evangelistic Church with a sanctuary that seats 5,100 was built. The church property covers most of the old block where once stood a ballpark.

Bibliography

BARTELL, RICHARD, AND MACHT, NORMAN. *Rowdy Richard*. North Atlantic Books, 1987.

BENSON, MICHAEL. *Ballparks of North America*. McFarland & Co., 1989.

DITMAR, JOSEPH J. *Baseball's Benchmark Boxscores*. McFarland & Co., 1990.

DOYLE, EDWARD F. *Baker Bowl, The National Pastime*. Society for American Baseball Research, 1995.

GERSHMAN, MICHAEL. *Diamonds, The Evolution of the Ballpark*. Boston: Houghton Mifflin, 1993.

HOLWAY, JOHN. *Blackball Stars*. Meckler Books, 1988.

KUKLICK, BRUCE. *To Every Thing a Season*. Princeton: NJ: Princeton University Press, 1991.

LEWIS, ALLEN. *Baseball's Greatest Streaks*. McFarland & Co., 1992.

LOWRY, PHILIP. *Green Cathedrals*. Addison-Wesley Publishing Co., 1992.

MEAD, WILLIAM, AND DICKSON, PAUL. *Baseball: The Presidents' Game*. Farragut Publishing Co., 1993.

NEMEC, DAVID. *The Beer and Whiskey League*. Lyons and Burford, 1994.

OREM, PRESTON. *Baseball: 1845–1881*. Preston D. Orem, 1961.

PEVERELLY, CHARLES. *Book of American Pastimes*, 1866.

REICHLER, JOSEPH. *Baseball's Great Moments*. Bonanza Books, 1983.

REIDENBAUGH, LOWELL. *100 Years of National League Baseball*. The Sporting News, 1976.

RHODES, GREG, AND ERARDI, JOHN. *The First Boys of Summer*. Road West Publishing, 1994.

ROMANOWSKI, REV. JEROME (THE BASEBALL PADRE). *The Mackmen*. 1979.

SHANNON, BILL, AND KALINSKY, GEORGE. *The Ballparks*. Hawthorn Books, 1975.

SMITH, RON. *The Sporting News Chronicle of Baseball*. BDD Illustrated Books, 1993.

STUMP, AL. *Cobb*. Algonquin Books, 1994.

WESTCOTT, RICH. *Diamond Greats*. Meckler Books, 1988.

WESTCOTT, RICH, AND BILOVSKY, FRANK. *The New Phillies Encyclopedia*. Philadelphia: Temple University Press, 1993.

OTHER SOURCES

The Baseball Encyclopedia. New York: Macmillan Publishing Co.

The World Series. The Sporting News.

PERIODICALS: *Phillies Report*, the *Evening Bulletin*, the *Philadelphia Inquirer*, the *Philadelphia Public Ledger*, the *Philadelphia Daily News*, the *Philadelphia Record*.

MISCELLANEOUS PUBLICATIONS: Phillies and Athletics yearbooks, Phillies media guides, Phillies and Athletics programs, commemorative programs—1909, 1970.

About the Author

*R*ich Westcott is the publisher and editor of *Phillies Report*, the nation's oldest, continuous team newspaper. He is the author of six other books, including *The Phillies Encyclopedia* with Frank Bilovsky, originally published in 1984, then updated and published by Temple University Press in 1993 as *The New Phillies Encyclopedia; Phillies '93, An Incredible Season; Diamond Greats* and *Masters of the Diamond,* two collections of interviews with former major league players, and *Mike Schmidt,* a children's book. Westcott has served as a writer and editor on the staffs of a variety of newspapers and magazines in the Philadelphia and Baltimore areas during his 35 years in publishing. Born and raised in Philadelphia, he is a graduate of the William Penn Charter School and Drexel University, and holds a master's degree from Johns Hopkins University.

Index

A

Adams, Bobby, 157
Adderly, Nat (Cannonball), 187
Adelis, Pete, 174
Aldrine Hotel, 149
Alert team, 10
Alexander, Grover Cleveland, 28, 41, 43, 51, 69, 70, 72, 73
Allen, Dick, 101, 125, 126, 131, 133, 160, 164
Allen, Ethan, 45, 82
Allen, John D., 75
All-Phillies team, 6
All-Star Game, 100, 145–147
Alpine Musical Bar, 97
Alpo dog food sign, 122
American Association, 1, 5, 6, 12, 31
American Baseball Club of Philadelphia, 107, 111
American Giants, 187
Ames, Red, 20
Andrews, Ed, 31
Angel, Joe, 166
Angott, Sammy, 185
Anson, Adrian (Cap), 5
Arellanes, Frank, 110
Aria, Austin, 43, 45, 47, 50, 56, 66, 81
Arnovich, Morrie, 96, 135
Ashbridge, Samuel, 18
Ashburn, Richie, 101, 103, 123, 127, 128, 132, 158, 170
Ashland Club, 12
Associated Press, 62, 86, 104, 168
Athletic Park, 4
Athletic Grounds Company, 104, 111
Atlantic & Pacific (A & P) store, 126

Atlantic City Bacharachs, 186
Atlantic City Press, 190
Atlantic Refining Company, 181
Atwood, Bill, 82, 96, 135
Avila, Bobby, 147

B

Baker, William, 40, 49, 70, 78, 92, 94
Baker, Frank (Home Run), 19, 100–102, 125, 136–138, 149–150, 173
Ball Hawk George, 56
Ballanfant, Lee, 170
Ballantine beer sign, 116
Baltimore Orioles, 22, 74, 151
Bancroft, Dave, 28
Banks, Ernie, 150
Barlick, Al, 170
Barr, George, 160
Barrett, Dick, 154
Barry, Jack, 102, 137, 151
Bartell, Dick, 28, 34, 43, 56, 62
Basie, Count, 187
Bastian, Charlie, 12
Bauer, Hank, 143
Baumgartner, Stan, 65, 96
Beck, Emil, 17, 25
Beck, Walter (Boom Boom), 81
Beck's Military Band, 31
Bednarik, Chuck, 183
Beebe, Kid, 63
Bell, Bert, 88
Bell, Cool Papa, 186
Bellevue-Stratford Hotel, 57
Bender, Chief, 17, 19, 21, 91, 100, 102, 136, 138, 151
Ben Franklin Hotel, 57
Benge, Ray, 50

Bengough, Bennie, 181
Benson, Gene, 186
Berger, Wally, 36
Berman, Reuben, 62
Bernhard, Bill, 17, 18
Bernstein, Ralph, 62, 64, 86, 88, 92, 168, 179, 190
Berry, Charlie, 184
Betts, Huck, 43, 93
Blackwell, Ewell, 132
Blankenburg, Rud, 70
Boley, Joe, 146, 153
Borden, Joe, 5
Boston Braves, 35, 41, 42, 71, 72, 73, 76, 134, 139
Boston Pilgrims, 20
Boston Red Caps, 5
Boston Red Sox, 69, 110, 149, 150, 152, 154
Boston Reds, 6
Bottomley, Jim, 32, 73
Boudreau, Lou, 174
Bowman, Joe, 41
Bowman baseball cards, 118
Brancato, Al, 90, 122, 131, 133, 171
Braves Field, 111
Brendley, Bill, 113–114, 125–126, 136, 162–163
Brennan, Bill, 58
Bresnahan, Roger, 57, 58
Brewerytown, 16
Bridge of Hope, 107
Brinton, Edwin, 110
Brissie, Lou, 102, 129, 177
Brooklyn Atlantics, 2, 3
Brooklyn Dodgers, 35, 39, 41, 50, 72, 81, 119, 120, 123, 142, 150, 155–157
Brown, Bobby, 143

Brown, Mordecai (Three-Finger), 136
Brown, Warren, 65
Brubeck, Dave, 187
Bucknell College, 138
Bull Durham, 35
Bulman, Jack, 53, 61
Bunning, Jim, 101
Burns, Ed, 70
Burtschy, Ed, 157
Bush, Joe, 102, 136, 137, 138, 149
Bush, Kenny, 164
Byron, Pete, 123

C

Cadillac sign, 122
Cadore, Leon, 72
Callison, Johnny, 102, 124, 126
Camilli, Dolph, 32, 33, 38, 41
Campbell, Bill, 61, 83
Carnera, Primo, 90
Carpenter, Bob, 103, 115, 167, 179, 191, 194
Carpenter, Ruly, 103, 132, 179, 191
Carter, Joe, 70
"Casey at the Bat," 13
Casey, Dan, 13
Casey, Hugh, 155
Cassidy, Art, 178–179
Cassidy, Pat, 164
Caster, George, 154
Castleman, Slick, 96
Casway, Jerrold, 10
Centennial Park, 10
Central High School, 89, 98
Cepeda, Orlando, 159
Chapman, Ben, 155
Chapman, Sam, 102, 127, 129
Chicago Bears, 88, 184
Chicago Cardinals, 181–183
Chicago Cubs, 72, 93, 136, 140, 157, 159, 160
Chicago White Sox, 19, 20, 122, 149
Chicago White Stockings, 31
Chiozza, Lou, 73
Christopher, Russ, 154
Church, Bubba, 157
City Series, 5, 12, 24, 25, 36, 51, 118, 122, 134
Cincinnati Reds, 73, 82, 119, 154, 155, 156, 157, 158
Cincinnati Red Stockings, 3
City Hall, 122
Civil War, 10
Clark, Andy, 164
Clements, Jack, 13, 28

Cleveland Indians, 119, 126, 151, 152, 153, 155, 174
Cleveland Naps, 22, 151
Cleveland Rams, 184
Coakley, Andy, 20
Cobb, Ty, 23, 94, 147–149, 151, 152, 173
Coca-Cola, 122, 166
Cochrane, Jimmy, 54, 55, 56, 162, 163
Cochrane, Mickey, 100, 101, 102, 140, 141, 153, 163
Cohan, George M., 154
Cohoksiak Creek, 28
Coleman, Jerry, 143
Coleman, John, 12
Collins, Eddie, 19, 100, 101, 102, 136, 138, 151
Collins, Eddie, Jr., 118
Collins, John, 67
Comiskey Park, 111
Coombs, Jack, 19, 101, 136
Cooper, Mort, 145
Corbett, Gene, 53
Corcoran, Tommy, 82
Coveleski, Harry, 72
Covington, Wes, 181
Cox, William, 103
Cravath, Gavvy, 28, 38, 64, 86
Crawford, Sam, 23, 24
Crompton, Yitz, 164
Cronin, Joe, 47, 154
Crosley Field, 111
Cross, Lave, 19, 21
Cross, Monte, 21, 23
Culver, George, 102

D

Dahlgren, Babe, 146, 154
Dailey, Hugh, 12
Daily, Ed, 13
Dark, Al, 158
Davis, Harry, 18, 20, 23, 24
Dean, Dizzy, 59, 158, 187
Deane, Bill, 39
Delahanty, Ed, 28, 37, 38, 51
Delaney, Jack, 185
Deliverance Evangelistic Church, 195
Detroit Tigers, 22, 149, 151, 153, 154
Detroit Wolverines, 31
Dewey, Thomas E., 188
Dickson, Paul, 142
Dilworth, Richardson, 114
DiMaggio, Joe, 143, 154, 172
DiMaggio, Vince, 35, 145
Divine, Father, 97

Dobbins Vocational High School, 162–163
Doerr, Bobby, 145
Doggett, Bill, 60
Donahue, Francis (Red), 42, 71
Donlin, Mike, 20
Donnelly, Harry, 174
Donnelly, Jackie, 123, 164
Donovan, Wild Bill, 23
Dooin, Charley (Red), 48, 58, 72, 82
Doolin, Mike, 43
Dooly, Bill, 95
Douthit, Taylor, 73
Doyle, Ed (Dutch), 30, 52, 61, 63, 84, 175
Duckett, Mahlon, 7
Duffy, Hugh, 72
Duggleby, Bill, 39
Duncan, Bill, 181
Duncan Park (Spartanburg), 195
Duross, George, 62, 64, 85, 89, 173
Dwyer, Bill, 179
Dygert, Jimmy, 19, 23
Dykes, Jimmy, 102, 140, 141, 152, 157

E

Earnshaw, George, 102, 140, 141, 148
Eastern Colored League, 7
Ebbets Field, 111, 142
Edwards, Hank, 126
Ehmke, Howard, 91, 102, 140, 142, 152
Eighth Ward of Lancaster, 91
Elephant Room, 121
Elia, Lee, 121
Elliott, Jumbo Jim, 53
Ennis, Del, 101, 123, 127, 128, 156, 157, 158
Erardi, John, 3
Equity, 10
Evans, Billy, 174
Evers, Charles, 125

F

Fabiani, Ray, 97
Fain, Ferris, 101, 123, 155, 187
Farrar, Geraldine, 12
Farrar, Sid, 12
Fatima cigarettes, 36
Federal League, 139
Feiner, Eddie, 185
Feller, Bob, 132, 150
Fenway Park, 32, 111, 140
Ferguson, Bob, 12

Ferguson, Charlie, 13, 14, 31
Ferguson, Maynard, 187
Ferrarese, Don, 159
Ferrick, Tom, 161, 168
Fidelity Trust Company, 104
Fillies, 11
Finneran, Bill, 72
Firpo, 61
Firpo, Luis, 91
First Boys of Summer, The, 3
First Regiment Band, 110
Fitzgerald, John F. (Honey Fitz), 139
Fitzsimmons, Bob, 90, 185
Fletcher, Art, 48, 50
Flowers, Ben, 149
Flying White Horse, 36
Fogarty, Jim, 13
Fogel, Horace, 58, 94
Forbes Field, 111
Forepaugh Circus, 6
Forepaugh Park, 1, 6
Forr, Ted, 164
Foster, George (Rube), 70, 187
Four Horsemen, 184
Foxx, Jimmie, 36, 100, 101, 125, 126, 140, 141, 153–155. 173
Fowler, Dick, 102, 148, 155
Frank, Charley, 166
Frankford Yellow Jackets, 89, 184
Frankhouse, Fred, 73
Fraser, Chick, 17, 18
Fryman, Woodie, 160

G

Galt, Mrs. Edith, 69, 70
Gamble, Oscar, 194
Gavilan, Kid, 185
Gears, Gary, 181
Gehrig, Lou, 102, 132, 147, 148, 173
Gettysburg College, 138
Giardello, Joey, 185
Gibson, Josh, 126, 186
Giles, Bill, 192–194
Glass, Tom, 152
Godfrey, George, 90
Goetz, Larry, 174
Goodwin, Charles, 62
Gordon, Joe, 154
Gottlieb, Eddie, 6, 60, 186
Grady, Sandy, 160
Graeff, Harry, 189–190
Graham, Bob, 181
Graham, George, 177
Graney, Jack, 151
Grange, Red, 88
Grant, Taylor, 54, 66, 80, 85

Grauley, Sig, 177
Green, Dallas, 123, 161–162
Greenberg, Reynold H., 94
Grimes, Burleigh, 141
Grove, Bob (Lefty), 100, 101, 140, 141, 153, 161

H

Haas, Mule, 140
Hafey, Chick, 73
Hall, George, 5
Hall, Irv, 155
Hallahan, Wild Bill, 141
Hamilton, Billy, 28, 38
Hamner, Granny, 102, 147
Hansen, Snipe, 45, 73
Harper, George, 74
Harridge, Will, 153
Hartsel, Topsy, 18
Hatters, 10
Hauser, Joe, 129
Hayes, Frankie, 153
Heath, Jeff, 154
Henline, Butch, 38
Herman, Babe, 32
Higbe, Kirby, 154
Higgins, Jimmy, 169
Higgins, Pinky, 153
Hilldale Daisies, Giants, 7, 91, 186
Hilldale Park, 7
Hoffman, Harry, 190
Holden, Joe, 34, 35, 41, 45, 74, 81
Hooper, Harry, 70
Hoopes, Bill, 164, 189
Hoover, Herbert, 141–142, 187
Hornsby, Rogers, 34, 37
Horwits, Al, 134
Hough, Frank, 104, 111
Houston Astros, 160
Howard University, 184
Hoyt, Waite, 141
Hubbell, Carl, 43, 59, 146, 154
Hudson, Tom, 164, 167, 173–174
Hulen, Bill, 28
Humphries, John, 154
Hurst, Don, 32

I

Irvin, Monte, 158
Isaminger, Jimmie, 177

J

Jackson, Grant, 160
Jackson, Joe, 19
Jackson, Larry, 130, 160

James, Bill, 140
Jefferson Park, 4, 5
Jeffries, Irv, 80
Jennings, Hugh, 151
Johnson, Arnold, 157
Johnson, Ban, 15, 104, 109
Johnson, Bob, 102, 153
Johnson, Judy, 7, 186
Johnson, Syl, 80
Johnson, Walter, 151
Jones, Sam, 102, 152
Jones, Samuel H., 104, 111
Jones, Willie, 102, 156
Joost, Eddie, 102, 172
Jordan, Pat, 97

K

Kansas City Monarchs, 7, 91
Kell, George, 155
Kelleher, Jack, 165
Keller, Charlie, 125
Kellner, Alex, 102, 126
Keltner, Ken, 145
Kendle, Samuel H., 110
Kennedy, Francis, 68
Kennedy, John F., 139
Kennedy, Moon, 63
Kennedy Brothers, 54
Kessler, Ace, 164
Kessler, Ted, 164
Keyborn, Mom's rooming house, 161
Keystone Park, 6
Keystones, 6
Kilbane, Johnny, 185
Kilroy's bar, 161
Kilroy, Bucko, 183
Kiner, Ralph, 129, 171
King and His Court, The, 185
Klein, Chuck, 28, 32, 34, 38, 39, 40, 41, 53, 56, 62, 73, 101, 134, 169
Klem, Bill, 72, 81, 82
Kline, Joe, 62
Kline, Patsy, 90
Knot-Hole Gang, 60, 175
Kofald, Jack, 57
Konstanty, Jim, 101, 102, 123, 142, 143, 157
Koufax, Sandy, 102, 150
Koy, Ernie, 39

L

Laabs, Chet, 145
Ladies Day, 171, 175
Lafata, Joe, 170
Lafayette College, 184
Lajoie, Napolean, 17, 18, 19, 28

Lamar, Bill, 174
Lamberton, Robert, 154
Lancaster, Tommy, 47, 97
Landis, Kenesaw Mountain, 59,
140, 141, 154, 175
Langdon, Dorothy, 179
Lanz, Charles, 85
Lapp, Jack, 149
La Salle College, 89
Lazzeri, Tony, 102, 148, 153
Lee, Cliff, 36
Lee, Hal, 36
League Park, 111
Leiber, Hank, 96
Lemon, Bob, 147
Leonard, Benny, 90, 185
Leonard, Buck, 186
Leonard, Dutch, 119, 145, 155
Lewis, Allen, vii-x, 37, 51, 59,
65, 177
Liberatore, Ed, 93
Lifebuoy, 35
Lincoln University, 184
Litwhiler, Danny, 102, 131, 161
Livingston, Mickey, 169
Lobert, Hans, 169
Lockman, Whitey, 146
Lombardi, Ernie, 34
Long, Dale, 149
Longines clock, 116
Lopez, Al, 35, 45, 84
Lorraine Hotel, 53, 161
Los Angeles Dodgers, 150, 188
Loughran, Tommy, 185
Lucchesi, Frank, 194
Luderus, Fred, 28, 32, 38
Lukens, Woods, 47
Lupien, Tony, 170–171
Lutheran Church, 98
Lynch, Jack, 60

M

Mack, Connie, 16, 17, 23, 24,
25, 94, 95, 100, 102–105,
112–115, 120, 122, 124, 130,
133, 134, 140–142, 149, 151,
154, 157, 161, 163, 164,
166–168, 174, 175, 186
Mack, Connie Jr., 164
Mack, Earle, 111, 164
Mack, Roy, 111, 164
Mackey, Biz, 7
Magee, Sherry, 28, 64, 72
Mahaffey, Art, 103, 129, 158,
159, 172
Mahaffey, Roy, 148
Maicher, Mike, 179–180
Majeski, Hank, 102, 172
Majestic Hotel, 53, 161

Mallon, Jack, 63
Mantle, Mickey, 125, 158
Marquard, Rube, 136, 137
Martin, Harry, 55
Martin, Hersh, 135
Martin, Pepper, 141
Master Plumbers Association,
75
Mathewson, Christy, 20, 21, 72,
136–138
Mauch, Gene, 102, 122, 123,
159, 191, 193
Maxwell, Tiny, 177
May, Pinky, 154
Mayer, Erskine, 70
Mays, Willie, 150
Mazeroski, Bill, 70
McCahan, Bill, 102, 155
McCall Post, 91
McCalley, Bill, 132
McCarthy, Joe, 140, 146, 163
McCarver, Tim, 194
McCormick, Charlie, 164, 175,
178
McCormick, Frank, 155
McCovey, Willie, 125
McDonnell, Maje, 129, 166
McDougald, Gil, 157
McFadden, George, 108
McGann, Dan, 21
McGinnity, Joe, 20, 21
McGraw, John, 20, 57, 136
McInnis, Stuffy, 102, 110
McLinn, Stoney, 177
McLoon, Hughie, 121
Mead, William, 142
Meadows, Lee, 72
Medwick, Joe, 34, 36, 132
Merckle, Fred, 138
Mertz Tours sign, 122
Meusel, Emil, 38
Meyer, Russ, 123
Miller, Bing, 102, 140
Miller, Dick, 36
Miller, Leo (Red), 71
Miller, Ralph, 71
Mills, Colonel A. G., 11
Minoso, Minnie, 147
Mitchell, Dale, 126
Mitchell, Fred, 24
Moken, Johnny, 73
Montella, Ernie, 172, 176
Montreal Expos, 191
Moore & White Tool Co., 52
Moore, Johnny, 28, 32, 34, 35,
38, 62, 64
Moore, Terry, 42, 43
Moran, Pat, 48
Moser, Nicholas, 77
Moses, Wally, 102

Mueller, Emmett, 39
Mueller, Les, 154
Mulcahy, Hugh, 35, 46, 83, 135,
171
Mulvey, Joe, 13
Murphy estate, 134
Murphy, Charles W., 93, 95
Murphy, Danny, 19, 23, 110,
137, 139
Murphy, Ed, 170
Murphy, Morgan, 83
Musial, Stan, 125, 146, 147
Muskert, Charles, 77

N

Nabors, Jack, 151
Nagurski, Bronko, 88
National Assocation, 2, 4, 5, 10
National Football League, 88,
181
Navin Field, 111
Neale, Earle (Greasy), 28, 182
Negro League, 6, 186
Nehf, Art, 36
Newcomb, Don, 156
New York Giants (baseball), 20,
21, 31, 42, 57, 58, 59, 72, 76,
95, 136, 150, 154, 157
New York Giants (football), 88,
183
New York Times, 22
New York *World-Telegram*, 142
New York Yankees, 120, 125,
128, 140, 142, 146, 148,
151–154, 157, 170, 174
Nicholls, Simon, 110
Nicholson, Bill, 125
Nixon, Richard, 188
Northeast General Hospital,
111
Northeast High School, 89
Northey, Ron, 102, 170
North Philadelphia Station, 163
Notre Dame University, 184
Nugent, Gerald, 49, 60, 63, 65,
68, 86, 103, 134
Nugent, Gerald, Jr., 64, 80, 84,
91, 93, 96, 174
Nugent, Mae, 94, 103, 134

O

Oakdale Park, 6
O'Brien, Davey, 183
O'Brien, Jack, 90, 185
O'Brien, Sherry, 123
O'Doul, Lefty, 33, 38, 41
Oeschger, Joe, 72
Oldring, Rube, 19
Olney High School, 89

O'Loughlin, Silk, 23
Omnibus Company, 75
Ott, Mel, 32, 96
Owen, George, 20

P

Packard Building, 134, 167
Paige, Satchell, 7, 91, 186
Paine, Don, 181
Parkinson, Fred, 73
Parvin & Company, 75
Paskert, Dode, 36, 38
Passeau, Claude, 28, 34, 43, 62, 96, 134, 135, 154
Passon Field, 6
Patkin, Max, 83, 91, 187
Payne, Sam, 42, 46, 47
Pearls, 5
Peck, Hal, 155
Peg and Dave's Luncheonette, 161
Penn Athletic Club, 91
Pennsylvania Railroad, 6, 84, 173
Pennsylvania Supreme Court, 18
Pennsylvania, University of, 6, 75
Peverelly, Charles, 3, 10
Philadelphia Board of Education, 97
Philadelphia Catholic League, 187
Philadelphia Centennials, 10
Philadelphia Daily News, 54, 180
Philadelphia Eagles, 88, 100, 130, 181–184, 195
Philadelphia Evening Bulletin, 31, 54, 75, 103, 111
Philadelphia Evening Item, 22
Philadelphia Evening Telegraph, 105, 110
Philadelphia Hospital for Contagious Diseases, 104
Philadelphia Inquirer, 18, 61, 65, 77, 96, 104
Philadelphia North American, 22
Philadelphia Public League, 134, 187
Philadelphia Public Ledger, 18, 54, 58
Philadelphia Record, 24, 65, 95
Philadelphia Pythians, 10
Philadelphia 76ers, 123
Philadelphia Stars, 6, 186
Philadelphia Sunday Item, 10
Philadelphia Transit Company, 98

Philadelphia Warriors, 60, 123, 186
Philco sign, 122
Philley, Dave, 127
Phillies Report, 10
Pickering, Ollie, 22
Pihos, Pete, 183
Pisciella, Anthony, 61
Pittsburgh Pirates, 70, 71, 127, 149, 154, 157, 187
Pittsburgh Steelers, 181
Plank, Eddie, 19, 20, 21, 22, 100, 110, 136–138, 140, 151
Players' League, 1, 6
Plover, Sky Joe, 47
Polo Grounds, 21, 42, 111, 135, 138
Portsmouth Spartans, 88
Potter, James, 76
Pottsville Maroons, 184
Powers, Maurice (Doc), 111
Presidents' Game, The, 142
Progressive Party, 188
Providence Grays, 14
Psorasi, Sam, 180
Purcell, Bill (Blondie), 12

Q

Quakers, 1, 5, 6
Quinn, John, 168, 193
Quinn's Tavern, 161

R

Radbourne, Charles (Old Hoss), 12
Raffensberger, Ken, 156
Raft, George, 55
Raschi, Vic, 143, 147
Reach, Al, 2, 10, 11, 13, 14, 16, 28, 32, 49, 75, 76, 78, 87, 104
Reach, George, 104
Reading Railroad, 29, 32, 84
Reagan, Frank, 183
Redding, Dick, 186
Reed, Howie, 195
Reese, Pee Wee, 155
Reilly, Tricky Charley, 74
Reyburn Park, 162–163
Reyburn, John, 109
Reynolds, Allie, 143
Rhodes, Greg, 3
Richardson, Paul, 194
Rigler, Charlie, 70
Ring, Jim, 173
Ring, Jimmy, 173
Rixey, Eppa, 28, 143
Roberts, Robin, 101, 102, 117, 142, 143, 147, 150, 156–158
Robinson, Eddie,147

Robinson, Frank, 159
Robinson, Jackie, 119, 146, 147, 150, 155
Robinson, Sugar Ray, 177, 185
Robison Field, 42
Rogell, Billy, 133, 153
Rogers, Colonel John, 11, 32, 76, 78, 87
Rojas, Cookie, 102, 160
Roman Catholic High School, 90, 149, 185
Rommel, Eddie, 140
Roosevelt, Franklin D.,187
Rossman, Claude, 23
Rowe, Schoolboy, 119, 153, 155, 156
Rudolph, Dick, 140
Ruiz, Chico, 159
Rush, Bob, 147
Russell, Unk, 164
Ruth, Babe, 69, 73, 102, 125, 133, 147, 148, 151, 153, 162, 186
Ryan, Connie, 157

S

Saam, By, 177
Sacony Vacuum Co., 36
Sain, Johnny, 157
St. Joseph's College, 89
St. Joseph's Home for Boys, 54, 167
St. Joseph's Prep, 90, 185
St. Louis Browns, 19, 153, 155, 187
St. Louis Cardinals, 37, 42, 59, 72, 73, 78, 127, 141
San Francisco Giants, 160
Santelle, Paul, 57
Sauer, Hank, 147
Sawyer, Eddie, 102, 118, 142, 143, 170
Schang, Wally, 138
Schlichter, H. Walter, 22
Schmeirer, Bob, 173
Schmidt's Beer, 35
Schreckengost, Ossee, 19
Schwartz, Fred, Jr., 78
Seerey, Pat, 102, 149
Selma, Dick, 194
Seminick, Andy, 102, 132, 156, 167, 172
Seybold, Ralph (Socks), 18, 22
Seymour, Harold, 62
Shantz, Bobby, 101, 102, 129, 146, 147, 172
Sharkey, Jack, 91
Shenk, Julie, 163
Shenk, Larry, 160, 163, 168
Shettsline, Billy, 47, 48, 77

Shibe, Benjamin F., 11, 16, 25, 103, 104, 115
Shibe, John, 104, 107
Shibe, Thomas, 104
Short, Chris, 102
Shotton, Burt, 44, 48
Siebert, Dick, 146
Simmons, Al, 100–102, 140, 141, 148, 152, 161, 175
Simmons, Curt, 102, 147
Simmons, Lew, 5
Sisler, Dick, 142
Sivess, Pete, 41, 43, 93
Skinner, Andy, 123
Smith, Edgar, 133
Smith, Red, 65, 95
South Catholic High School, 90
Southern High School, 90
South Street, 47
Sports Illustrated, 57
Sportsman's Park, 32, 135
Stainback, Tuck, 135
Stallings, George, 83, 139
Stanley, Joe, 76
Stark, Dolly, 179
State Police, 87, 97
Steele, Joseph N., 104
Steele, Williams and Sons Company, 106, 112
Steinberg, Seymour, 165–166, 175
Stengel, Casey, 28, 34, 81, 142
Stevens, Johnny, 91
Stoneman, Bill, 102
Stovey, Harry, 5
Stowe, Grafley, 62
Strange family, 91
Strunk, Amos, 102
Stuhldreher, Harry, 184
Suder, Pete, 157
Sullivan, Frank, 164
Sunday, Billy, 28
Swift, Bill, 187
Swiftfoot team, 10

T

Tabor, Jim, 149, 154
Taft, Mrs. William Howard, 93
Tastykake, 181
Taylor, Tony, 102, 192
Teeter, Lucky, 97
Temple University, 89
Tendler, Lew, 91
Terry, Bill, 32
Tesreau, Jeff, 42
Thayer, Ernest, 13
Third Regiment Band, 110
Thompson, Sam, 28, 38
Thompson, Tommy, 183

Thomson, Bobby, 123
Thorpe, Jim, 89
Titus, John (Tight Pants), 58
Todd, Al, 80
Toronto Blue Jays, 70
Travers, Aloysius, 151
Triplett, Coaker, 154
Trosky, Hal, 153
Trucks, Virgil, 132
Turner, Gil, 185
Turner, Tuck, 38

U

Unholy Seven (or The Big Seven), The, 54, 162
Union Association, 2, 6
Union League, 6
United Drug Store, 57
United States Supreme Court, 78
Urbanski, Bill, 74

V

Valo, Elmer, 102, 124, 127, 132, 155
Van Buren, Steve, 182–183
Vander Meer, Johnny, 145
VanZandt, Lou, 121
Verban, Emil, 102
Vernon, Mickey, 120, 124, 132
Villanova University, 89, 184
Virdon, Bill, 127
Volstead Act, 142

W

Waddell, Rube, 17, 19, 20, 22, 23, 24
Wagner Free Institute of Science, 4
Waitkus, Eddie, 150, 157
Wakefield, Dick, 145
Walberg, Rube, 140
Walker, Harry, 101, 155
Walker, Mickey, 91
Walker, Tilly, 101
Wallace, Henry, 188
Walters, Bucky, 30, 34, 41, 58, 84
Waner, Paul, 32
Wasdell, Jimmy, 170
Washington Senators (or Nationals), 18, 119, 151, 155, 157
Waterfield, Bob, 184
WCAU, 66
Weart, William, 105
Weinert, Eugene, 85
Weintraub, Phil, 96

Wentz-Olney, 91
Werber, Bill, 128
West Catholic High School, 89, 185
Western League, 15, 16
West Philadelphia High School, 89
WFIL-TV, 181
White, Bill, 169
White Stockings, 5, 10
Whitney, Pinky, 80, 135
Whiz Kids, 102, 120, 136, 142
Wiechec, Frank, 167
Wiechec, Frank, Jr., 176
Wilkie, Wendall, 188
Williams, Cy, 28, 32, 33, 34, 38, 73
Williams, Edgar, 61, 64, 65, 83
Williams, Ike, 185
Williams, Joe, 142
Williams, Ted, 102, 125, 147, 148, 154
Wilson, Frank, 78
Wilson, Hack, 34, 81, 140
Wilson, Jimmie, 28, 42, 44, 48, 78, 81, 82, 96, 135
Wilson, Woodrow, 69, 70
Winona, 10
WIP, 66
Wise, Rick, 160
Wistert, Al, 183
Witt, Whitey, 128, 152
Wolfe, Art, 193
Wolman, Jerry, 195
Wood, George, 31
Worcester Brown Stockings, 11
World Series, 20, 21, 69, 70, 92, 100, 113, 135–144
Wright, George, 109
Wright, Harry, 3, 5, 13, 31, 48, 109
Wrightstone, Russ, 78
Wrigley Field, 32, 111, 140
Wyrostek, Johnny, 102

Y

Yale University, 5
Yankee Stadium, 32, 116, 135
Yeutter Frank, 179
Yockel, Frederick, 110
York, Rudy, 145
Young, Cy, 22

Z

Zeisler, Anne, 172
Zernial, Gus, 101, 169
Ziegler brothers, 174
Ziegler, Ray, 24
Zinkoff, Dave, 123